Lecture Notes in Computer Science　　11260

Commenced Publication in 1973
Founding and Former Series Editors:
Gerhard Goos, Juris Hartmanis, and Jan van Leeuwen

More information about this series at http://www.springer.com/series/7410

Eric Luiijf · Inga Žutautaitė
Bernhard M. Hämmerli (Eds.)

Critical Information Infrastructures Security

13th International Conference, CRITIS 2018
Kaunas, Lithuania, September 24–26, 2018
Revised Selected Papers

 Springer

Editors
Eric Luiijf 🆔
TNO (retired) and Luiijf Consultancy
Zoetermeer, The Netherlands

Bernhard M. Hämmerli
Hochschule Luzern/Acris GmbH
Wettingen, Switzerland

Inga Žutautaitė 🆔
Vytautas Magnus University
Kaunas, Lithuania

ISSN 0302-9743   ISSN 1611-3349   (electronic)
Lecture Notes in Computer Science
ISBN 978-3-030-05848-7   ISBN 978-3-030-05849-4   (eBook)
https://doi.org/10.1007/978-3-030-05849-4

Library of Congress Control Number: 2018952640

LNCS Sublibrary: SL4 – Security and Cryptology

This Springer imprint is published by the registered company Springer Nature Switzerland AG
The registered company address is: Gewerbestrasse 11, 6330 Cham, Switzerland

Preface

This volume contains the proceedings of the 13th International Conference on Critical Information Infrastructures Security (CRITIS 2018). The conference was held at the Vytautas Magnus University, Kaunas, Lithuania during September 24–26, 2018. The conference was organized by the Lithuanian Energy Institute and Vytautas Magnus University.

CRITIS 2018 continued the well-established series of successful CRITIS conferences. The conference contained the following keynote lectures:

- "Protecting Critical Information Infrastructure on National and EU Level – Lithuanian Approach" by Edvinas Kerza (Vice-Minister, Ministry of National Defense of the Republic of Lithuania)
- "Bridging the Gap Between ICS and Corporate IT Security: Finding Common Culture and Views" by Stefan Lüders (Head of Computer Security at CERN, Switzerland)
- "Comparison of Nordic and Continental Europe Grids from the Cyber Resilience Perspective" by Hayretdin Bahşi (Center for Digital Forensics and Cyber Security, Tallinn University of Technology, Estonia)

The main theme of the conference concerned the challenges for the energy sector as national and multinational critical infrastructure. Two special sessions addressed the technological and policy challenges for energy operators, policymakers, and other stakeholders. The following sessions were introduced by invited speakers:

- "The Necessity of Synchronization of the Baltic States' Electricity Network with the European System" by Ramūnas Bikulčius (Head of Strategy and Research Division, AB Litgrid, Lithuania)
- "Building a Network of Trust Among European Utilities to Foster Proactive Security Though Info Sharing" by Massimo Rocca (Enel Security representative and EE-ISAC Chair, Enel, Italy)
- "Securing BKW's Electrical Power Production and Distribution: A 3D Approach to Cyber Threats" by Ivo Maritz (Head, Cyber Security (CSO/CISO), BKW Group, Switzerland)
- "Emerging Threats for Energy Security" by Egidijus Purlys (Vice-Minister, Ministry of Energy of the Republic of Lithuania)
- "Cybersecurity in the Energy Sector – The EU Perspective" by Michaela Kollau (European Commission, Directorate-General for Energy)
- "Implications of Political and Policy Decisions to Energy Security" by Einari Kisel (Regional Manager for Europe, World Energy Council, Estonia)
- "Role of Public – Private Partnership in Critical Energy Infrastructure Protection: NATO ENSEC COE Perspective" by Artūras Petkus (Head of Strategic Analysis Division, NATO ENSECCOE, Lithuania)

Panel discussions led by the session chairman Marcelo Masera (European Commission, Joint Research Centre, Petten, The Netherlands) between these invited speakers and interactions with the audience stimulated the long-term debate between energy domain stakeholders and the research community.

As in previous years, the Program Committee received a large set of paper submissions. The Program Committee provided insightful reviews and comments to the authors of 51 papers. At least three, on average 4.6 independent reviews per submission took place resulting in the acceptance of 16 full papers. Therefore, the acceptance rate was 31%. Another three submissions were accepted as short papers. All these papers are published in this proceedings volume.

The selected reviewed papers and their presentations were grouped in the conference program under the topic sections "Advanced Analysis of Critical Energy Systems", "Strengthening Urban Resilience", "Securing Internet of Things and Industrial Control Systems", "Need and Tool Sets for Industrial Control System Security", "Advancements in Governance and Resilience of Critical Infrastructures", and "Short papers". The same outline can be found in this volume.

To stimulate international collaboration and exchange of ideas, the program chairs invited work-in-progress projects for a short presentation and poster session. There were three candidates for the Young CRITIS Award (YCA): Luca Faramondi, Davide Fauri, and Anamitra Pal. The intention of the YCA is building a virtual international community that allows junior researchers in the C(I)I domain to interact and network with peers and experienced researchers in the C(I)I domain. This stimulates faster and better research results and may also lead to further joint international research. The fifth YCA was presented by Marco Santarelli (Scientific Director ReS On Network, Italy) as chair of the YCA commission to Anamitra Pal (Pal Lab, SECEE, Arizona State University) for his contribution to the paper "Health Monitoring of Critical Power System Equipments Using Identifying Codes".

Organizing a conference like CRITIS entails an effort that is largely invisible to the participants. We, therefore, want to acknowledge the personal commitment of the local organizing team, general chairs, the contributions by the keynote speakers and invited speakers, as well as the support of the host organizations Vytautas Magnus University and the Lithuanian Energy Institute. The Program Committee chairs express their gratitude to the Technical Program Committee members who volunteered their services and devoted considerable time in preparing insightful reviews and comments to the authors of the papers. Together with the contributions to the discussions and interactions between all conference participants, this resulted in a very successful and stimulating CRITIS 2018.

November 2018   Eric Luiijf
                                                   Inga Žutautaitė
                                            Bernhard M. Hämmerli

CRITIS 2018

13th International Workshop on Critical Information Infrastructures Security

Vytautas Magnus University, Kaunas, Lithuania
September 24–26, 2018
Organized by
The Lithuanian Energy Institute

Executive Committee

Programme Chair

Eric Luiijf	Luiijf Consultancy, The Netherlands

Supporting Chairs

Marcelo Masera	European Commission/Joint Research Centre, The Netherlands
Marianthi Theocharidou	European Commission/Joint Research Centre, Italy
Grigore Havarneanu	International Union of Railways, France
Simin Nadjm-Tehrani	Linköping University, Sweden
Erich Rome	2E!SAC; Fraunhofer IAIS, Germany
Enrico Zio	Politecnico di Milano, Italy; Ecole Centrale Paris, France
Sokratis K. Katsikas	Norwegian University of Science and Technology, Norway; University of Piraeus, Greece

Local Co-chairs

Inga Žutautaitė	Lithuanian Energy Institute, Lithuania
Ričardas Krikštolaitis	Vytautas Magnus University, Lithuania

Young CRITIS Award Chair

Marco Santarelli	Res on Networks, Italy

Honorary Chair

Algirdas Avižienis	Vytautas Magnus University, Lithuania; University of California, Los Angeles, USA

Publicity Chairs

Cristina Alcaraz	University of Malaga, Spain
Rolandas Urbonas	Lithuanian Energy Institute, Lithuania

Program Committee

Cristina Alcaraz	University of Malaga, Spain
John Andrews	University of Nottingham, UK
Juozas Augutis	Vytautas Magnus University, Lithuania
Fabrizio Baiardi	University of Pisa, Italy
Robin Bloomfield	CSR City University London, UK
Arslan Brömme	GI Biometrics Special Interest Group (BIOSIG), Germany
Emiliano Casalicchio	Blekinge Institute of Technology, Sweden
Simona Cavallini	Fondazione FORMIT, Italy
Michal Choras	ITTI Ltd., Poland
Gregorio D'Agostino	ENEA, Italy
Myriam Dunn	ETH Center for Security Studies Zurich, Switzerland
Mohamed Eid	CEA, France
Dimitris Gritzalis	Athens University of Economics and Business, Greece
Stefanos Gritzalis	University of the Aegean, Greece
Bernhard M. Hämmerli	Lucerne University of Applied Sciences and Arts, ACRIS GmbH, Switzerland
Chris Hankin	Imperial College London, UK
Grigore M. Havarneanu	International Union of Railways, France
Sokratis Katsikas	Center for Cyber and Information Security, NTNU, Norway
Elias Kyriakides	University of Cyprus, Cyprus
Marieke Klaver	Netherlands Organisation for Applied Scientific Research TNO, The Netherlands
Vytis Kopustinskas	European Commission/Joint Research Centre, Italy
Panayiotis Kotzanikolaou	University of Piraeus, Greece
Rafal Kozik	Institute of Telecommunications, UTP Bydgoszcz, Poland
Ričardas Krikštolaitis	Vytautas Magnus University, Lithuania
Javier Lopez	University of Malaga, Spain
Eric Luiijf	TNO (retired) and Luiijf Consultancy, The Netherlands
Jose Martí	UBC, Canada
Linas Martišauskas	Lithuanian Energy Institute, Lithuania
Raimundas Matulevičius	University of Tartu, Estonia
Richard McEvoy	NTNU and HPE Ltd., Norway
Hypatia Nassopoulos	EIVP, France
Eiji Okamoto	University of Tsukuba, Japan
Gabriele Oliva	Università Campus Bio-Medico di Roma, Italy
Evangelos Ouzounis	ENISA, Greece

Stefano Panzieri	Roma Tre University, Italy
Peter T. Popov	City University London, UK
Sigitas Rimkevičius	Lithuanian Energy Institute, Lithuania
Brendan Ryan	University of Nottingham, UK
Erich Rome	Fraunhofer IAIS, Germany
Vittorio Rosato	ENEA, Italy
Andre Samberg	i4-Flame OU (LLC), Estonia
Maria Paola Scaparra	Kent Business School, University of Kent, UK
Dominique Sérafin	CEA, France
Andrea Servida	European Commission/DG Connect, Belgium
Roberto Setola	Università Campus Bio-Medico di Roma, Italy
George Stergiopoulos	Athens University of Econ and Business, Greece
Nils Kalstad Svendsen	Gjøvik University College, Norway
André Teixeira	Uppsala Universitet, Sweden
Marianthi Theocharidou	European Commission, Joint Research Centre, Italy
Alberto Tofani	ENEA, Italy
Eugenijus Ušpuras	Lithuanian Energy Institute, Lithuania
Simona Louise Voronca	Transelectrica, Romania
Stephen D. Wolthusen	Royal Holloway, University of London, UK; Norwegian University of Science and Technology, Norway
Christos Xenakis	University of Piraeus, Greece
Jianying Zhou	Singapore University of Technology and Design, Singapore
Enrico Zio	Politecnico di Milano, Italy
Urko Zurutuza	University of Mondragón, Spain
Inga Žutautaitė	Lithuanian Energy Institute, Lithuania

Local Organizing Committee CRITIS 2018

Juozas Augutis	Vytautas Magnus University, Lithuania
Sigitas Rimkevičius	Lithuanian Energy Institute, Lithuania
Rolandas Urbonas	Lithuanian Energy Institute, Lithuania
Inga Žutautaitė	Lithuanian Energy Institute, Lithuania
Ričardas Krikštolaitis	Vytautas Magnus University, Lithuania
Linas Martišauskas	Lithuanian Energy Institute, Lithuania
Rūta Užupytė	Vytautas Magnus University, Lithuania
Simona Staskevičiūtė	Vytautas Magnus University, Lithuania

Steering Committee

Chairs

Bernhard M. Hämmerli	Lucerne University of Applied Sciences and Arts, ACRIS GmbH, Switzerland
Javier Lopez	University of Malaga, Spain
Stephen D. Wolthusen	Royal Holloway, University of London, UK; Norwegian University of Science and Technology, Norway

Members

Robin Bloomfield	City University London, UK
Sandro Bologna	AIIC, Italy
Gregorio D'Agostino	ENEA, Italy
Grigore Havarneanu	International Union of Railways, France
Sokratis K. Katsikas	Norwegian University of Science and Technology, Norway; University of Piraeus, Greece
Elias Kyriakides	University of Cyprus, Cyprus
Eric Luiijf	Luiijf Consultancy, The Netherlands
Marios M. Polycarpou	University of Cyprus, Cyprus
Reinhard Posch	Technical University Graz, Austria
Saifur Rahman	Advanced Research Institute, Virginia Tech, USA
Erich Rome	2E!SAC; Fraunhofer IAIS, Germany
Antonio Scala	IMT – CNR, Italy
Roberto Setola	Università Campus Bio-Medico, Italy
Nils Kalstad Svendsen	Gjøvik University College, Norway
Marianthi Theocharidou	European Commission, Joint Research Centre, Italy

Contents

Need and Tool Sets for Industrial Control System Security

**Advancements in Governance and Resilience
of Critical Infrastructures**

Short Papers

Advanced Analysis of Critical Energy Systems

Node Importance Analysis of a Gas Transmission Network with Evaluation of a New Infrastructure by ProGasNet

Pavel Praks[(✉)]📶 and Vytis Kopustinskas

European Commission, Joint Research Centre (JRC),
Directorate for Energy, Transport and Climate, Energy Security,
Distribution and Market Unit, E. Fermi 2749, TP440, 21027 Ispra, VA, Italy
pavel.praks@gmail.com, Vytis.Kopustinskas@ec.europa.eu

Abstract. We present a probabilistic approach for identification and ranking of important gas network components from the security of supply point of view. We perform a probabilistic risk analysis of a regional European gas transmission network under selected attack scenarios. Moreover, in order to evaluate security of supply consequences of a new gas infrastructure project, this analysis is performed twice: before and after the infrastructure project. The results of 1 million of Monte-Carlo simulations under the attack scenarios clearly indicate various gas supply consequences. Thus, the obtained list of most critical components includes suitable candidates for the protection of infrastructure.

Keywords: Gas transmission network modelling · Network reliability
Network resilience · Monte-Carlo methods

1 Introduction

After a number of energy supply disturbances in Europe, for example the Russian-Ukrainian natural gas dispute of January 2009, the European Commission (EC) reacted by adopting the EU Reg. 994/2010 concerning measures to safeguard security of gas supply [1]. This regulation was repealed in October 2017 by a new EU Reg. 2017/1938 concerning measures to safeguard security of gas supply [2]. For reducing security of supply consequences of potential future disruptions, the Regulation requires Member States to perform risk assessments of their gas infrastructure and establish preventive and emergency plans. Further steps contain the EC funded Connecting Europe Facility which supports trans-European networks and infrastructures in energy and other sectors.

In order to support the Regulation EC Reg 2017/1938, JRC develops a number of in-house natural gas transmission system modelling tools, ProGasNet being one of them. The ProGasNet is a versatile Matlab based probabilistic transmission gas network simulator that can be used for risk assessment, reliability and vulnerability analysis, evaluation of a new infrastructure and bottleneck analysis [3, 4]. The Pro-GasNet model is based on maximum flow algorithm of graph theory [7]. In order to simulate a gas crisis, a priority supply pattern of gas networks is assumed. The aim is to

© Springer Nature Switzerland AG 2019
E. Luiijf et al. (Eds.): CRITIS 2018, LNCS 11260, pp. 3–16, 2019.
https://doi.org/10.1007/978-3-030-05849-4_1

maximize volume of flow entering the demand nodes among functions respecting the given pipeline capacities and conserving flow over inner network elements, which might randomly fail according to the Monte Carlo sampling. A risk ratio is used for security of supply quantification of a new gas infrastructure [3]. Study of flow networks behaviour including reliability, optimisation or security of supply aspects are among popular topics in the research of infrastructure networks [8, 9].

The paper [5] was the first attempt to rank importance of the gas network elements by probabilistic measures. We used Risk Achievement (RA) similar to those used in the PSAs for ranking components (Fussell-Vesely, Birnbaum, Risk Achievement Worth, etc....), see [10, 16].

In this paper, we evaluate an importance measure based on average gas deficit and RA for the selected attack scenarios. The security of supply results of these attack scenarios are automatically analysed, in order to obtain information, how the gas network can optimally react under various constrains (component failures) and under various (loss of) supply scenarios. Moreover, in order to evaluate security of supply consequences of a new gas infrastructure project, we compare a gas network reaction of two different infrastructure models to the attack scenarios: Model P and Model F. Model P describes a situation in the past, whereas Model F represents a future development of the gas network under the gas infrastructure project.

Thus, we can clearly quantify security of supply consequences of the new gas infrastructure project: We present a sorted list of attack scenarios with largest security of supply consequences for both models. Finally, we compare these two lists, in order to check, how the new gas infrastructure project helps to reduce the security of supply consequences of these attacks. Fortunately, majority of attacks will have smaller or close to zero security of supply consequences. However, we still detect a limited number of attack strategies with large security of supply consequences.

2   Importance Modelling for Networked Systems

Importance measures for networks are studied in the literature. The paper [11] presents two novel component importance measures for a stochastic flow network system with random edges capacities: system availability improvement potential of the component and expected unutilized capacity of the component.

The paper [12] provides two resilience-based component importance measures, which quantify the potential adverse impact on system resilience from a disruption affecting a selected link, and potential positive impact on system resilience when the selected link cannot be disrupted, respectively. Authors assume that recovery time is the same for any positive value of vulnerability.

Authors [13] present composite importance measures (CIM) for multi-state systems with multi-state components (MSMC). Experimental results show that the proposed CIM can be used as an effective tool to assess component criticality for MSMC.

The recent paper [15] includes a review on modelling of the operation of gas transmission networks in abnormal operating conditions. Novel approaches for critical infrastructure modelling and the search for the most important elements from the standpoint of system health are presented and discussed. Finally, authors suggest considering each facility whose failure to operate causes relative gas undersupply to consumers in the amount of 5% and more of the total demand for gas throughout the system as critically important. This value is substantiated by multi-iterative simulation studies and allows speaking of a small amount of potential critical facilities.

In this paper, we present a probabilistic approach for automated identification and ranking of important network elements of a European transmission gas network by ProGasNet. Moreover, in order to evaluate security of supply consequences of a gas infrastructure project, this analysis is performed twice: before and after the infrastructure project.

2.1 ProGasNet Methodology

ProGasNet is currently used for experimental simulation-based security of supply analyses of selected European gas transmission networks. Software runs well on a parallel multi-core computer, as the Monte-Carlo simulations can be independently evaluated.

We use a stochastic network representation for modelling reliability and capacity constraints of gas transmission networks. Each node and pipeline may randomly fail by a given probabilistic failure model. These component failures are sampled by the Monte-Carlo method. In each Monte-Carlo simulation, a maximum-flow optimization problem with a user defined priority of supply pattern is solved.

In order to model consequences during potential gas crises, a user given priority supply pattern is assumed for probabilistic reliability modelling of gas networks. Usually, the algorithm uses a priority supply pattern based on distances from source nodes: nodes geographically closer to the gas source are served first. This supply pattern was observed in gas transmission networks during previous European gas crises [3].

Let us describe the ProGasNet algorithm. In each Monte-Carlo simulation step, firstly component failures, it means failures of key gas network components (pipelines, LNG terminals and compressor stations), are sampled according to a given probabilistic law [6]. Then, an optimal maximum flow response of the gas network to the user-defined attack scenarios is evaluated and stored in a multidimensional flow matrix. For flow modelling, we use a maximum flow algorithm with multiple sources and sinks [7]. Moreover, a user defined priority of supply pattern is applied. Finally, the stored flow matrix is statistically analysed.

Of course, the flow model can be easily tuned if a prior flow information is available. For example, the maximum pipeline capacity at the cross-border connection point together with pipeline diameters can be taken from a transmission system operator (TSO) reports. A pipeline failure probability is modelled according to the EGIG report [14].

During gas supply crises, there is a necessary to maximize usage of gas sources and transmission elements under the given gas supply. Fortunately, the used maximum flow algorithm solves an optimization task, which guaranties an optimal solution, a maximum flow.

2.2   Component Importance Modelling in ProGasNet

According to [10], a risk importance measure gives an indication of the contribution of a certain component to the total risk. In this paper, we use two measures for calculation of the component importance: average gas deficit (AGD) and Risk Achievement (RA).

The average gas deficit on the i-the demand node of the given attack scenario is computed as:

$$AGD_i = demand_i - average(flow_i), \tag{1}$$

where $demand_i$ denotes the demand on the i-the demand node, whereas $average(flow_i)$ represents an average value of flow at the given attack scenario on the i-the demand node. The both mentioned values are expressed in million of cubic meter per day dimension (mcm/d). Thus, the average gas deficit is also expressed in mcm/d.

Risk Achievement for the j-th attack scenario is computed as

$$RA = R(x_j = 1) - R(base). \tag{2}$$

Here $R(x_j = 1)$ represents the increased risk level, in which the components from the j-th attack scenario are failed (i.e. $x_j = 1$ with probability 1), whereas the remaining components might fail by the given probabilistic law. The symbol R(base) denotes the present risk level (i.e. the base scenario), in which all components may fail with the given probabilistic law.

In our implementation, Risk Achievement is estimated as the non-delivery probability on the assumed attack scenario minus the non-delivery probability of the base-scenario (a "business as usual" scenario). In this study, we present results of probabilities that the gas delivery at selected demand node will be less than 80% of demands, i.e. RA < 0.8D. Results are discussed in Sect. 4.

When the both non-delivered probabilities are the same on the selected network node, the corresponding risk achievement is zero. It means that there is no security of supply impact of the selected attack scenario on the network node and the given risk level. Thus, the attack scenario is not important for the selected node and the risk level.

Average gas deficit is fast in identifying of dangerous attack scenarios. Then, Risk Achievement is used for more detailed analyses on the given risk level.

3   Definition of the Gas Network

Figure 1 represents an anonymized gas network topology of the gas network Model P. The here analysed gas network is based on a European gas transmission network. The model has representative supply and demand data. However, the graph topology is anonymized.

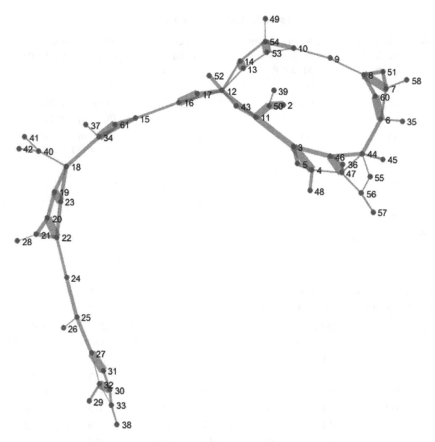

Fig. 1. Anonymized topology of the analyzed European gas network. The linewidth is proportional to the pipeline capacity.

For simplicity, the Fig. 1 and Table 1 do not include virtual nodes (namely the virtual source represented by node 1 and the virtual sink represented by node 64, respectively. These virtual nodes are required for the maximum flow algorithm with multiple sources and multiple sinks [7]. Moreover, also nodes 59 and 62 are hidden, because these nodes represent purely new gas sources, which are connected only in Model F, see Tables 1 and 3. The detailed description of gas network Model P, for example properties of connected elements of the gas network (capacities and pipeline lengths) are available in [3].

Table 3 presents a comparison between Model P and Model F, respectively. The table includes list of improved pipeline sections with a positive capacity increase in mcm/d and the length of new pipelines in km. If length of a new pipeline is zero, it means that no new pipeline has been added: The reported capacity increase is due to an enhancement of the network in this case. For example, the pipeline connecting node 15 with node 16 is not new (i.e. represented by 0 km pipeline length). On the other hand, the pipeline capacity has been increased by 6 mcm/d: as a result of the new gas infrastructure project.

Table 1. List of gas sources.

Node	Limit for Model P (mcm/d)	Yearly failure frequency for Model P	Limit for Model F (mcm/d)	Yearly failure frequency for Model F
2	31	0	31.2	0
10	10.5	0.15	10.2	f(C = 0) = 0.083; f(C = 5) = 0.125
19	25	0.1	26	f(C = 0) = 0.046; f(C = 15) = 0.0625
29	4	0	4.3	0
38	0	0	2.3	0
59	0	0	7.1	0
62	0	0	7	0
Total	70.5		88.1	

Table 2. List of non-zero demand nodes. The gas demand is represented by mcm/d. Node 64 represents the total demand in the network (Total).

Node	D(P) (mcm/d)	D(F) (mcm/d)	Diff (mcm/d)	Node	D(P) (mcm/d)	D(F) (mcm/d)	Diff (mcm/d)
4	0.1	0.1	0	36	4.2	4.2	0
5	3.2	3.2	0	37	1.3	0.5	0.8
6	0.1	0.1	0	39	0.3	0.3	0
8	0.1	0.1	0	40	0	0.5	−0.5
9	0.1	0.1	0	41	0.6	0.8	−0.2
10	1	1	0	42	0.6	0.2	0.4
13	0.5	0.5	0	43	0.2	0.2	0
17	0.1	0.1	0	44	0.7	0.7	0
18	8.5	7.8	0.7	45	1.3	1.3	0
20	0.6	0.8	−0.2	47	0.1	0.1	0
25	0.5	0.1	0.4	48	1.8	1.8	0
26	0.8	0.1	0.7	49	0.2	0.2	0
27	3	3.4	−0.4	51	7	8.4	−1.4
28	6	0	6	52	0.6	0.6	0
30	0.5	0.8	−0.3	53	0.1	0.1	0
33	0.5	0.7	−0.2	55	0.2	0.2	0
34	0.5	2	−1.5	57	0.2	0.2	0
35	0.1	0.1	0	58	0.3	0.3	0
				64	45.9	41.6	4.3

Table 3. A comparison between Model P and Model F: List of improved pipeline sections with a positive capacity increase in mcm/d and the length of new pipelines in km.

From node	To node	Capacity (mcm/d)	Length (km)
4	11	12.11	29
4	56	12.11	59
15	16	6	0
18	61	12.11	43
22	24	3	0
31	59	12.11	50
44	60	12.11	11.6
56	62	12.11	65

The network encloses various gas network elements: pipelines, LNG terminal (node 10), gas storage (node 19) and compressor stations (nodes 11, 12). Properties of gas sources are presented at Table 1. All numbers have million of cubic meter per day dimension. Let us remind that probabilistic modelling of new infrastructure projects, especially a reliability quantification of redundancy of gas supply, was studied in [3].

According to literature indications [3], we set for Model P the monthly failure frequency of the LNG terminal to $f_{LNG} = 0.15/12 = 1.25E-2$ and the monthly failure frequency of the gas storage (node 19) to $f_{storage} = 0.1/12 = 8.33E-3$, respectively. In contrary to Model P, we use a more detailed multi-state representation of these two gas sources for Model F, see Table 1. Here symbol C denotes the gas source limit expressed by mcm/d. For example, C = 0 means that the gas source is disconnected. The remaining gas sources are modelled as statistically reliable sources.

Finally, Table 2 shows a list of demand nodes for Model P and for Model F represented by the column D(P) and D(F), respectively. All demand numbers are expressed by mcm/d, too. A difference between these demands is summarized in the column 'Diff', which is also expressed by mcm/d. We can see that the largest positive difference is for node 28: 6 mcm/d, whereas the largest negative difference is for node 51: −1.4 mcm/d. Let us remind that probabilistic modelling of new infrastructure projects with constant demand was studied in [3–6].

The gas network elements can fail according to a given probabilistic model. For example, a pipeline failure is modelled by the reduction of the pipeline capacity to zero. According to the EGIG report [14], the average failure frequency of a European gas transmission pipeline is 3.5E−4 per kilometer-year. Let us assume that 10% of the reported failures cause complete rupture of a pipeline. The assumed 10% represents the pipeline rupture, according to the EGIG report. As a result, we set the pipeline failure frequency as 3.5E−5 per kilometer-year [3]. The model uses annual failure data (probability of failure per year), however when simulations are performed, one month interval is considered.

Table 4 provides list of 31 attack scenarios used for the importance modelling. These attack scenarios include high-capacity pipelines, which forms a back-bone of the transmission gas network. In some network areas, the back-bone is formed by a single high-capacity pipeline, whereas in different network areas, the back-bone is formed by

Table 4. List of attack scenarios.

Scen.	From	To	From	To
S1	29	32		
S2	27	32	30	31
S3	25	27		
S4	24	25		
S5	22	24		
S6	20	21	21	22
S7	21	28		
S8	19	20	22	23
S9	18	19	18	23
S10	18	34	18	61
S11	15	34	15	61
S12	12	17	12	16
S13	12	13	12	14
S14	13	53	14	54
S15	10	53	10	54
S16	9	10		
S17	8	9		
S18	7	51	8	51
S19	6	7	8	60
S20	6	44	44	60
S21	44	46	44	47
S22	36	46	36	47
S23	3	46	4	47
S24	3	5	4	5
S25	3	11	4	11
S26	11	50		
S27	2	50		
S28	11	12	12	43
S29	11	43	12	43
S30	1	19		
S31	1	10		

two parallel pipelines, which are geographically very close to each other. For example, attack scenario S1 includes a disruption of single pipeline connecting node 29 with node 32, whereas attack scenario S23 includes a simultaneous disruption of two pipelines: The first pipeline connects node 3 with node 46, whereas the second pipeline connects node 4 with node 47.

In the next section, we will evaluate, how important is each segment of the backbone for security of gas supply. We will evaluate security of supply consequences of these selected attack scenarios by the Monte-Carlo method.

4 Results of Simulations

In this section, we will describe results of 1 million of Monte-Carlo simulations applied to 31 attack scenarios of the transmission gas network back-bone. In order to highlight the most important reliability aspects, we will analyse the overall security of supply situation in the network and also security of supply situation on the selected 7 demand nodes.

Table 5 presents selected results of Monte-Carlo simulations for Model P: rows represent the attack scenarios, whereas columns represent the importance measures: the average gas deficit in the network (AGD in mcm/d) and estimated risk achievement that the gas delivery at selected demand node will be less than 80% of demands, i.e. RA < 0.8D. The column "Total" presents RA scores of the total supply in the network (45.9 mcm/d). Then, RA scores at 4 selected aggregated demand nodes (regions) Reg1, Reg2, ... Reg4) are presented. The table also presents demand data for RA-columns expressed in mcm/d. For example, Region1 has demand 15.5 mcm/d. In order to highlight the most important security of supply consequences, results are sorted by the average gas deficit and then by risk achievement results. Only top 18 attack scenarios with the largest security of supply consequences are presented for Model P, see the column "Importance(P)". It is because the 18th Scenario (S29) has the average gas deficit close to zero: only 0.32 mcm/d.

Table 5. Sorted results for Model P: Selected attack scenarios vs. average gas deficit and estimated risk achievement that the gas delivery at selected demand nodes will be less than 80% of demands. Negative values indicate a positive energy supply impact, and vice versa.

Importance (P)	Scen/Node	AGD (mcm/d)	RA < 0.8D				
			Total	Reg1	Reg2	Reg3	Reg4
			45.9	15.5	12.1	5.3	7
1	S25	16.79	9.9E−01	1	0	0	1
2	S30	13.41	9.9E−01	1.5E−04	9.9E−01	9.9E−01	2.8E−04
3	S23	11.69	9.9E−01	1	0	0	1
4	S8	7.95	1.4E−03	0	1.0E−06	9.9E−01	0
5	S18	7.12	6.9E−05	0	0	0	1
6	S27	6.75	1.4E−02	2.3E−02	0	0	1
7	S26	6.45	1.4E−02	2.2E−02	0	0	1
8	S6	6.07	2.5E−04	0	0	0	0
9	S7	6.07	2.5E−04	0	0	0	0
10	S21	5.85	1.0E−06	0	0	0	1
11	S9	5.57	4.6E−04	1.5E−04	9.9E−01	0	2.8E−04
12	S20	4.99	1.0E−06	6.4E−05	0	0	1
13	S19	4.79	1.0E−06	6.4E−05	0	0	1
14	S22	4.32	1.0E−06	1	0	0	−1.0E−06
15	S24	3.32	0	1	0	0	−1.0E−06
16	S4	1.41	0	0	0	9.9E−01	0
17	S5	1.41	0	0	0	9.9E−01	0
18	S29	0.32	0	0	0	0	0

First, let's us analyze the summary of supply (column 'Total') results. Security of supply consequences of attack scenarios can be grouped on the following three categories:

1. Scenarios S25, S30 and S23 with average gas deficit larger than 10 mcm/d and with RA < 0.8D for demand node Total ∼ 1
2. Scenarios S8 and S18 with average gas deficit between 7 and 8 mcm/d
3. Scenarios S26, S27 with average gas deficit close to 6.5 mcm/d and with RA < 0.8D for demand node Total ∼ 0.014, which corresponds to a failure rate of gas source at node 10
4. The remaining scenarios with average gas deficit 6.07 mcm/d or less

The largest security of supply consequences has Scenario S25, which represents a failure of node 3 to node 11 pipeline and a failure of node 4 to node 11 pipeline (only for Model F). However, only demand nodes Region1 and Region4 are highly affected, as their RA scores are close to 1. The second largest consequence has Scenario S30, i.e. disruption of source node 19 (a second largest gas source in the network). We can also see that only demand nodes Region2 and Region3 are highly affected. On the other hand, the security of supply situation at Region1 and Region4 is almost not affected: RA scores are close to zero (E-04 order).

Attack scenarios S26 and S27 represent cases in which the largest gas source (node 2) is partially or fully lost. Risk achievement for demand node Total for these cases is around 1.4E−2. This value is related mainly to the failure frequency of gas source at node 10. Thus, a failure of the largest gas source can be compensated in these two attack scenarios by the gas source at node 10. However, the gas deficit mainly affects Region4, which demands 7 mcm/d.

Let us analyse a situation at selected regions. Region4 represents the most vulnerable part of the network: 8 of top 18 attack scenarios have RA ∼ 1, namely S18-S21, S23, S25−S27. Fortunately, the rest of scenarios lead to risk achievement scores, which are close to zero. In contrary to Region4, Region1 and Region3 are much less vulnerable to analysed attacks: 4 of 15 scenarios have RA ∼ 1. In contrary to Region3, Region1 is partially sensitive to above mentioned S26 and S27 attacks. However, these two attacks lead to a relative small risk achievement for Region1: around 2.2E−2. Finally, Region2 is quite resilient to attacks, as only 2 scenarios have RA scores close to 1: S9 and S30. Consequently, importance of the second largest gas source (node 19) is evident for Region2.

Table 5 include also 'paradoxes': negative RA values for Region4. These values indicate a fact, that Region4 can profit, when an attack scenario occurs. However, these situations occur very rarely, as negative risk achievement values are very close to zero (order of 1E−6).

Table 6 presents selected Monte-Carlo results for Model F. In order to highlight the most important security of supply consequences, results are again sorted by the average gas deficit and by risk achievement values. Only results of top 15 attack scenarios with largest energy supply consequences are presented, as the rest of attacks have AGD very close to zero.

Table 6. Sorted results for Model F: Selected attack scenarios vs. average gas deficit and estimated risk achievement that the gas delivery at selected demand nodes will be less than 80% of demands. Negative values indicate a positive energy supply impact, and vice versa.

Importance(F)	Scen/Node	AGD (mcm/d)	RA < 0.8D				
			Total	Reg1	Reg2	Reg3	Reg4
			41.6	15.5	12.6	5.1	8.4
1	S25	11.07	1	8.3E−04	0	0	1
2	S23	9.74	1	6.1E−04	0	0	1
3	**S18**	**8.40**	**1**	**0**	**0**	**0**	**1**
4	**S21**	**7.13**	**1.2E−03**	**1.6E−05**	**0**	**0**	**1**
5	**S20**	**6.27**	**5.1E−04**	**1.6E−05**	**0**	**0**	**1**
6	**S19**	**6.07**	**4.5E−04**	**1.6E−05**	**0**	**0**	**1**
7	S22	4.20	5.6E−05	1	0	0	−3.0E−05
8	S24	3.20	1.0E−04	1	0	0	−1.9E−05
9	S29	0.20	0	0	0	0	4.8E−05
10	S27	0.08	3.8E−03	8.1E−05	8.2E−05	0	1.1E−02
11	S9	0.08	4.2E−03	7.7E−05	4.3E−03	0	4.1E−03
12	S26	0.08	3.8E−03	7.8E−05	8.2E−05	0	1.1E−02
13	S28	0.05	4.2E−03	1.7E−03	3.7E−05	0	4.1E−03
14	S30	0.05	4.2E−03	7.7E−05	9.3E−05	0	4.1E−03
15	S10	0.05	4.2E−03	7.6E−05	1.2E−05	0	4.1E−03

Let us compare number of scenarios with average gas deficit larger than 1 mcm/d. Model P includes 17 scenarios, whereas Model F includes only 8 scenarios. Let us analyse these most critical attack scenarios.

For Model F, the scenario S25 remains on the top. However, the average gas deficit has been reduced from 16.79 mcm/d to 11.07 mcm/d, i.e. by 5.72 mcm/d. Thus, the relative deficit reduction is 34%, see Table 7.

The second most critical scenario for Model P was S30. However, this scenario is ranked on 14-th place for Model F, as the average gas deficit is very close to zero for Model F: only 0.05 mcm/d. Thus, the average gas deficit has been reduced by 13.36 mcm/d, i.e. by 99.6%, see Table 7. This result clearly indicates positive security of supply effects of the new infrastructure project.

Scenario S23 remains on the top 3 critical list, but the average deficit has been reduced from 11.69 mcm/d to 9.74 mcm/d, i.e. by 16.7%, see Table 7.

On the other hand, Table 6 includes 4 scenarios, in which the average gas deficit has been increased: see results of scenarios S18–S21. The lines corresponding to these scenarios are highlighted **in bold**, see Tables 6 and 7. The reason why the average gas deficit has been increased is simple: Demand of Region4 has been increased from 7 mcm/d (Model P) to 8.4 mcm/d in Model F. We can see from Table 6 that risk achievement of Region4 for attacks S18–S21 is equal to 1 also in Model F.

Table 7. A comparison of top 18 attack scenarios of Model P with Model F results by the average gas deficit.

ImportanceP	Scen	AGD(P) (mcm/d)	ImportanceF	AGD(F) (mcm/d)	Deficit reduction (mcm/d)	Relative deficit reduction (%)
1	S25	16.79	1	11.07	5.72	34
2	S30	13.41	14	0.05	13.36	99.6
3	S23	11.69	2	9.74	1.95	16.7
4	S8	7.95	26	0	7.95	99.9
5	**S18**	**7.12**	**3**	**8.4**	**−1.28**	**−18**
6	S27	6.75	10	0.08	6.67	98.8
7	S26	6.45	12	0.08	6.37	98.8
8	S6	6.07	30	0	6.07	99.9
9	S7	6.07	31	0	6.07	99.9
10	**S21**	**5.85**	**4**	**7.13**	**−1.28**	**−21.9**
11	S9	5.57	11	0.08	5.49	98.5
12	**S20**	**4.99**	**5**	**6.27**	**−1.28**	**−25.7**
13	**S19**	**4.79**	**6**	**6.07**	**−1.28**	**−26.8**
14	S22	4.32	7	4.2	0.12	2.7
15	S24	3.32	8	3.2	0.12	3.6
16	S4	1.41	24	0.01	1.4	99.3
17	S5	1.41	25	0.01	1.4	99.3
18	S29	0.32	9	0.2	0.12	37.5

Although the total limit of gas sources has been increased from 70.5 mcm/d to 88.1 mcm/d (see Table 1) and the total network demand has been reduced from 45.9 mcm/d to 41.6 mcm/d (Table 2), Model F is not fully able to respond to the increased demand of Region4. The reason is that Region4 represents a geographically remoted consumer, in which the transmission network capacity is limited by a bottleneck. In the other words, although there are gas sources available, there is not enough transmission capacity to pump gas to Region4, even a new infrastructure project has been implemented.

In contrary to Model P, Model F reduced the average gas deficit almost to zero in 9 attack scenarios: S4–S9, S26, S27 and S30. Let us remind that S30 was the scenario with the second largest average gas deficit in Model P: 13.41 mcm/d.

Finally, there are 5 scenarios, in which the average gas deficit has been partially reduced: S22–S25 and S29. In these scenarios, the average deficit reduction is between 0.12 mcm/d (for S22, S24 and S29) and 5.72 mcm/d (for S25).

5 Conclusions

We presented a probabilistic approach for identification and ranking of important gas network elements. We used a combination of two measures for calculation of the component importance: average gas deficit and Risk Achievement. In order to evaluate security of supply consequences of a new gas infrastructure project, this analysis was performed twice: before and after the infrastructure project.

The results of 31 selected attack scenarios under 1 million of Monte Carlo steps were automatically analysed and compared in ProGasNet, in order to obtain information, how the gas network can optimally react under various constrains (random component failures) and under the given attack scenarios. Results indicate that the new infrastructure project was very helpful for the analysed gas network, as the number of attack scenarios with a large gas deficit (1 mcm/d or more) has been reduced from 17 to 8. However, we identified 4 scenarios, in which the average gas deficit is larger than before. Even when a new infrastructure project has been implemented, the network is not able to transfer enough gas to Region4, because of a network bottleneck, as demand of Region4 increased.

On the other hand, majority of failure consequences of the largest gas source can be reliably compensated by the third largest gas source. Moreover, simulated results clearly show that the gas network is not critically sensitive to disruptions leading to disconnection (or a failure) of the second largest gas source, when the new gas infrastructure is implemented.

The ProGasNet approach for identification and ranking of important gas network elements by a combination of two measures for calculation of the component importance was very useful for large number of attack scenarios.

References

1. EU Regulation: Regulation No. 994/2010 of the European Parliament and of the Council of 20 October 2010 concerning measures to safeguard security of gas supply and repealing Council Directive 2004/67/EC. Official Journal of the European Union, L295, 53, 1–22 (2010)
2. EU Regulation: Regulation (EU) 2017/1938 of the European Parliament and of the Council of 25 October 2017 concerning measures to safeguard the security of gas supply and repealing Regulation (EU) No 994/2010. Official Journal of the European Union, L 280/1, 60, 1–57 (2017)
3. Praks, P., Kopustinskas, V., Masera, M.: Probabilistic modelling of security of supply in gas networks and evaluation of new infrastructure. Reliab. Eng. Syst. Saf. **144**, 254–264 (2015)
4. Kopustinskas, V., Praks, P.: Bottleneck analysis of the gas transmission network using ProGasNet simulator. In: ESREL 2015, pp. 1259–1266 (2015)
5. Praks, P., Kopustinskas, V.: Identification and ranking of important elements in a gas transmission network by using ProGasNet. In: ESREL 2016, pp. 1573–1579 (2016)
6. Praks, P., Kopustinskas, V., Masera, M.: Monte-Carlo-based reliability and vulnerability assessment of a natural gas transmission system due to random network component failures. Sustain. Resilient Infrastruct. **2**(3), 97–107 (2017)

7. Deo, N.: Graph Theory with Applications to Engineering with Computer Science. Prentice Hall, Englewood Cliffs (2008)
8. Todinov, M.T.: The same sign local effects principle and its applications for risk reduction. Int. J. Reliab. Saf. **9**(4), 311–329 (2015)
9. Rømo, F., Tomasgard, A., Hellemo, L., Fodstad, M.: Optimizing the Norwegian natural gas production and transport. Interfaces **39**(1), 46–56 (2009)
10. van der Borst, M., Schoonakker, H.: An overview of PSA importance measures. Reliab. Eng. Syst. Saf. **72**(3), 241–245 (2001). https://doi.org/10.1016/S0951-8320(01)00007-2. ISSN 0951-8320
11. Aven, T., Østebø, R.: Two new component importance measures for a flow network system. Reliab. Eng. **14**(1), 75–80 (1986). https://doi.org/10.1016/0143-8174(86)90091-0. ISSN 0143-8174
12. Barker, K., Ramirez-Marquez, J.E., Rocco, C.M.: Resilience-based network component importance measures. Reliab. Eng. Syst. Saf. **117**, 89–97 (2013). https://doi.org/10.1016/j.ress.2013.03.012. ISSN 0951-8320
13. Ramirez-Marquez, J.E., Coit, D.W.: Composite importance measures for multi-state systems with multi-state components. IEEE Trans. Reliab. **54**(3), 517–529 (2005)
14. EGIG report: 8th Report of the European gas pipeline incident data group; Groninge (2011)
15. Senderov, S.M., Edelev, A.V.: Formation of a list of critical facilities in the gas transportation system of Russia in terms of energy security. Energy, 10 November 2017 (in press). https://doi.org/10.1016/j.energy.2017.11.063
16. Vesely, W.E., et al.: Measures of risk importance and their applications, NUREG/CR-3385 (1983)

In-Cycle Sequential Topology Faults and Attacks: Effects on State Estimation

Ammara Gul[1](✉) and Stephen Wolthusen[1,2]

[1] Information Security Group, Royal Holloway University of London,
Egham, Surrey TW20 0EX, UK
ammara.gul.2015@live.rhul.ac.uk, stephen.wolthusen@rhul.ac.uk
[2] Norwegian Information Security Laboratory,
Gjovik University College, Gjovik, Norway

Abstract. Monitoring and state estimation as well as ultimately higher-order tasks in power networks require timely and accurate measurements arising from a wide area network. Knowledge of the current topology of the network is crucial to interpret any such measurements and is also required for state estimators to obtain correct results. As both faults and deliberate actions such as opening breakers may alter the topology, an important step in any state estimator is *topology processing* to obtain an accurate view for a given set of measurements. This, however, is conventionally performed prior to state estimation. We argue that this gives adversaries an opportunity to stealthily induce and possibly revert topology changes within a single scan cycle, resulting in some results being influenced by the intermittent changes as conventional models rely on the abstraction that all measurements to arrive instantly and synchronously. We provide a formal model of the attack and formulate an optimisation problem to minimise the cost to attackers and determine the effects of induced topology faults, resulting in denial of service attacks up to loss of observability and study recoverability. Finally, we compare our approach to conventional contingency analysis and offer simulation results based on the standard IEEE-14 and IEEE-30 test cases.

Keywords: Power system · Smart grid · State estimation
Sequential topology change · Scan cycle · Topology processing

1 Introduction

Monitoring and state estimation require accurate knowledge of the underlying topology of the power network to take effective control actions in addition to raw measurements. A substantial body of work exists on vulnerabilities of such systems to malicious false data injection, but this tends to assume that the underlying power network topology is known and static for the duration of both operation and attack; the conventional approach for state estimation being to perform *topology processing* [1] prior to state estimation.

© Springer Nature Switzerland AG 2019
E. Luiijf et al. (Eds.): CRITIS 2018, LNCS 11260, pp. 17–28, 2019.
https://doi.org/10.1007/978-3-030-05849-4_2

However, modern power networks are likely to be more dynamic as particularly generators based on renewable energy may have intermittent availability and can also be configured in the form of virtual power stations; this renders contingency case analysis more problematic already even in the absence of active attackers. In this paper we concentrate on studying the effects of topology faults, particularly when introduced deliberately.

Information on how generators and loads are connected via buses, transformers, tie and transmission lines are obtained from equipment state information in the form of binary state or that can be further corroborated by other analogue measurements (phase, voltage, current), and are commonly subjected to topology processing, which seeks to eliminate errors based on wrongly recorded equipment state as well as the presence of faults.

Topology changes may include tripping of generators, accidental line failures, or deliberate attacks; the former is commonly handled based on contingency analyses, but combinatorial limits prevent this from extending beyond single line failures.

Topology processors identify the network, connectivity, and location of measurement devices. *Conventional topology processing* is performed before state estimation and functions such as observability analysis and bad data processing take place. Once the network topology is known, state estimation assumes that this topology is correct and proceeds to estimate the state and identify analogue bad data. *Generalized topology processing* extends this with explicit modelling of switches, but is not widely deployed [1].

The research reported in this paper is motivated by the relative paucity of work on topology-related attacks compared to the body of research on bad data injection and related data-based attacks. Earlier work has studied single and double topology modifications, including induced double line faults and analyse the effects on state estimators in terms of possible state forcing or also state estimator divergence [2]. On the other hand, here we formulate a mechanism for finding optimal conditions for resource-constrained attacker and compare the results with conventional contingency cases while *explicitly including the non-simultaneous capture of measurements*, abandoning the abstraction of atomic measurements across the entire power system.

The main contribution of the present paper is therefore an analysis of the effects of *transient* faults and attacks, and we explicitly analyse a topology change taking place during a scan cycle. This way, the state of the topology remain unchanged in the beginning and the end of the measurement taking process therefore, making the attack sufficiently undetectable. We derive a metric to analyse the attack impact on state estimation motivated by the fact that there are some lines which have negligible effect on state estimation upon inclusion/removal, and on the other hand the possible existence of a small number of few other branches and lines whose addition/withdrawal may result in a catastrophic attack.

The remainder of this paper is structured as follows: Background and related work are briefly described in Sect. 2 followed by a description of the system models used in state estimation, bad-data detection, and identification in Sect. 3. Our novel topology attack model is presented in Sect. 4, along with the necessary conditions to make the attack feasible. In Sect. 5, simulation results are shown for the introduced attack on IEEE bus systems and feasibility of our proposed attack is also discussed. We provide conclusions as well as ongoing work in Sect. 6.

2   Related Work

Bad data injection attacks and their detection/mitigation is a widely researched area in power system state estimation, with a large body of work emerging since study of bad data injection was proposed in work by Liu et al. in [3]. However, substantially less attention has been paid to the other main cause of the faults namely topology errors.

Hines et al. [4] elaborated topological and electrical structure of the power grid while proposing a graph theoretic method for generating random networks similar to the power grid to better notice topology changes. Monitoring of power system topology in real-time is achieved currently by observing the circuit breaker's (CB) operation and statuses by using Remote Transmission Units (RTUs) of a SCADA system. However, changes such as trip conditions, etc. cannot be determined solely by this SCADA approach. Kezunovic proposed a solution based on a new CB Monitor (CBM) which would be permanently connected to the substation CBs [5]. This CBM scheme can be extended to the system level, but deployment cost cannot be ignored.

In [6], Lu et al. proposed a rule-based topology error/change detection method in which all analogue data are screened before applying the heuristic rules to detect the errors. Although the results are appealing but, it is computationally expensive approach. Lefebrve et al. [7] proposed a pre-processing method for detecting and identifying topology errors and bad measurements before a state estimation solution. This incurs the drawback that every time a change in topology occurs, the system has to go through this whole process. Another different, yet complicated approach, is to take the status of switching devices as new state variables estimated together with usual ones while considering three state variables for one switch status [8].

Steady state simulations of power system with changes in topology are shown in [9] by collecting all the possible topologies as a result of isolation of transmission lines from the system. In principle detection and identification of topology changes in power systems by using PMUs is becoming more attractive as PMUs are more widely deployed. Placing PMUs at strategic points can help quickly detecting topology changes caused by events such as lines going down or large voltage drops [10]. A quick change algorithm is proposed to be applied on the data provided by high-speed PMUs to detect the change-point that corresponds to the system topology change instant [11]. A systematic bus selection scheme is presented for the minimum required PMUs. Taking into account the load dynamics and measurement error, the topology detection algorithm is constructed based on data from micro-synchrophasors or μPMUs [12]. [13] proposed that the minimal difference between measured and calculated voltage angle or magnitude indicates the actual topology and hence a method based on multiple μPMUs is devised.

Topology changes can be caused deliberately by the adversary to harm the power network. The attack as a result of topology change is known as hidden topology attack, where the attacker may need to change the status of just one circuit breaker at a transmission line and suppress the corresponding alert or measurements to make it hidden [14]. Frequent topology changes in today's power system have raised a big challenge of assessing the system protection and security afterwards [15]. Further, an impact analysis of the topology change on relay settings is conducted.

A joint cyber and physical attack is analysed where the adversary attacks a zone by physically disconnecting some of the power lines and then blocking the information flow from the attacked zone to the control center [16]. Information recovery model following such attack is proposed to retrieve the data about the disconnected lines. The vulnerability of grid to such attacks is analysed and an efficient EXPOSE algorithm to detect and recover missing information is proposed [17]. Furthermore, the properties of the cascade and introduce algorithms to identify the cascading failure evolution and vulnerable lines in a linearized power-flow model are studied [18]. Classes of attacks including single and double topology modifications are studied and the effects on state estimators including possible state forcing or also state estimator divergence are analysed [2].

Lourenco et al. in [19] presents a method for processing real-time data error in generalized state estimation while considering both type of errors namely topology and analogue data errors. [20] reviews the most relevant works that have investigated robustness in power grids using Complex Networks (CN) concepts. Undetectable attacks on network topology of a smart grid are considered with a strong assumption that the adversary can observe all the meter and network data for existence of an undetectable attack [21].

Woodward in his report last year [22] quoted a research that 10.8% of all links in the US and Southern Canada are at risk of cascade event. Results imply that the same disturbance in a given power grid can lead to disparate outcomes under different conditions–ranging from no damage to a large-scale cascade is proposed by Wang et al. in [23]. It indicates that the topological and geographical properties of the vulnerable set is a major factor determining whether the failures spread widely. Xiao and Yeh study the problem of cascading link failures in power grids and model these failures by graph theoretic approach [24] while considering the fact that links fail according to a probability which depends on the neighbouring links.

3 Power System State Estimation and Topology Identification

Currently in our power grids, the control center receives two kinds of data from the metering devices throughout the system. Binary data $\mathbf{s} \in \{0, 1\}^d$ corresponds to the switch status and circuit breakers knowledge and can be represented as a string of binary numbers denoting the on/off states of the switches/breakers. Analogue numbers are taken for real and reactive flows, injections, voltage and current measurements and we denote it by the measurement vector $\mathbf{z}$. When there is no attack or sensor error, $\mathbf{s}$ corresponds to a true switch/breaker states. Each $\mathbf{s}$ provides a network topology and we denote that topology by a directed graph $\mathcal{G} = (\mathcal{V}, \mathcal{E})$ with a set of $\mathcal{V}$ buses and $\mathcal{E}$ transmission lines. The state of the power network is $\mathbf{x}$ which is a vector of voltage magnitude and phasors on all the buses of the network. When there is no attack, the measurements collected by SCADA, $\mathbf{z}$, the system state $\mathbf{x}$ and the topology defined above $\mathcal{G}$ are related by the AC power flow model

$$\mathbf{z} = h(\mathbf{x}, \mathcal{G}) + \mathbf{e} \tag{1}$$

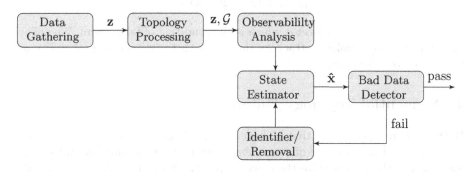

Fig. 1. Real-time modelling of a power network: conventional state estimation

where $\mathbf{z}$ is measurement vector consist of both real and reactive measurements, $\mathbf{x}$ is the state vector, h is the non-linear measurement function of $\mathbf{x}$ and $\mathcal{G}$ and $\mathbf{e}$ is the noise vector having zero mean and known co-variance $\mathbf{R}$ of order $m \times n$ where there are m measurements and n state variables ($m > n$). As described by Monticelli, the control center executes state estimation with network information and meter readings as inputs [1]. Figure 1 represent this SE where network and meter data are $(\mathbf{s}, \mathbf{z})$. It checks both the network information and the measurement data for errors. If the bad data test in SE detects some inconsistencies in the data and the estimates, it refines the data by removing the outliers and then searches for the topology and the estimates that matches the best with the data. Our aim of an undetectable topology attack is achieved when one may pass through bad data test without raising an alarm.

If $(\mathbf{s}, \mathbf{z})$ is the input to state estimation under the AC model given by (1) and $\mathbf{s}$ corresponds the topology $\hat{\mathcal{G}}$, the control center acquire the Weighted Least Square (WLS) estimate by

$$\hat{\mathbf{x}} = \operatorname{argmin}(\mathbf{z} - h(\mathbf{x}, \hat{\mathcal{G}}))^t \mathbf{R}^{-1}(\mathbf{z} - h(\mathbf{x}, \hat{\mathcal{G}})) \tag{2}$$

where $\hat{\mathcal{G}}$ is network topology when there is no attack and $\bar{\mathcal{G}}$ when there is a topology attack. Although Weighted Least Absolute Value (WLAV) method for state estimation is more robust and stable in the sense that it is able to reject bad data efficiently but it has some major drawbacks i.e., it involves time consuming Linear Programming (LP) technique and slow convergence rate among others. Therefore, WLS, although not that effective in presence of bad data, is considered as the most widely used method to SE problems (see [25] for details).

Once the states $\hat{\mathbf{x}}$ are estimated, bad data analysis is done. Generally, control center uses residue error for bad data detection. In $J(\hat{\mathbf{x}})$, the WLS error

$$J(\hat{\mathbf{x}}) = (\mathbf{z} - h(\hat{\mathbf{x}}, \hat{\mathcal{G}}))^t R^{-1} (\mathbf{z} - h(\hat{\mathbf{x}}, \hat{\mathcal{G}}))$$

is used and a statistical threshold τ is used

$$\begin{cases} \text{bad data} & \text{if } J(\hat{\mathbf{x}}) > \tau \\ \text{good data} & \text{if } J(\hat{\mathbf{x}}) \leq \tau \end{cases} \tag{3}$$

where τ is determined to meet α which is the condition of false alarm. We define the undetectable topology attack as the one with the detection probability as low as rate of false alarm.

4 Sequential Topology Failures

With a dynamic power grid that we have today, it is fair to expect frequent topology changes. The expertise of power engineers rely on the smooth and steady operation of the grid despite these recurrent changes in topology. Deployment of Phasor Measurement Units (PMUs) is allowing topology change detection schemes to be more accurate and significantly faster [7,10]. Hundreds of PMUs are being deployed round the globe to increase the redundancy in measurement vector and help getting topology changes detected, therefore contributing to more secure power grid. The major issue related to this advancement is the cost of these advanced devices. Due to this constraint, there are still thousands of branches with no PMUs leaving room for the attackers. Even if it is possible to have PMUs at every line, there is still a potential chance for the attacker such as by aiming at GPS, a time reference signal upon which generally all PMUs rely. Spoofing of such signals is very common and inexpensive source to create confusion about the correct signals in the control centre.

To make a clear understanding about how the power grid responses towards such changes we need to report some preliminaries from previous works. An attack (error) that can pass through the system without being noticed by the bad data test is called an **undetectable attack**. Such attacks (errors) can be classified further as data-based or topology-based, both of which require some criterion to get the desired impact. Undetectable false data injection attacks on state estimation as introduced by Liu et al. [3] have a necessary condition of undetectability as: *Suppose the original measurements* $\mathbf{z}$ *can pass the bad measurement detection. The malicious measurements* $\bar{\mathbf{z}} = \mathbf{z} + \mathbf{a}$ *can pass the* *bad measurement detection if* **a** *lies in a column space of H i.e.,* $\mathbf{a} \in Col(H)$. On the other hand, for a topology-related attack, Kim and Tong proposed a similar undetectability condition as *Suppose the original measurement set* $(\mathbf{z}; \mathbf{s})$ *can pass the bad measurement detection. The malicious measurements* $\bar{\mathbf{z}} = \mathbf{z} + \mathbf{a}$ *can pass the bad measurement detection if* $\bar{\mathbf{z}}$ *lies in a column space of* $\bar{H}$ *where* s *denotes the topological data and* $\bar{H}$ *is the measurement matrix after topology attack* $\bar{\mathcal{G}}$ [21].

Details of the undetectable single/multiple topology attack and the related possibilities for the attacker to create misconception among the operators can be found in [2]. Here, we are introducing a novel **sequential topology attack** that goes undetected due to its reverse nature. In addition, in both of our works i.e., the previous and the present one, we consider these faults as a result of deliberately induced error. However, such errors can also emerge due to some natural reasons for example thunderstorms, earthquakes, floods, or even high winds that are not under the scope of this paper.

4.1 Adversary Model

In this section, we intend to analyse the attack model for transient topology changes in a single scan cycle. There are usually two scenarios when SCADA systems transmit the measurement data collected from sensors i.e., (I) the devices will sent a message if something interesting/unusual happens and (II) SCADA systems need to complete its scan/poll cycle despite of some changes. Theoretically, former is correct as protocols allow one to perform it but such a synchronization is relatively uncommon. Contrarily, later is common traditionally which is a deterministic real-time behaviour where every deadline is maintained within a certain time period.

As an attacker, we are considering the most widely used behaviour of SCADA systems where SCADA take a definite amount of time after coming back to the same sensor. In fact some sensors are slightly slower or faster compared to others. In other words, there must be an interval between each time the measurements being integrated leaving a possibility for the attacker. As long as the attacker maintains operation(s) within that frame of single scan cycle while keeping itself hidden, the attack can be made successful.

The attacker aims to change the current topology $\mathcal{G}$ to a desired topology $\bar{\mathcal{G}} = (\mathcal{V}; \bar{\mathcal{E}})$ and then reverses that change before the completion of the scan cycle such that the final topology $\bar{\bar{\mathcal{G}}} = (\mathcal{V}; \bar{\bar{\mathcal{E}}})$ would be same as it was in the start i.e., $\bar{\bar{\mathcal{G}}} = \mathcal{G}$. This attack only involves line faults, therefore, the number of vertices $\mathcal{V}$ (bus-bars) will remain the same during the attack but the number of edges $\mathcal{E}$ (transmission lines) will become $\bar{\mathcal{E}}$ or $\bar{\bar{\mathcal{E}}}$ where $\mathcal{E} \subset \bar{\mathcal{E}}$, $\mathcal{E} = \bar{\bar{\mathcal{E}}}$. The lines that are not common between $\mathcal{E}$ and $\bar{\mathcal{E}}$ and between $\bar{\mathcal{E}}$ and $\bar{\bar{\mathcal{E}}}$ are called attacked lines in the first and second attack intervals respectively. Similarly, all the buses with which target/attacked lines are connected are called attacked buses (Fig. 2).

As a prerequisite, the attacker must have the knowledge of few of the time windows in between two scan cycles where the success probability is maximum.

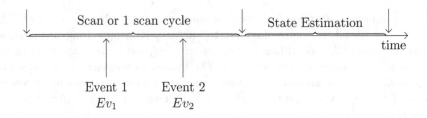

Fig. 2. Sequential topology attack model

In the beginning of a particular scan cycle, the attacker closes already open circuit breakers/switches. The corresponding measurements from the relative sensor changes themselves due to the change in topology. Before the end of the same cycle, the attacker switch the statuses back to its original (open) position such that the topology now $\bar{\bar{\mathcal{E}}}$ is same as was before the manipulation i.e., $\bar{\bar{\mathcal{E}}} = \mathcal{E}$. To launch such a sequential or a two-stage attack, the attacker at first, needs to change the status of a single breaker from $0 \rightarrow 1$ and then within the scan of measurements, the attacker needs to reverse that change i.e., $1 \rightarrow 0$.

$$\bar{s} = s + a, \quad a \in \{0,1\}$$
$$\bar{\bar{s}} = \bar{s} + b, \quad b \in \{0,1\} \tag{4}$$

where a and b are the topology changes at first and second stage of the sequential attack respectively. The attacker is limited in resources in terms of time availability and therefore, the necessary but not sufficient condition for the attacker about time limitation will be

$$\bar{s} - \bar{\bar{s}} \leq T, \quad \bar{s} \in \bar{\mathcal{G}}, \bar{\bar{s}} \in \bar{\bar{\mathcal{G}}} \tag{5}$$

where $\bar{\bar{s}} - \bar{s}$ is the length of the attack. This constraint limit the attacker such that he must launch and complete the attack before the next scan cycle starts. There is no proper attack vector in both stages of this attack as the amount of topology change induced by the attacker is reversed inside the same scan cycle. It is important to mention that the above model can be seen as a more realistic extension of [3] where Liu et al. introduced a as an amount of change in the true measurement data. The difference here is of the resources available to the attacker along with very low detection probability and the similarity is the ultimate data fault caused by the attacker.

The measurement vector can be seen as a collection of measurements at three instants, (1) before attack, (2) after first attack and (3) after second sequential attack

$$
\mathbf{z}^* = \begin{bmatrix} 1 \\ 1 \\ \vdots \\ 1 \\ 0 \\ 0 \\ 0 \\ \vdots \\ 0 \end{bmatrix} \cdot \mathbf{z}' + \begin{bmatrix} 0 \\ \vdots \\ 0 \\ 1 \\ \vdots \\ 1 \\ 0 \\ \vdots \\ 0 \end{bmatrix} \cdot \mathbf{z}'' + \begin{bmatrix} 0 \\ 0 \\ 0 \\ \vdots \\ 0 \\ 1 \\ 1 \\ \vdots \\ 1 \end{bmatrix} \cdot \mathbf{z}''' \tag{6}
$$

where $\mathbf{z}^*$ is the manipulated measurement vector. After the attack, states can be determined by Eq. 2 as

$$
\hat{\mathbf{x}}^* = \mathrm{argmin}(\mathbf{z}_A^* - \hat{H}\mathbf{x})^t \mathbf{R}^{-1}(\mathbf{z}_A^* - \hat{H}\mathbf{x}) \tag{7}
$$

where $\hat{\mathbf{x}}^*$ is the false state vector.

The success of the attack lies on how bad is its influence on the measurements in between such sequential change and then how the compromised measurements impact the state estimation process. If the topology before the scan cycle would not match the topology after it, the operators could simply reject the corresponding data and go for contingency analysis. However, even if it not a sequential attack, the first attack alone can cause damage to the system but here, the adversary is aiming for its desired impact or at most DoS attack.

The least cost attack can be seen as the one with the most impact $\mathcal{I}$ on the operation of power grid such as

$$
\max \; \mathcal{I} \; = \qquad\qquad \| \bar{\mathbf{z}} - \bar{\bar{\mathbf{z}}} \|_0 \tag{8a}
$$
$$
\text{subject to} \qquad\qquad \| \bar{\mathbf{z}} - \bar{\bar{\mathbf{z}}} \|_1 \leq \alpha, \tag{8b}
$$
$$
z_{km} = \infty \text{ if } \bar{\mathbf{s}} : 1 \to 0. \tag{8c}
$$

where $\bar{\mathbf{z}}$ and $\bar{\bar{\mathbf{z}}}$ are the manipulated and true measurements respectively. $\| \cdot \|_0$ is the total number of non-zero entries in a vector and $\| \cdot \|_1$ is the magnitude. Equation 8 is a an optimization problem with an objective function maximizing the impact of the proposed topology attack by finding the optimum for the number of modifications required. The impact $\mathcal{I}$ depends on the total number of measurements between the two stages of the attack i.e., $\bar{\mathbf{s}}$ and $\bar{\bar{\mathbf{s}}}$. Constraint 8b denotes that the magnitude of change is bounded while Eq. 8c shows the stealth condition. z_{kl} is the line impedance for kl where k and l denote the end buses.

5   Results and Discussions

We note that we seek to consider undetectable topology attacks on conventional centralised state estimation. In this section, we discuss the performance of the above mentioned state estimation model as a result of sequential topology errors by simulations on IEEE 14 and 30-bus systems. The technique used to estimate the state is WLS and MATPOWER is used for loading the data for AC model. Note that, without any topology attack both systems take 4 iterations to converge.

Our sequential attack is composed of two stages to be completed in a single scan cycle. It is worth mentioning here that we consider the same transmission line in both stages i.e., first stage of attack is opening a line while the second stage is closing the same line. Table 1 shows that there is always an impact no matter which line is under attack. After N simulations for each bus system, where N is the total number of lines in a system we notice that our attack model remain successful whether it is about the error in estimated states or delayed convergence.

Table 1. Sequential faults in 14 and 30-bus system

Test case	Failed line	Convergence (iterations)		Error (MSE)	
		Single LF	Sequential LF	Single LF	Sequential LF
14-bus system	1–2	4 iterations	4 iterations	83.19	3.455
	2–3	4 iterations	5 iterations	0.0003	0.6424
	5–8	4 iterations	7 iterations	0.0013	0.4731
	3–14	4 iterations	5 iterations	0.0001	0.287
30-bus system	1–2	4 iterations	5 iterations	0.0001	6.159
	2–4	diverge	6 iterations	∞	108.12
	4–12	4 iterations	4 iterations	0.0001	6.53
	24–25	diverge	6 iterations	∞	6.16

In above table, the first and second columns are for the considered test systems and the attacked lines respectively. We test all the lines of both systems but only showing few of them in table chosen randomly. We make a comparison between a single topology attack (base case) and the proposed one. *Single LF* column represents a single line failure as a result of an undetectable attack whereas *Sequential LF* column shows the proposed attack where the attacker opens and closes the breaker sequentially during measurement taking process. The mean-square error (MSE) between two vectors is simply a squared Euclidean distance between them, normalized by the length of the vectors. It can be seen for the two transmission lines in 30-bus system, i.e., 2–4 and 24–25 that the system diverge due to singularities after removing these lines. Even for such critical lines (a transmission line between a pair of buses whose removal leave the system disconnected), the proposed attack (Sequential LF) outperforms the single LF by forcing the state estimator and not just breaking down the system. It is mainly due to the fact that the proposed method can avoid detection because the topology state of the system remains the same before and after the measurement process. Table 1 illustrates that the proposed model works better than the basic one in almost every respect and shows even better results for the larger grid.

6 Conclusion

The frequent topology changes make our grid more vulnerable to topology attacks where the operator can think of the attack as the usual unplanned change. We propose a transient topology attack involving sequential failures during a single scan cycle. This way, the state of the topology remains same in the beginning and the end of the process of collecting measurements therefore, making the attack adequately undetectable. Finally, an optimization problem for the least cost attack is formulated.

Results show adequate success of the model and our ongoing work includes understanding the behaviour and criticality of these faults in different topologies and different systems. We will possibly be looking at if same might be true for PMU measurements as they often consider as equality constraints and don't have to go through bad data detection.

References

1. Monticellii, A.: State Estimation in Electric Power System: A Generalized Approach. Business and Economics Series. Springer, US (1999). https://doi.org/10. 1007/978-1-4615-4999-4
2. Anonymised for Review
3. Liu, Y., Ning, P., Reiter, M.K.: False data injection attacks against state estimation in electric power grids. In: Proceedings of 16th ACM Conference on Computer and Communications Security, pp. 21–32 (2009)
4. Hines, P., Blumsack, S., Cotilla, E., Barrows., C.: Topological and electrical structure of power grids. In: Proceedings of the 43rd Hawaii International Conference on System Sciences (HICSS), pp. 1–10 (2010)
5. Kezunovic, M.: Monitoring of Power System Topology in Real-Time. In: Proceedings of the 39th Hawaii International Conference on System Sciences (HICSS), pp. 1–10 (2010)
6. Lu, C.N., Teng, J.H., Chang, B.S.: Power system network topology error detection. In: Proceedings of the Generation, Transmission and Distribution, pp. 623–629. IEEE (1994)
7. Lefebvre, S., Prevost, J.: Topology error detection and identification in network analysis. Electr. Power Energy Syst. **28**(5), 293–305 (2005)
8. Korres, G., Manosakis, N.: A state estimation algorithm for monitoring topology changes in distribution systems. In: Proceedings of Power and Energy Society General Meeting. IEEE (2012)
9. Abidin, A.A.Z., Nagi, F.H., Ramasamy, A.K., Abidin, I.Z.: Steady state simulation of power systems with change in topology. Int. J. Electr. Comput. Energ. Electron. Commun. Eng. **7**(8), 1046–1049 (2013)
10. Vander Weil, S., Bent, R., Casleton, E., Lawrence, E.: Identification of topology changes in power grids using phasor measurements. Appl. Stoch. Model. Bus. Ind. **30**(6), 740–752 (2014)
11. Jiang, X.: Real-Time Power System Topology Change Detection and Identification. Ph.D. Thesis from University of Illinois (2013)
12. Cavraro, G., Arghandeh, R., Poolla, K., Von Meier, A.: Data-driven approach for distribution network topology detection. In: Proceedings of IEEE PES General Meeting (2015)

13. Arghandeh, R., Gahr, M., Von Meier, A., Cavraro, G., Ruh, M., Andersson, G.: Topology Detection in Micro-grids with Micro-Synchrophasors (2015)
14. Deka, D., Baldick, R., Vishwanath, S.: One breaker is enough: hidden topology attacks on power grids. In: Proceedings of the 2015 IEEE Power and Energy Society General Meeting, pp. 1–5. IEEE (2015)
15. Tasdighi, M., Kezunovic, M.: Impact analysis of network topology change on transmission distance relay settings. In: Proceedings of the Power and Energy Society General Meeting, pp. 48–59. IEEE (2015)
16. Soltan, S., Yannakakis, M., Zussman, G.: Power grid state estimation following a joint cyber and physical attack. IEEE Trans. Control Netw. Syst. 5(1), 499–512 (2016)
17. Soltan, S., Zussman, G.: EXPOSE the line failures following a cyber-physical attack on the power grid. IEEE Trans. Control of Netw. Syst. (2017)
18. Soltan, S., Mazauric, D., Zussman, G.: Analysis of failures in power grid. IEEE Trans. Control Netw. Syst. 4(2), 288–300 (2017)
19. Lourenco, E., Coelho, E., Pal, B.: Topology error and bad data processing in generalized state estimation. IEEE Trans. Power Syst. 30, 3190–3200 (2015)
20. Cuadra, L., Sanz, S., Ser, J., Fernández, S., Geem, Z.: A critical review of robustness in power grids using complex networks concepts. Energies 8, 9211–9265 (2015)
21. Kim, J., Tong, L.: On topology attack of a smart grid: undetectable attacks and countermeasures. J. Sel. Areas Commun. 31(7), 1294–1305 (2013)
22. Woodward, A.: Weak links in US power grid vulnerable in event of catastrophe. In: DAILY NEWS, 16 November 2017
23. Wang, W., Sun, Z., Zhu, B.: Modelling the seismic impacts on communication networks in smart grid. Int. J. Distrib. Sens. Netw. 11(2), 587–640 (2015)
24. Xiao, H., Yeh, E.: Cascading link failure in the power grid: a percolation-based analysis. In: International Conference on Communications Workshops (ICC). IEEE (2011)
25. Abur, A., Exposito, A.G.: Power System State Estimation: Theory and Implementation. CRC Press, Boca Raton (2004)

Health Monitoring of Critical Power System Equipments Using Identifying Codes

Kaustav Basu[1]([✉]), Malhar Padhee[2], Sohini Roy[1], Anamitra Pal[2], Arunabha Sen[1], Matthew Rhodes[3], and Brian Keel[3]

[1] NetXT Lab, SCIDSE, Arizona State University, Tempe, USA
{kaustav.basu,Sohini.Roy,asen}@asu.edu
[2] Pal Lab, SECEE, Arizona State University, Tempe, USA
{Malhar.Padhee,Anamitra.Pal}@asu.edu
[3] Salt River Project, Tempe, USA
{Matthew.Rhodes,Brian.Keel}@srpnet.com

Abstract. High voltage power transformers are one of the most critical equipments in the electric power grid. A sudden failure of a power transformer can significantly disrupt bulk power delivery. Before a transformer reaches its critical failure state, there are indicators which, if monitored periodically, can alert an operator that the transformer is heading towards a failure. One of the indicators is the signal to noise ratio (SNR) of the voltage and current signals in substations located in the vicinity of the transformer. During normal operations, the width of the SNR band is small. However, when the transformer heads towards a failure, the widths of the bands increase, reaching their maximum just before the failure actually occurs. This change in width of the SNR can be observed by *sensors*, such as phasor measurement units (PMUs) located nearby. Identifying Code is a mathematical tool that enables one to *uniquely* identify one or more *objects of interest*, by generating a *unique signature* corresponding to those objects, which can then be detected by a sensor. In this paper, we first describe how Identifying Code can be utilized for detecting failure of power transformers. Then, we apply this technique to determine the fewest number of sensors needed to *uniquely* identify failing transformers in different test systems.

Keywords: Transformer health · Identifying codes · PMU placement

1 Introduction

The electric power grid is arguably the most critical of all the infrastructures as other infrastructures, such as, communication, transportation and finance are heavily dependent on it. Similarly, high voltage (HV) power transformers, generators, and transmission lines are the most critical components of the electric power grid. Therefore, an untimely loss of HV transformers can be catastrophic

E. Luiijf et al. (Eds.): CRITIS 2018, LNCS 11260, pp. 29–41, 2019.
https://doi.org/10.1007/978-3-030-05849-4_3

for not only the electrical infrastructure, but also the other critical infrastructures that depend on it. Accordingly, it will be helpful if it can be recognized before the event, that a transformer is heading towards a failure, so that corrective measures can be undertaken. Fortunately, before a transformer reaches its critical failure state, there are "cues"(or indicators) which, if monitored periodically, can alert an operator that the transformer is heading towards a failure. One of the indicators is the signal to noise ratio (SNR) of the voltage and current signals in substations located in the vicinity of the transformer. During normal operations, the width of the SNR bands are small. However, when the transformer heads towards a failure, the widths of the bands increase, reaching their maximum just before the failure actually occurs. This change in width of the SNR can be observed by phasor measurement units (PMUs) located nearby.

Identifying Code is a mathematical tool that enables one to *uniquely* identify one or more *objects of interest*, by generating a *unique signature* corresponding to those objects, which can then be detected by a sensor. In this paper, the objects of interest are HV transformers. When a transformer is heading towards failure, it generates "indicators", which, if monitored by some "sensors", may provide information to an operator in the control center about the impending failure of the transformer. Since the number of transformers in the grid is large, and the sensors are expensive, one would like to deploy as few sensors as possible (fewer than the number of transformers) and yet retain the capability that, when a transformer is heading towards a failure, it can be *uniquely* identified.

PMU is a device that can be utilized as a "sensor" for monitoring the health of transformers. When placed on a generator, load, or zero injection bus, in the power grid, PMUs give the voltage of that particular bus, as well as the currents flowing in the branches (lines or transformers) incident on that bus (while being subjected to the PMU's measurement channel limitations). Since a power transformer can *only* be placed between two buses, a judicious placement of a few PMUs (sensors) can effectively monitor health of all the transformers, and in case a transformer heads towards a failure, the sensors can create a *unique fault signature* that enables the operator to identify the troubled transformer.

In this paper, we, (i) describe the Rudd power transformer failure incident that motivated this study, (ii) describe how Identifying Code can be utilized for *unique* identification of the transformers that are heading towards a failure, and, (iii) provide a technique to compute the fewest number of sensors to be deployed, to ensure *unique* identification of the transformers that are heading towards a failure in standard test systems.

2   Related Work

Prior research on health monitoring using PMUs have been mostly directed towards improving security and stability of the power system [1]. In addition, a number of studies have focused on placement of PMUs [2,3] to realize a variety of objectives. The problem under study in this paper can also be viewed as a PMU placement problem as it computes the fewest number of PMUs and their locations, so that the *unique* identification capability is realized. It is important to highlight here that none of the PMU placement strategies proposed so far had the unique identification capability as the objective for PMU deployment.

Karpovsky *et al.* introduced the concept of Identifying Codes in [4] and provided results for Identifying Codes for graphs with specific topologies, such as binary cubes and trees. Using Identifying Codes, Laifenfeld *et al.* studied covering problems in [5]. A special case, where only a subset of nodes needs a unique code, can be modeled with a bipartite graph, and was studied as "Discriminating Codes" in [6]. This special case is relevant for our study as we focus on finding unique signatures for a subset of nodes, instead of all the nodes, as is done in Identifying Codes.

3 Lessons Learnt from Rudd Power Transformer Failure

During the early hours of June 1, 2016, a large power transformer at the Rudd substation of Salt River Project (SRP), a large utility company in Arizona, suddenly caught fire. A 27,000-gallon tank of mineral oil used as a transformer coolant, burned, and spewed thick smoke over a large area. A few snapshots are illustrated in Figs. 1(a) and (b) [7]. The cause of the failure was identified to be bushing failure. Due to the redundancy present in the system design as well as the fact that the fire broke out during low-load conditions (system load is small in early morning), no power outages occurred. This incident highlights the need for better monitoring techniques for these critical and expensive equipments.

(a)   (b)

Fig. 1. Transformer fire at Salt River Project (SRP)'s Rudd substation in Avondale [7].

SRP shared their operational data leading up to the failure of this transformer with us for analysis. Because causes of such failures gradually build-up over time, if one is paying attention, the signs of an impending failure may be observable "days" before the actual failure event. PMUs continuously produce outputs at a very fast rate (typically 30 samples per second). When placed near transformers, PMUs, through their measurements, can serve as *sensors* to monitor the health of the transformer, and capture degradation in the health of a transformer over time. It may be noted that a PMU provides complex voltage and current measurements at the bus where it is placed. If the PMU has to serve as a sensor for monitoring transformer health, it must have a way to measure it with a "cue" (or indicator or metric). This metric should be independent of the "unit" of the measured quantity (either voltage or current), so that a proper comparison can be made. Signal to noise ratio (SNR), a classical measure of the quality of a signal, can serve as this desired metric. It compares the level of a signal to the level of background noise that is present in it. Mathematically, the SNR of a signal can be expressed as reciprocal of the coefficient of variation, i.e., the ratio of its mean to its standard deviation, as shown in Eq. 1.

$$SNR \ (in \ dB) = 10 * log\frac{\mu}{\sigma} \tag{1}$$

In Eq. 1, μ is the signal mean or expected value and σ is the standard deviation, or an estimate thereof. It is difficult to directly compare different signals (such as voltages and currents). However, SNR (in decibels) is a relative metric and therefore, it can be used to compare diverse signals and create alerts/alarms. The Rudd transformer failure data obtained from SRP, comprises of PMU readings (voltages and currents) one year away from the day of the failure (June 1, 2016) up to the data collected only a few hours prior to the actual failure event.

Two important pieces of observation were made from the SRP data.

Observation 1: A steady growth in the width of the SNR bands (computed from the voltage magnitude measurements obtained from neighboring substations), was observed over a period of time, till the transformer failed. The observations for three instances of time, as it approached the actual time of failure, are shown in Fig. 2. Since the growth was similar in all three phases, it was concluded that the SNRs were capturing an event that was affecting all three phases, and not due to a single phase failure event, contributed by a current or a potential transformer failure. Moreover, as the width was uniform over the observed time period (an hour worth of data), it is clear that the captured event was *not* a random transient event.

Observation 2: In observation 1, we noted that the width of the SNR band at a specific PMU (sensor) location, increases as time approaches the actual failure event. From the data it was also clear that, as the distance of the PMU (sensor/monitoring device), from the transformer (monitored device) increased, the width of the observed SNR decreased. Figure 3 shows the decrease in the width of the SNR bands as a function of the electrical distance (termed as hops) from the Rudd transformer. The data was collected from eight substations (S1, ..., S8) that neighbor Rudd, and had PMUs placed on them. It may be noted that the Rudd substation itself did not have a PMU on it during the time of failure.

Given that the deteriorating condition of a transformer can be noticed by PMUs located within a certain distance of the transformer, signals indicating the deteriorating condition, can be utilized to deploy effective monitoring strategies, so that an alarm is generated *before* a transformer reaches a critical failure state. *Identifying Code* is a mathematical tool that can be used for monitoring transformers in the power grid. Using this technique, the fewest number of sensors needed to enable an operator to *uniquely* identify the failing transformer before it reaches a critical failure state can be computed.

4   Overview of Identifying and Discriminating Codes

The notion of *Identifying Codes* [4] has been established as a useful concept for optimizing sensor deployment in multiple domains. In this paper, we use Identifying Code of the *simplest form* and define it as follows. *A vertex set V' of a graph $G = (V, E)$ is defined as the Identifying Code Set (ICS) for the vertex set V, if for all $v \in V$, $N^+(v) \cap V'$ is unique where, $N^+(v) = v \cup N(v)$ and $N(v)$ represents the set of nodes adjacent to v in $G = (V, E)$.* The *Minimum Identifying Code Set* (MICS) problem is to find the Identifying Code Set of *smallest cardinality*. The vertices of the set V' may be viewed as *alphabets* of the code, and the *string* made up with the alphabets of $N^+(v)$ may be viewed as the unique "code" for the node v. For instance, consider the graph $G = (V, E)$ shown in Fig. 4. In this graph $V' = \{v_1, v_2, v_3, v_4\}$ is an ICS as it can be seen from Table 1 that $N^+(v) \cap V'$ is *unique* for all $v_i \in V$. From the table, it can be seen that the code for node v_1 is v_1, the code for v_5 is v_1, v_2, the code for v_{10} is v_3, v_4, etc.

Table 1. $N^+(v) \cap V'$ results for all $v \in V$ for the graph in Fig. 4

$N^+(v_1) \cap V' = \{v_1\}$	$N^+(v_2) \cap V' = \{v_2\}$
$N^+(v_3) \cap V' = \{v_3\}$	$N^+(v_4) \cap V' = \{v_4\}$
$N^+(v_5) \cap V' = \{v_1, v_2\}$	$N^+(v_6) \cap V' = \{v_1, v_3\}$
$N^+(v_7) \cap V' = \{v_1, v_4\}$	$N^+(v_8) \cap V' = \{v_2, v_3\}$
$N^+(v_9) \cap V' = \{v_2, v_4\}$	$N^+(v_{10}) \cap V' = \{v_3, v_4\}$

Graph Coloring with Seepage (GCS) Problem: The MICS computation problem can be viewed as a novel variation of the classical Graph Coloring problem. We will refer to this version as the *Graph Coloring with Seepage (GCS)* problem. In the classical graph coloring problem, when a color is *assigned* (or injected) to a node, only that node is colored. The goal of the classical graph coloring problem is to use as few distinct colors as possible such that (i) every node receives a color, and (ii) no two adjacent nodes of the graph have the same color. In the GCS problem, when a color is assigned (or injected) to a node, not only does that node receive the color, but also the color *seeps* into all the adjoining nodes. For example, if a node v_i is adjacent to two other nodes v_j and v_k in the graph, then if the color red is injected to v_j, not only v_j will become red, but also v_i will become red as it is adjacent to v_j. Now if the color blue is injected to v_k, not only v_k will become blue, but also the color blue will seep in to v_i as it is adjacent to v_k. Since v_i was already colored red (due to seepage from v_j), after color seepage from v_k, it's color will be a *combination of red and blue*

34   K. Basu et al.

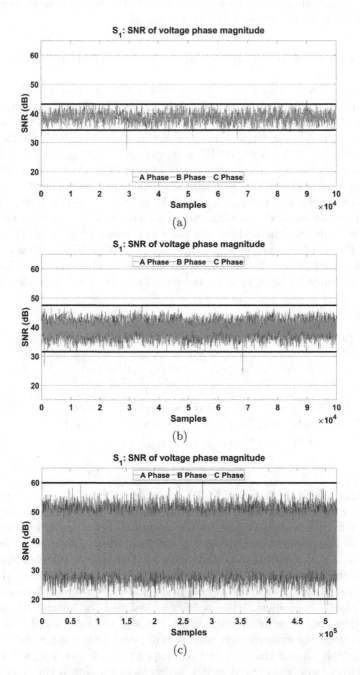

Fig. 2. Variation in width of SNR as one moves closer (in time) to instant of failure.

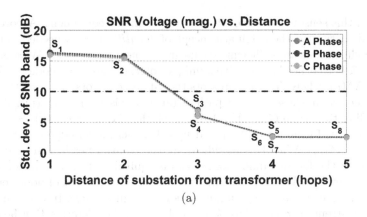

Fig. 3. Standard deviation of width of SNR as one moves (spatially) away from the failing equipment.

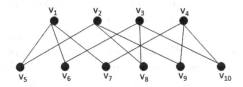

Fig. 4. Graph with Identifying Code Set $\{v_1, v_2, v_3, v_4\}$

(purple). At this point, all three nodes v_j, v_k, and v_i will have "distinct" colors red, blue, and purple, respectively. *The color assigned to a node may be due to: (i) only injection at that node, (ii) only seepage from other adjoining nodes and (iii) a combination of injection and seepage.* The colors injected at the nodes are referred to as *atomic* colors. The colors formed by the combination of two or more atomic colors are referred to as *composite* colors. The colors injected at the nodes (atomic colors) are all *unique.* The goal of the GCS problem is to inject colors to as few nodes as possible, such that (i) every node receives a color, and (ii) no two nodes of the graph have the same color.

Suppose that the node set V' is an ICS of a graph $G = (V, E)$ and $|V'| = p$. In this case if p distinct colors are injected to V' (one distinct atomic color to one node of V'), then by the definition of ICS for all $v \in V$, if $N^+(v) \cap V'$ is unique, all nodes of $G = (V, E)$ will have a unique color (either atomic or composite). Thus computation of MICS is equivalent to solving the GCS problem.

Identifying Code is useful when the goal is to monitor all nodes of the graph (i.e., each node is required to have a unique signature). However, in this paper our focus is on monitoring the health of only power transformers. Moreover, in Identifying Code a color can be injected at any node of the graph (i.e., a sensor can be placed at any node of the graph). However, in the health monitoring problem, a sensor placed far away from the equipment to be monitored, may not be useful as "cues" (signals) indicating failing state of the equipment, may not even reach this sensor because of its distance from the equipment. Accordingly, some modification to the original concept of *Identification* is needed. The following modifications are sufficient to capture the new scenario: (i) We identify a subset $V' \subseteq V$ that needs to receive a unique color; (ii) For each node $v \in V'$, we compute $N^k(v)$, where $N^k(v)$ represents the k-hop neighbors of v (i.e., the set of nodes in the graph whose shortest path distance to v is at most k); (iii). We construct a Bipartite graph $G' = (V_1 \cup V_2, E)$ such that (a) $V_1 = V'$, (b) $V_2 = \cup_{v \in V_1} N^k(v)$, and (iii) for nodes $v_i \in V_1$ and $v_j \in V_2$, there is an edge $e \in E$, if and only if $v_j \in N^k(v_i)$. With this modification, the transformer health monitoring problem with the fewest number of sensors is equivalent to computation of the smallest subset $V_2' \in V_2$ such that injection of colors to this set of nodes ensures that each node in V_1 receives a unique color through *seepage*. In this study, we restrict our attention to $k = 1$ or $k = 2$ only, as cues of deteriorating health of transformer may not be observable at distances $k \geq 3$ (See Fig. 3).

A variation of Identification Code when restricted to Bipartite graphs is known as *Discriminating Code* [6], and is defined as follows: Let $G = (V_1 \cup V_2, E)$ be an undirected bipartite graph and let $N(v)$, denote the neighborhood of v, for any $v \in V_2$, a subset $V_2' \subseteq V_2$ is called the Discriminating Code of G if $\forall v \in V_1, N(v) \cap V_2'$ is unique. We will refer to critical equipment health monitoring problem, with the fewest number of sensors, as the *Monitoring Critical Equipment* (MCE) problem, which may be stated formally in the following way: **MCE Problem:** Find the smallest subset $V_2' \subseteq V_2$, such that injection of colors at these nodes, ensures that each node $v \in V_1$, receives a unique color through seepage.

5   Problem Formulation

In this section, we formalize the problem of computing the fewest number of sensors to be deployed to monitor all critical equipments (HV transformers) in the power grid, so that, if they show signs of potential failure, then an operator in the control room, can uniquely identify them. Once the failing equipment is identified, corrective measures can be undertaken, such as a planned shutdown.

From our discussion in Sect. 4, it is clear that Identifying Code relates to an underlying graph. In order to use Identifying Code to find the fewest number of sensors to be deployed to monitor critical equipments, we first have to construct a graph from the single line diagram (SLD) of the power system. Consider the IEEE 14 Bus System shown in Fig. 5. We construct a graph $G = (V, E)$ from the SLD, where each node represents either a bus or a transformer, and two nodes are connected by an edge if the corresponding buses, or bus and transformer are connected. The Fig. 6 shows the graph $G = (V, E)$ constructed from the IEEE 14 Bus SLD, shown in Fig. 5. In Fig. 6, the buses are represented by black circular nodes and the transformers by red square nodes. In power systems, the monitoring devices (such as the PMUs) can be placed on the ends of the transmission lines, next to the buses [2]. In Fig. 6, the potential locations where a monitoring device can be deployed are shown by small green squares.

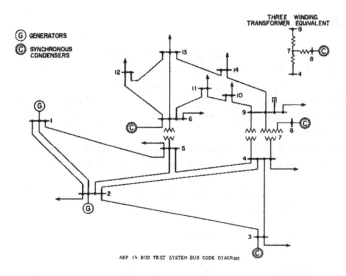

Fig. 5. IEEE 14 Bus Test System

The goal of this exercise is to determine the health of the red squares (transformers) before they reach a critical state. Signal of failing health of a red square reaches only up to a certain distance from the location of the red square, where distance is measured in terms of number of hops. The monitoring devices can only be placed at the green squares. If we assume that the signal of failing health of a red square can reach k hops, then all green squares within k hop distance of the red square will recognize that particular red square (transformer) is failing. This can be captured in a bipartite graph $G = (V_1 \cup V_2, E)$, where each node $v \in V_1$ represents a red square and each node $v \in V_2$ represents a green square. There is an edge $e \in E$ connecting nodes $v_i \in V_1$ and $v_j \in V_2$ if the signal from the red square r_i, represented by node v_i in Fig. 6, can reach the green square g_j, represented by node v_j in Fig. 6. Such graphs corresponding to the IEEE 14 Bus System, with $k = 1$ and $k = 2$, are shown in Fig. 7 and Fig. 8, respectively. Since the IEEE 14 Bus System has 5 transformers (red squares in Fig. 6), the vertex set V_1 in the bipartite graphs shown in Figs. 7 and 8 has 5 nodes. Since, in the IEEE 14 Bus System, there are 40 potential locations for placement of sensors (green squares), in Fig. 6, the vertex set V_2, in the bipartite graphs shown in Figs. 7 and 8, has 40 nodes (numbered from 6–45), denoted by green circles. It may be noted that when $k = 1$, only 21 out of 40 potential locations are viable locations for placement of sensors as the other 19 locations are not within 1-hop neighborhood of the transformers. However, when $k = 2$, all 40 nodes are viable locations for placement of sensors, as all of them are within the 2-hop neighborhood of the transformers. It may be noted that some of the nodes in Figs. 7 and 8, are labeled with strings such as "A", "AC", etc. The explanation and significance of these strings are given in Sect. 7.

6 Problem Solution

In this section, we provide an Integer Linear Programming (ILP) formulation for solving the MCE problem, as stated below.

Instance: $G = (V_1 \cup V_2, E)$, an undirected bipartite graph.

Problem: Find the smallest subset $V_2' \subseteq V_2$, such that injection of colors at these nodes, ensures that each node $v_i \in V_1$, receives a unique color (either atomic or composite) through seepage.

We use the notation $N(v_i)$ to denote the neighborhood of v_i, for any $v_i \in V_1 \cup V_2$. Corresponding to each $v_i \in V_2$, we use an indicator variable x_i,

$$x_i = \begin{cases} 1, \text{ if a color is injected at node } v_i, \\ 0, \text{ otherwise} \end{cases}$$

Objective Function: $\qquad\qquad$ Minimize $\sum_{v_i \in V_2} x_i$

Coloring Constraint: $\qquad\qquad \sum_{v_i \in N(v_j)} x_i \geq 1, \qquad\qquad \forall v_j \in V_1$

Unique Coloring Constraint: $\sum_{v_i \in \{N(v_j) \oplus N(v_k)\}} x_i \geq 1, \ \forall v_j \neq v_k, \in V_1$

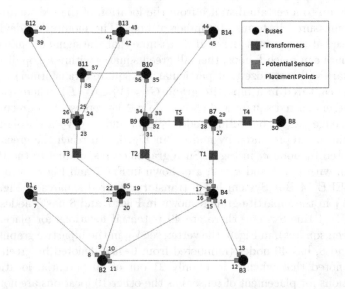

Fig. 6. Potential sensor placement locations in IEEE 14 Bus System (Color figure online)

$N(v_j) \oplus N(v_k)$ denotes the Exclusive-OR (symmetric set difference) of the node sets $N(v_j)$ and $N(v_k)$. It may be noted that the objective function ensures that the fewest number of nodes in V_2 are assigned a color. The Coloring Constraint

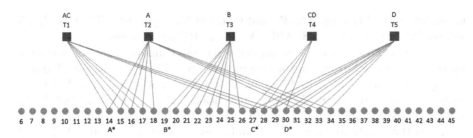

Fig. 7. Bipartite graph corresponding to IEEE 14 bus system with for k = 1 (Color figure online)

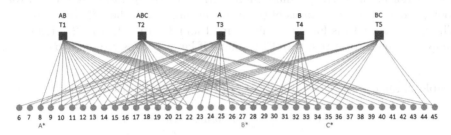

Fig. 8. Bipartite graph corresponding to IEEE 14 bus system with for k = 2 (Color figure online)

ensures that every node in V_1 receives at least one color through seepage from the colors injected at nodes in V_2. A consequence of the Coloring Constraint is that, a node in V_1 may receive more than one color through seepage from the colors injected at nodes in V_2. The Unique Coloring Constraint ensures that, for every pair of nodes (v_j, v_k) in V_1, at least one node in the node set $N(v_j) \bigoplus N(v_k) \subseteq V_2$ is injected with a color. This guarantees that v_j and v_k will not receive identical colors through the color seepage from the nodes in V_2.

7 Experimental Results and Discussion

In this section, we present the results of our technique on standard power system test cases, such as IEEE 14, 30, 57, 118, PEGASE 89 bus, and Polish 2383 bus systems. As discussed in Sect. 5, the IEEE 14 bus system has 5 transformers and 40 potential locations for placement of sensors. The bipartite graphs for the IEEE 14 bus system for $k = 1$ and $k = 2$ are shown in Figs. 7 and 8. Our results obtained from the solution to the ILP show that the 5 transformers can be monitored with 4 sensors when $k = 1$, and 3 sensors when $k = 2$. As shown in Fig. 7, for $k = 1$, if 4 sensors are deployed at nodes 14, 19, 27, and 30 (equivalently 4 colors A, B, C, and D are injected at these nodes, shown in Fig. 7 by A*, B*, C*, and D*), the 5 transformers T1 through T5 will receive *unique* colors AC, A, B, CD, and D, respectively. Similarly, for $k = 2$, if 3 sensors are deployed at nodes 8, 27, and 35 (equivalently 3 colors A, B, and C are injected at these nodes, shown in Fig. 8 by A*, B*, and C*), the 5 transformers T1 through T5 will receive *unique* colors AB, ABC, A, B, and BC respectively.

The significance of each transformer receiving a unique color (or a unique signature), is the following. In the example shown in Fig. 8, if colors A, B and C are injected at nodes 8, 27 and 35 (i.e., PMUs A, B, and C are placed at these locations, among the 40 (6–45) potential locations), the transformers T1-T5 will receive colors AB, ABC, A, B, and BC, respectively. Suppose that the control room has three indicator lamps, 1, 2, and 3, corresponding to PMUs A, B, and C, respectively. As long as the width of the SNR ratio is within the normal range, the lamps are green. As soon as the width of the SNR ratio exceeds the normal range, the corresponding lamps turn red. An operator, at the control room, can interpret the status of the five transformers, in the following way: (i) The transformer T1 is failing if only lamps 1 and 2 turn red, (ii) T2 is failing if lamps 1, 2 and 3 turn red, (iii) T3 is failing if lamp 1 turns red, and so on.

Table 2. No. of sensors needed in IEEE, PEGASE, and Polish systems for $k = 1, 2$.

Bus system	No. of transformers	No. of sensors	
		$k = 1$	$k = 2$
IEEE 14	5	4	3
IEEE 30	7	6	4
IEEE 57	14	13	10
PEGASE 89	10	10	6
IEEE 118	9	9	5
Polish 2383	155	155	106

Our results for power system test cases are tabulated in Table 2. The results show that the number of sensors needed to monitor all the transformers are fewer than the number of transformers. On an average there were 6.90% and 37.90% savings in the number of sensors using our technique for $k = 1$ and $k = 2$, respectively. From Fig. 3, it can be seen that the difference in the width of the SNR band in dB at substations S_1 and S_2 (1 and 2 hop distance away respectively, from the transformer) is minimal. Accordingly, we can use $k = 2$ results, which implies that significant savings (37.90%) can be realized using our technique. The ILPs for the test cases were computed using GUROBI for python. An Intel Core i5-6300HQ CPU with 2.30 GHz and 32 GB RAM was used for our experiments. The computation time varied from 0.17 s, for the smallest test case ($|V_1| = 5$, $|V_2| = 40$, $|E| = 36$, $k = 1$), to 25.18 s ($|V_1| = 155$, $|V_2| = 5,772$, $|E| = 3,655$, $k = 2$) for the largest. As the computation times for these test cases were only a few seconds, we expect that for larger systems involving thousands of buses and hundreds of transformers, the problem can still be solved within a short period of time.

8 Conclusion

We present a novel technique involving PMU-based metrics and Identifying Code to find the least number of sensors to monitor the health of the critical equipments, such as HV power transformers. In the future, we plan to investigate (i) a fault tolerant monitoring system, where the system will be able to *uniquely* identify a failing critical equipment, even when one or more of the sensors are malfunctioning, and (ii) multiple simultaneous failure of critical equipments, in the sense that, not only failure of individual equipments will have a *unique* signature, but also failure of a set of equipments will have a *unique fault signature*.

References

1. Salehi, V., Mohamed, A., Mazloomzadeh, A., Mohammed, O.A.: Laboratory-based smart power system, part II: control, monitoring, and protection. IEEE Trans. Smart Grid **3**(3), 1405–1417 (2012)
2. Pal, A., Vullikanti, A.K.S., Ravi, S.S.: A PMU placement scheme considering realistic costs and modern trends in relaying. IEEE Trans. Power Syst. **32**(1), 552–561 (2017)
3. Pal, A., Mishra, C., Vullikanti, A.K.S., Ravi, S.S.: General optimal substation coverage algorithm for phasor measurement unit placement in practical systems. IET Gener. Transm. Distrib. **11**(2), 347–353 (2017)
4. Karpovsky, M.G., Chakrabarty, K., Levitin, L.B.: On a new class of codes for identifying vertices in graphs. IEEE Trans. Inf. Theory **44**(2), 599–611 (1998)
5. Laifenfeld, M., Trachtenberg, A.: Identifying codes and covering problems. IEEE Trans. Inf. Theory **54**(9), 3929–3950 (2008)
6. Charbit, E., Charon, I., Cohen, G., Hudry, O.: Discriminating codes in bipartite graphs. Electron. Notes Discrete Math. **26**, 29–35 (2006)
7. Transformer explodes into fireball at SRP substation in Avondale. http://www.azfamily.com/story/32111291/transformer-explodes-into-fireball-at-srp-substation-in-avondale

Strengthening Urban Resilience

Towards Computer-Aided Security Life Cycle Management for Critical Industrial Control Systems

Florian Patzer[1]([⊠]), Ankush Meshram[2], Pascal Birnstill[1], Christian Haas[1], and Jürgen Beyerer[1,2]

[1] Fraunhofer Institute of Optronics, System Technologies and Image Exploitation (IOSB), Karlsruhe, Germany
{florian.patzer,pascal.birnstill,christian.haas,
juergen.beyerer}@iosb.fraunhofer.de
[2] Vision and Fusion Laboratory (IES), Karlsruhe Institute of Technology (KIT), Karlsruhe, Germany
{ankush.meshram,juergen.beyerer}@kit.edu

Abstract. Critical infrastructure experienced a transformation from isolated towards highly (inter-)connected systems. This development introduced a variety of new cyber threats, causing high financial damage, threatening lives and affecting the society. Known examples are Stuxnet, WannaCry and the attacks on the Ukrainian power grid. To prevent such attacks, it is indispensable to properly design, assess and maintain countermeasures and security strategies throughout the whole life cycle of the critical systems. For this, security has to be considered and assessed for every system design and redesign. However, common assessment tools and methodologies are not executed on a detailed system knowledge and therefore they are enhanced with penetration tests. Unfortunately, performing only abstract assessments is inadequate and penetration tests endanger the availability of the tested systems. Therefore, the latter cannot be performed on live systems executing critical processes. In this paper, we address these issues for Industrial Control Systems and explain how new concepts for continuous security-by-design or model-based system monitoring and automated vulnerability assessments can resolve them by exploiting new Industry 4.0 developments.

Keywords: ICS security · Critical infrastructure security
Security-by-design · Automated vulnerability assessment
Security life cycle management · Defense-in-depth · Knowledge base

1 Introduction

Many industrial systems (hereafter referenced as Industrial Control Systems (ICS)) are classified as critical infrastructure. Due to high costs of down-times or the respective risk for safety and public health, interruption of their processes

© Springer Nature Switzerland AG 2019
E. Luiijf et al. (Eds.): CRITIS 2018, LNCS 11260, pp. 45–56, 2019.
https://doi.org/10.1007/978-3-030-05849-4_4

is usually unacceptable. Consequently, in contrast to office IT, the prioritized security objective for ICS is availability and not confidentiality.

Unfortunately, ICS are generally very vulnerable to cyber attacks. One reason for this situation is that the applied technologies were not designed to fulfill security requirements, since the systems in question were isolated from the outside world for decades and thus isolated from many kinds of attacks. As a consequence, the need for security has not been strong enough to support the development of more secure technologies. In addition, the life time of ICS components tends to be much longer than that of components in other domains. Thus, insecure technology is still common in ICS. However, the mentioned isolation does not exist anymore and most ICS operators have realized that to maintain availability and safety of their systems, they have to apply countermeasures which will prevent attackers from endangering the systems.

Additionally, governments have reacted to the new threats by submitting new laws which try to force the ICS operators to improve their systems' security. For example, by building security management systems and performing respective security audits. To support the ICS operators at the design and implementation of these measures, standard collections such as IEC 62443[1] and NIST SP 800-82 - Guide to Industrial Control Systems (ICS) Security[2] have been elaborated.

Among others, the standards contain measures to maintain the security management systems and to ensure their effectiveness. This includes periodic vulnerability assessments, which are typically performed via "pen and paper" approach and supplemented with penetration tests. However, pen and paper assessments often cannot rely on a detailed technological view of the system (1). The available analyzing and testing techniques applied in penetration tests on the other hand can lead to malfunctioning and outage of the systems under test (2). To avoid such disruptions, in ICS penetration tests can be either omitted or just performed on isolated test systems. The former is very dangerous, since there is not even an indication for the effectiveness of the applied security measures, for existing vulnerabilities or for system design-flaws. Thus, such issues are often first recognized, once an attacker has already exploited them. To avoid this, the common solution is the analysis and penetration of isolated testbeds [3]. Nevertheless, we argue that due to differences in configuration, state and in- or outbound interfaces of the perimeter the test systems are not identical to the real systems. Thus, this approach is generally inaccurate (3). In modern flexible plants, such rather static testbeds would even be incomparable to the real system.

Moreover, the security of a system has to be assessed and improved over its whole life cycle, meaning planning, engineering, deployment, operation, maintenance, adaptation and decommissioning of the system and its components. In terms of security-by-design this includes not only every system design but also every redesign. Such ongoing security evaluations and assessments require current knowledge about the evolving system and do not scale without proper

---

[1] https://isa99.isa.org/ISA99%20Wiki/Home.aspx.

[2] https://csrc.nist.gov/publications/detail/sp/800-82/rev-2/final.

computer-aided security analysis. To the best of our knowledge, solutions supporting these necessary processes are currently not available for ICS (4).

Leveraging new Industry 4.0 concepts, such as digital twins (cf. Sect. 3) and interoperable data exchange protocols for ICS devices, new and enhanced security applications can be realized. These applications operate on detailed technological information about the respective critical system without stressing the system's components and networks while providing comprehensive security analysis and security life cycle management. We argue that with such security applications the above mentioned issues (1)–(4) can be resolved.

In this work-in-progress paper, we introduce first concepts and results of our research regarding such security applications (cf. Sects. 2.1, 2.2, 2.3 and 2.4). All these applications rely on a computer-readable system knowledge base (i.e. a digital twin). Moreover, we describe what kind of information is needed to be collected by the knowledge base and how it is collected (cf. Sect. 2). Afterwards, we discuss similar work and applicable related Industry 4.0 concepts (cf. Sect. 3). Finally, we provide a discussion about specific issues and pitfalls which arise when such a knowledge base is implemented for the ICS domain (cf. Sect. 4).

2   System Knowledge Base

Each device of an ICS comprises different types of security-relevant information. Such information can be a device's network configuration, software details, applied security measures or available hardware interfaces. These classes can further consist of subclasses. For example, a network configuration can contain static information (e.g. a MAC address) and dynamic information, e.g open ports. Open ports relate to services which can be described with static information, like the type of a service and its version. In our concept, we let each device (further called *Device of Interest* (*DoI*)) of the ICS hold a semantically described model containing this information. Periodically or when certain values have changed, the device updates its model's corresponding values and offers this model to the knowledge base (see Fig. 1). We call this process *self-disclosure*. By building the knowledge base from this information, a digital copy of the real system is generated and maintained. The Platform Industry 4.0 consortium[3] is currently developing the Asset Administration Shell [12] which will implement such a self-disclosure strategy (cf. Sect. 3) and should ideally be implemented on every future component.

A second source of information are models sent by a user (user-based information). As an example, this user could be an engineer creating a system design or redesign using engineering tools. As output, these tools can generate a semantic representation of the designs, e.g. as AutomationML model [15] or OPC UA node set [1,7] which then embodies a model that can be taken as input by the knowledge base.

Using these two types of information, the knowledge base consists of a representation of the real system and another of the system's design. These two

---

[3] https://www.plattform-i40.de/I40/Navigation/EN/Home/home.html.

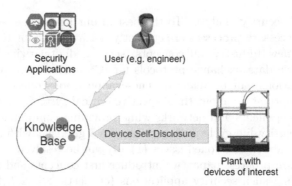

Security
Applications

User (e.g. engineer)

Knowledge
Base

Device Self-Disclosure

Plant with
devices of interest

Fig. 1. A system knowledge base interacting with different agents

representation types can now be used by different security applications. Certainly, such a knowledge base can also be used by other types of applications, but in this publication we concentrate on the security domain.

In the following sections, we describe the security applications we deem most important to provide a high level of security in ICS. All these applications exploit the knowledge base.

2.1 System Flaws and Continuous Security-by-Design

The first new security application is a vulnerability analysis tool for a type of vulnerability we classify as *system flaw*. This class consists of vulnerabilities which are not found in common vulnerability databases and are not zero-day exploits. Instead, system flaws are flaws within an ICS that can have a negative impact on its security, for example, missing security measures like firewalls, or a flawed network segmentation due to wrong VLAN affiliations, or undesired conduits through dual homed computers. Further examples are policy violations within a security zone due to firewall misconfiguration or hardware interfaces that are not allowed, but nevertheless available. A *System Flaw Analyzer* (cf. Fig. 2) can look for such a vulnerability by retrieving relevant information from the knowledge base. It can then transform this information into facts (knowledge facts) (e.g. Prolog facts[4]). The vulnerability being searched also gets described as facts (vulnerability facts). The analyzer can use these facts as input for a reasoner (e.g. Prolog) which will calculate whether all these facts can be true simultaneously. As a simplified example, the knowledge fact $is\_open(device, port)$ and the vulnerability fact $not(is\_open(device, port))$ cannot be true at once. Thus, the System Flaw Analyzer can find these issues. The vulnerability facts can consist of facts describing attack vectors, which formally describe what conditions the attack would exploit, and facts representing security policies, describing what conditions are allowed (or not allowed). This idea is mainly motivated by the

---

[4] www.cse.unsw.edu.au/~billw/cs9414/notes/prolog/intro.html#facts.

vulnerability analysis of MulVal ([11], cf. Sect. 3) which uses this approach but neither semantic models nor ICS applicable data exchange protocols.

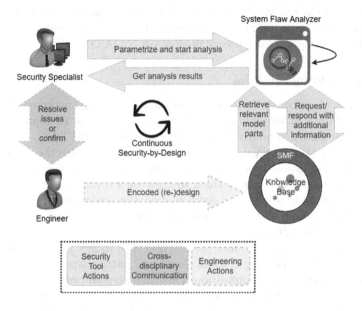

Fig. 2. The concept of continuous security-by-design

Until now the System Flaw Analyzer has only used the ICS representation. However, by adding another step of intelligence to the analyzer, it can be used for a concept we call *continuous security-by-design*, which can be seen in Fig. 2. For this, the aforementioned engineer submits the model of a partial redesign to the knowledge base. As described before, this can be created using common engineering tools. Let's assume the redesign model consists of a certain device reconfiguration, namely a new IP address (this is a very simplified example for better understanding). The System Flaw Analyzer can then be configured by a security specialist to use the main model and apply the redesign to it. Subsequently, the analyzer proceeds as described before but with one exception. Every time it requests information from the knowledge base's ICS representation to build the knowledge facts, it replaces the retrieved information with the corresponding information of the redesign. In our example, it would replace the device's current IP address with the one specified in the redesign. As a result, the analyzer would calculate on facts, representing the system as it will be when the redesign is applied. The security specialist can then use the analyzer's output to identify necessary changes and measures. He can then assist the engineer to improve the security of the redesign, which afterwards can be resubmitted to the knowledge base. This process can then be repeated until the security specialist has no more concerns about the changes. This allows a detailed computer-aided assessment of the real ICS **before** it gets adapted. Thus, in contrast to common automated vulnerability assessment concepts, our approach is able to find security vulnerabilities before they exist in the real system and does not endanger the system at any point in time.

Moreover, if the analyzed system model has the granularity of device configurations, it can even be used to (re-)configure the devices of interest accordingly, as it is already common for network devices via NETCONF [5].

2.2 Known Vulnerabilities

Another type of vulnerability can also be identified using the knowledge base, namely the *known vulnerabilities*. These vulnerabilities can be found in public databases like the Open Source Vulnerability Database (OSVDB[5]). The already referenced application MulVal [11] uses such databases. It sends the vulnerability precondition descriptions, retrieved from such databases, to the devices which use special scanners to compare them to their own configuration and state. If this comparison results in a successful match, the device notifies the MulVal main application about the match, which can then conclude that the device has the respective vulnerability.

Such applications can minimize the reaction time to new exploits and help to manage them, e.g. by keeping track of them until patches are available. Thus, it is desirable to support such applications for ICS. This goal can be achieved, when the application (e.g. MulVal) queries the knowledge base for devices matching the preconditions, instead of asking every device to perform a self-check for the preconditions. The result would contain the vulnerable devices.

2.3 System Model Monitoring

In every complex ICS, the original design and the actual system tend to diverge from each other as the time proceeds. In modern plants, this is even intended since more and more flexibility within the system composition is introduced, e.g. by Plug-and-Produce concepts [4]. Especially from a security point of view this development is dangerous, since security measures cannot be maintained accurately if the available view of the system is outdated. For example, firewall rules might not be updated correctly, when the removal or addition of a device which communicates through the firewall is not recognized.

However, when the knowledge base contains the representation of the design and the real system, a security application, we simply call *System Model Monitoring*, can compare these models to each other (e.g. on every update of the knowledge base) and raise alerts when they differ. This enables the engineer and security specialist to timely react to the issue.

2.4 Testbed Synchronization

We already argued why testbeds are important for ICS. Furthermore, as mentioned before their main disadvantage is their disability to represent the real

---

[5] https://blog.osvdb.org.

system properly. The knowledge base consists of the information necessary to synchronize a testbed with the real system. If the testbed devices support the necessary protocols (cf. NETCONF Sect. 2.1), their configuration can be updated by the knowledge base, or an additional synchronization application. As a result, tests can be performed on a testbed, which is more comparable to the real system.

There are even more security-related applications being out of scope for this paper. Examples are the context provision for intrusion detection systems, the improvements of pen and paper security assessments or the retrieval of crystal box knowledge when penetration tests are being applied after all.

2.5   Modeling Language

The two types of models, self-disclosure- and user-based, are the core of the knowledge base. Nevertheless, we did not define the modeling language which is required to create and encode semantic models. A number of languages are available to build such a model. Unfortunately, the available modeling languages either support some of the necessary semantics but cannot be applied for reasoning (i.e. they are not directly convertible into facts, cf. Sect. 2.1) or they do not support the necessary semantics but do support reasoning. However, various available ICS devices already support protocols for information disclosure, focusing on interoperability and therefore providing own modeling strategies. As an example, industrial devices often support either OPC UA or oneM2M[6], whereas for network devices NETCONF with YANG [2] is more common. Since the resource restrictions of the DoIs will usually inhibit the simultaneous existence of multiple such protocol stacks and it would be futile to expect vendors of different domains to deploy a common protocol stack only used for the here described concepts, the knowledge base should be able to communicate with the DoIs using various protocols. Thus, a transformation from different languages into a common one, which is also supported by reasoners, is inevitable. For example, our current implementation of the knowledge base is connected to the DoI's via OPC UA (cf. Fig. 3) using the protocol's own information model. The received data gets then converted into OWL 2 DL[7] to be able to perform reasoning and leverage the strong tool support for OWL 2 DL. Nevertheless, the here described concept of the knowledge base is not restricted to any certain modeling language.

3   Related Work

Critical processes within ICS will be more and more equipped with so called *digital twins* [14]. Digital twins are digital representations of their physical "twin system". They do not have to consist of simulations or visual representations.

---

[6] http://www.onem2m.org/.
[7] https://www.w3.org/TR/owl2-primer/.

```
<UAVariable BrowseName="1:Destination" DataType="String" NodeId="i=11320" ParentNodeId="i=11316">
  <DisplayName>Destination</DisplayName>
  <Description>Destination</Description>
  <References>
    <Reference ReferenceType="HasModellingRule">i=78</Reference>
    <Reference IsForward="false" ReferenceType="HasComponent">i=11316</Reference>
    <Reference ReferenceType="HasTypeDefinition">i=63</Reference>
  </References>
  <Value>
    <uax:String>anywhere</uax:String>
  </Value>
</UAVariable>
<UAVariable BrowseName="1:Source" DataType="String" NodeId="i=11321" ParentNodeId="i=11316">
  <DisplayName>Source</DisplayName>
  <Description>Source</Description>
  <References>
    <Reference ReferenceType="HasModellingRule">i=78</Reference>
    <Reference IsForward="false" ReferenceType="HasComponent">i=11316</Reference>
    <Reference ReferenceType="HasTypeDefinition">i=63</Reference>
  </References>
  <Value>
    <uax:String>anywhere</uax:String>
  </Value>
</UAVariable>
```

Fig. 3. Example snipped of an OPC UA-based self-disclosure as XML export which shows the source and destination fields of an IP Tables entry.

Instead a digital twin can consist of only a semantic model of a system. Depending on the use case, it can be composed of data with different focus. Common digital twin concepts often focus on physical or process-related data. Based on this data, applications like simulations, analysis or monitoring can be performed without having to alter, endanger or stress the real system. The knowledge base described in Sect. 2 is therefore a digital twin of critical systems, concentrating on security-relevant information.

Although network components already support self-disclosure for years (e.g. NETCONF or OF-config for Software-Defined Networking [10]), PLCs, human machine interfaces (HMIs), industrial PCs or smart sensors either do not support similar concepts or only for process-related data. However, the trend towards such technology is already visible. For example, flexible and self-orchestrated production concepts like the Asset Administration Shell (AAS) [12] and concrete protocols like OPC UA have been developed. The AAS is a concept designed precisely to empower devices to provide the service of self-disclosure. It even consists of a security view, which should provide security-related information as desired for security assessments. The amount of important industrial partners of the AAS project shows the need for such a technology and strengthens the impression that a wide range of future industrial components will support this technology. Unfortunately, the concept and its implementations are not yet sufficiently mature to be applicable for our approach. In the future, AAS implementations might provide a suitable self-disclosure solution for the here described concept (cf. Sect. 2).

Automated vulnerability assessment tools, like OpenVAS[8], have been available for years. However, most of these tools perform the same scans and penetration techniques as manual penetration tests. As argued before, these are not

---

[8] http://www.openvas.org/index.de.html.

applicable for critical systems and are therefore not further considered. More relevant approaches are explained in the next paragraphs.

The Open Vulnerability Assessment Language (OVAL[9]) is a language to encode configuration and vulnerability details for vulnerability assessments. An OVAL scanner running on the device under test, can perform automated vulnerability assessments by receiving OVAL-encoded vulnerability and related configuration descriptions from a remote OVAL main application and comparing them to its system's configuration. However, due to their local view of the device, OVAL scanners are limited to device vulnerabilities. Thus, they are not applicable for the System Flaw Analyzer concept of Sect. 2.1. Even though to the best of our knowledge no scanners and schemes exist, which can be applied to common industrial components, it might, for example, be reasonable to support OVAL as a language to interact with the knowledge base and use the OVAL Systems Characteristics Schema to describe device configurations (cf. Sect. 2.5).

A system analysis approach using OVAL scanners is MulVal [11]. MulVal is a concept which gathers vulnerabilities of devices by using OVAL scanners. Additionally, network information is captured via routers and firewalls. All this information is sent to a host running the main application. This application transforms the information into Datalog, which is a subset of Prolog and can therefore be transformed into Prolog facts directly. The same main application receives a list of rules, written in Datalog as well, which define semantics of different kinds of exploits, compromise propagation, whitelist access policies and multihop network access. As a result, Prolog can be run as a reasoner given the facts derived from the device/network information and the facts representing the rules. The idea of letting the devices provide security relevant information to a system by themselves and running reasoners on that information is similar to our approach in Sect. 2.1. However, MulVal is not designed for ICS, collects facts instead of building semantic models and the reasoning concentrates on attack graphs given the device vulnerabilities instead of analyzing the facts for compliance to best practice. In contrast to the MulVal assumptions, in the industrial domain various data formats and protocols have to be supported for information gathering, and simultaneously a variety of different applications will use this knowledge base (e.g. our security applications, digital twin implementations or inventory tools). Even though in [13] the authors claim to propose a MulVal-related solution for ICS, we could not find any evidence for that in the paper, since the solution does not consider any of the typical ICS devices, architectures or operating systems.

Further publications are available, either similar to MulVal [17], or extending it to perform risk assessments using game theory [8], or focusing on the model refinement [16]. The latter is an approach similar to our Unknown Vulnerability Analyzer concept. It conceptually leverages automated scanning, which is not recommended for ICS, as already mentioned, but can be used for our knowledge base approach as well.

---

[9] https://oval.mitre.org/language/.

A similar approach to MulVal was recently initiated in a series of IETF drafts and RFCs by the IETF Security Automation and Continuous Monitoring (SACM) working group[10]. The SACM WG describes a basic concept which consists of an OVAL-scanner-like as well as a self-disclosure approach. Currently, their work concentrates on endpoint security and the respective knowledge base is a software inventory. In addition, they do not yet consider reasoning on the captured data and do not take the peculiarities of the ICS domain into account. However, the working group is still active and intends to elaborate and specify further parts of the overall idea. Thus, in the future they might address more issues which could support the implementation and adaptation of our concept.

Model-based vulnerability assessments like [6] and [9] try to benefit from abstract models of the system (e.g. modelled in SysML[11]) in order to run automated vulnerability assessments. These approaches are not using real configurations and system states, which forces them to operate on a higher abstraction layer than our approach. Due to this abstract view, most vulnerabilities that could be identified on the knowledge base are not visible at the high level of SysML models or similar models. In other words, approaches based on such models have the issue of not representing the real system, but only an abstract plan or view of the system with no guarantees of validity. However, the strategies to identify vulnerabilities on high-level models might be useful to develop respective strategies for our concept. Moreover, it might be reasonable to use such abstract approaches in early design phases to support the planning of initial security measures and to use our approach afterwards.

4   Discussion

Since the knowledge base captures security relevant information about the DoIs, it can make the ICS even more vulnerable by providing an additional sweet spot for attackers. Hence, each communication with the knowledge base has to ensure confidentiality, integrity and authenticity of the data providing this information. Furthermore, we strongly advice that every knowledge base instance supports at least a level of security which is as high as the highest level of security provided by any of its DoIs. In addition, the same security level needs to be provided by the applications using the knowledge base and their respective environment. Moreover, the knowledge base should be hardened and tested intensively to ensure that no data can leak.

Most embedded devices currently do not support security algorithms such as en-/decryption, or signing and verifying messages. Therefore, they do not have the resources and dependencies (e.g. libraries) such mechanisms would require. Thus, our concept suffers from the same issue as the AAS, namely the infeasibility to deploy the necessary security on such devices. This sets a limit for the self-disclosure and respectively the knowledge base. To alleviate this issue, such

---

[10] https://tools.ietf.org/wg/sacm/.
[11] https://sysml.org.

devices can be reported by neighbored DoIs. Afterwards, additional information can be added by users manually to include the devices.

While developing applications using the data captured from self-disclosure, it is important to keep in mind that this data is only as trustworthy as the DoIs themselves. For some information e.g. regarding network interfaces this is actually a disadvantage of the here described self-disclosure approach which common network mapping techniques do not suffer from. However, for most information this issue remains regardless of what information gathering technique is applied.

5   Future Work

In this paper, we presented our concepts for ICS security life cycle management. For these concepts we currently implement a system knowledge base following the described approach of Sect. 2. As already mentioned, the current version of our implementation already supports OPC UA and a partial transformation to OWL 2 DL. Additionally, we are working on a first version of the System Flaw Analyzer for continuous security-by-design. This includes the evaluation of several reasoning and ontology based analysis techniques and a rich transformation from security best practices into logical statements. These implementations will help us to evaluate and improve our here explained concepts further.

6   Conclusion

In this paper we motivated the advantages of a new system knowledge base concept and how it improves and enables security applications. These security applications accomplish a level of security for critical systems which is currently not achievable. Unfortunately, currently available solutions of other domains are not applicable for critical ICS due to specific requirements, such as to attain technological compatibility to industrial protocols and modeling languages, security of the handled information, and feasibility of the knowledge base integration. Thus, we expect our current work to be essential for the future of ICS security.

References

1. PLCopen and OPC Foundation: OPC UA Information Model for IEC 61131–3. Standard, OPC Foundation, March 2010
2. Bjorklund, M.: YANG - A Data Modeling Language for the Network Configuration Protocol (NETCONF). RFC 6020, RFC Editor, October 2010. https://rfc-editor.org/rfc/rfc6020.txt
3. CPNI: Cyber security assessments of industrial control systems: A good practice guide, April 2011
4. Dürkop, L., Imtiaz, J., Trsek, H., Wisniewski, L., Jasperneite, J.: Using OPC-UA for the auto configuration of real-time ethernet systems. In: 2013 11th IEEE International Conference on Industrial Informatics (INDIN), pp. 248–253, July 2013. https://doi.org/10.1109/INDIN.2013.6622890

5. Enns, R., Bjorklund, M., Schoenwaelder, J., Bierman, A.: Network Configuration Protocol (NETCONF). RFC 6241, RFC Editor, June 2011. https://tools.ietf.org/html/rfc6241

6. Holm, H., Sommestadt, T., Ekstedt, M., Nordström, L.: Cysemol: Atool for cyber security analysis of enterprises. In: 22nd International Conference and Exhibition on Electricity Distribution (CIRED 2013), p. 1109. IEEE, Piscataway (2013). https://doi.org/10.1049/cp.2013.1077

7. OPC Unified Architecture - Part 1: Overview and Concepts. Standard, International Electrotechnical Commission, November 2016

8. Ji, Y., Wen, D., Wang, H., Xia, C.: A logic-based approach to network security risk assessment. In: 2009 ISECS International Colloquium on Computing, Communication, Control, and Management, pp. 9–14. IEEE, September 2009. https://doi.org/10.1109/CCCM.2009.5267887

9. Lemaire, L., Vossaert, J., Jansen, J., Naessens, V.: Extracting vulnerabilities in industrial control systems using a knowledge-based system. In: 3rd International Symposium for ICS & SCADA Cyber Security Research 2015. Electronic Workshops in Computing, BCS Learning & Development Ltd (2015). https://doi.org/10.14236/ewic/ICS2015.1

10. ONF: Of-config 1.2 - openflow management and configuration protocol - onf ts-016. Tech. rep., Open Networking Foundation (2014). https://www.opennetworking.org/images/stories/downloads/sdn-resources/onf-specifications/openflow-config/of-config-1.2.pdf

11. Ou, X., Govindavajhala, S., Appel, A.W.: Mulval: a logic-based network security analyzer. In: Proceedings of the 14th Conference on USENIX Security Symposium, vol. 14. USENIX Association, Berkeley, CA, USA (2005). http://dl.acm.org/citation.cfm?id=1251398.1251406

12. Plattform Industrie 4.0: Structure of the administration shell, April 2016. https://www.plattform-i40.de/I40/Redaktion/EN/Downloads/Publikation/structure-of-the-administration-shell.pdf?__blob=publicationFile&v=7

13. Rakshit, A., Ou, X.: A host-based security assessment architecture for industrial control systems. In: 2nd International Symposium on Resilient Control Systems, pp. 13–18. IEEE (2009). https://doi.org/10.1109/ISRCS.2009.5251378

14. Rosen, R., von Wichert, G., Lo, G., Bettenhausen, K.D.: About the importance of autonomy and digital twins for the future of manufacturing (2015). https://doi.org/10.1016/j.ifacol.2015.06.141

15. Schmidt, N., Lüder, A.: AutomationML in a Nutshell. AutomationML - The Glue for Seamless Automation Engineering, November 2015

16. Wolf, J., Wieczorek, F., Schiller, F., Hansch, G., Wiedermann, N., Hutle, M.: Adaptive modelling for security analysis of networked control systems. In: Proceedings of the 4th International Symposium for ICS & SCADA Cyber Security Research 2016. BCS Learning & Development Ltd., Swindon, UK (2016)

17. Zhang, S., Ou, X., Homer, J.: Effective network vulnerability assessment through model abstraction. In: Holz, T., Bos, H. (eds.) DIMVA 2011. LNCS, vol. 6739, pp. 17–34. Springer, Heidelberg (2011). https://doi.org/10.1007/978-3-642-22424-9_2

A Measure for Resilience of Critical Infrastructures

Sandra König[1]([✉]) [iD], Thomas Schaberreiter[2], Stefan Rass[3] [iD],
and Stefan Schauer[1] [iD]

[1] Center for Digital Safety & Security, Austrian Institute of Technology GmbH,
Vienna, Austria
{sandra.koenig,stefan.schauer}@ait.ac.at
[2] Faculty of Computer Science, University of Vienna, Vienna, Austria
thomas.schaberreiter@univie.ac.at
[3] Institute of Applied Informatics, System Security Group, Universität Klagenfurt,
Klagenfurt, Austria
stefan.rass@aau.at

Abstract. While risk in many areas of science and security is quantitatively understood as expected loss, resilience is a frequently used but much less formalized term. Defining the term plainly as the probability of outage appears as an oversimplification of practical matters, since precautions towards resilience typically target at impacts and may be without influence on any likelihoods of outage at all. We thus propose a quantitative definition of resilience inspired by and in alignment with the understanding of risk as the product of likelihood and impact. Our measure is based on the same ingredients as risk measures, but takes the level of preparedness as an additional variable into account. We discuss the embedding of this measure in the landscape of security risk management, as well as we point out issues and possibilities to the finding of the inputs from which resilience can be computed. A worked example illustrates and corroborates our proposed method.

Keywords: Critical infrastructure protection · Resilience
Interdependent critical infrastructures

1 Introduction

The functionality of critical infrastructures (CIs) is essential for both society and economy. Recent incidents have demonstrated that the impact of a disruption of a CI may be huge and involves cascading effects that have not been expected at first. For example, the blackout in Italy in 2003 was triggered by failure of two power lines in Switzerland according to a report of UCTE [35]. As interdependencies between critical infrastructures increase the analysis of an incident and its consequences gets more complex. Especially, the list of potential attacks and thus the list of available countermeasures will always be incomplete. Further,

© Springer Nature Switzerland AG 2019
E. Luiijf et al. (Eds.): CRITIS 2018, LNCS 11260, pp. 57–71, 2019.
https://doi.org/10.1007/978-3-030-05849-4_5

the effect of an attack involves a lot of uncertainty since it can never be perfectly predicted due to the many influencing factors that cannot be controlled, such as the current condition of CI, weather conditions or legal restrictions. In order to capture this uncertainty, we apply a probabilistic model to describe the (random) interaction between CIs and the consequences of a failure of one CI on the other CIs.

Several recent reports, for example by the Royal Academy of Engineering [25], the Lloyd's Register Foundation [18] or Arup together with the University College London (UCL) [34], have highlighted the importance of resilient infrastructures for the functioning of modern society and economy. Furthermore, the resilience of an infrastructure or network of infrastructures is an important measure, for example for coordination of first responders in case of an incident or crisis situation. It is important for the coordinator of the response action to have a realistic estimate of what infrastructures are at risk of failure either as a direct effect of an incident or due to critical dependencies. While there are several examples of how to estimate risk in the context of risk management, like the widely accepted definition in ISO 31000 [11], a similar metric for resilience seems to be missing in the literature.

Our notion of resilience is based on the estimated impact deduced from the probabilistic model as well as on the countermeasures a CI takes to protect itself (which will be described through a variable termed preparedness). Both the impact and the preparedness are risk-specific, i.e., these values can only be determined in a given context. An overall measure of resilience is then obtained by considering a collection of risks and combining the results of the risk-specific analyses. We demonstrate how to include all the parameters that are commonly associated with resilience, yet operate at a level that combines those parameters in an intuitive way, and is thus designed for suitability as a resilience management metric similar to the ISO 31000 risk management considerations. Furthermore, we will show how the relevant parameters can be obtained in a way that reflects the complexity of critical infrastructure networks and is able to take dependencies into account. We illustrate our approach with the running example of a hospital depending on electricity, water and a transportation system.

Paper Outline

The remainder is organized as follows: after a recap of the current research situation in Sect. 2, Sect. 3 introduces our model for resilience of a critical infrastructure inside a network of interdependent CIs. Section 4 shows a computational example. Finally, we provide concluding remarks in Sect. 5.

2   Related Work

Since the early work on critical infrastructure dependencies presented by Rinaldi, Peerenboom and Kelly [24], a lot of research has been carried out to better understand and model dependencies between critical infrastructures and simulate the interactions that influence the security and safety of those infrastructures. For example, Setola et al. [27] propose a model to assess cascading effects through critical infrastructure dependencies using the input-output inoperability model (IMM), D'agostino et al. present an approach based on extended Leontief models [6]. Svendsen and Wolthusen [29] propose a graph based model to understand critical infrastructure interdependencies and Theocharidou et al. [31] present a risk assessment methodology for critical infrastructures with a focus on dependencies. Schaberreiter et al. [26] present an interdependency modeling and simulation approach for on-line risk monitoring in interdependent critical infrastructures based on a Bayesian network. With a few exceptions, critical infrastructure interdependency research has been conducted to better understand risks and threats. Critical infrastructure resilience has not been the main focus of this research so far, especially in the context of organizational resilience management.

Various definitions of the term resilience exist in the literature in different areas [33], e.g., an overview on different definitions in the field of supply chains is given in [12]. In [16], Hollnagel et al. provide an excellent overview to resilience and resilience engineering in the safety context. The report presented in [20] builds on those definitions to argue about how resilience can be applied on an operational level to interdependent infrastructure systems. While significant initial work is identified, it is concluded that scientific research in the field of resilience is still in its infancy, and that the integration of institutional elements that define the complexity of real-world interdependent infrastructures, as well as the current lack of universally applicable resilience metrics, are two main factors that need to be further substantiated.

Shen and Tang [28] propose a resilience assessment framework for critical infrastructure systems. They identified three resilience capacities for CI systems: The absorptive capacity (the ability of systems to absorb incidents) the adaptive capacity (the ability of systems to adapt to an incident) and the restorative capacity (the ability of systems to be repaired easily). The resilience framework however does not rely on those parameters, it is rather based on the interplay between two random variables: The severity of an event and the recovery time of an infrastructure system. While such a framework can provide a high level estimate of resilience, it seems to lack the modeling depth required to understand the complex interactions in CI environments. Creese et al. [4] take a top-down modeling approach on resilience that allows a high degree of flexibility and modularity since elements can be incrementally refined to the required level of detail. External events can be taken into account, and the framework should encourage joint risk mitigation for a more resilient CI network. The framework is based on an identification of assets and internal/external dependencies on the enterprise, information, technology and physical layers. The actual dependency assessment is based on the creation of a dependency graph, capturing the different relations nodes in the graph can have. Resilience determination is achieved via what-if analysis based on this graph. Hromada and Ludek [19] argue the importance of the resilience of critical infrastructure systems when evaluating resilience of those systems. They state that the two main positive influences on the resilience of a systems are the preparedness of the system against a threat and the resilience of the system against this threat, and that resilience is mainly influenced by the structural resilience and the security resilience. The authors illustrate how to derive those two resilience coefficients using a case from the energy sector.

Liu and Hutchison [17] propose to achieve resilience through situational awareness. Building on a situational awareness system, the authors argue that by observing specified classes of network characteristics, a decision maker can derive counter measures for discovered problems based on a holistic understanding of the system gained with situational awareness, and improve the resilience of the network in the process. Gouglidis et al. [9] propose a similar approach to improve critical infrastructure resilience, basing the situational awareness considerations on threat awareness. In this context, a set of metrics is derived for a European utility network in [10].

Many proposed resilience models are specific to a CI sector, to a concrete use case or to a specific threat. For example, Tokgoz and Gheorghe [32] present a resilience model for residential buildings in case of hurricane winds. Panteli et al. [23] propose resilience metrics for the energy sector with a focus on quantifying high impact low probability events. Cuisong and Hao [5] propose resilience measures for water supply infrastructure with a focus on the effects of rapidly changing urban environments on the supply system. While those examples of resilience measures based on specific sectors or concrete use cases can give valuable insight into the resilience requirements of the different sectors, our approach aims to capture infrastructure resilience on a higher conceptual level, taking into account the influences dependent infrastructures have on the resilience. We argue that a trade-off between modeling depth and abstraction is required to achieve this goal.

While the resilience research so far includes both framework based approaches and use cases, none of these works has proposed a resilience metric aimed at resilience management, similar to the risk management metric proposed in ISO 31000, taking into account the risks critical dependencies pose on resilience. The advantage of such a metric is its applicability to the diverse and vastly different set-ups in critical infrastructures or complex organizational set-ups, useful to both the management of such infrastructures to be able to better direct investment in resilience enhancing measures, and to first responders to better direct and coordinate response actions in case of an incident. Such a measure should be in line with state-of-the art cybersecurity efforts like the NIST cybersecurity framework [21], or on a European level, the legislative requirements for critical infrastructures implemented in the network and information security (NIS) directive [30]. The additional effort to derive a resilience metric based on regular organizational risk management according to ISO 31000 (or other methodologies like OCTAVE [1], CRAMM [36], ISRAM [13]) should be kept minimal.

3   A Model for Resilience of a Critical Infrastructure

Definitions of resilience are manifold and mostly qualitative. Among the proposals are [20]: "the capacity of the system to return to its original state after shocks", or an amended version thereof calling it the"possibility of reaching a new stable state, possibly different from the original state", up to more recent ones [16]: "system that can sustain its function by constantly adjusting itself prior, during and after shocks" and "how the system can function under different scenarios", as well as [25]: "the capacity of a system to handle disruptions to operation" and [18]: "the ability to withstand, respond and/or adapt to a vast range of disruptive events by preserving and even enhancing critical functionality". All these understandings are sufficiently similar to admit a common denominator upon which we propose a way to *measure* the resilience of a critical infrastructure for a specific situation. Hereafter, we shall understand *resilience* as the ability of an infrastructure to maintain operation despite the realization of a risk scenario. That is, the extent to which an impact of incident affects the infrastructure on providing its input to other dependent CIs and to the society.

In an increasingly interconnected world, resilience of a critical infrastructure does not only depend on external incidents interrupting the normal operation and on available countermeasures inside the CI but also on the condition of other CIs on which the CI under consideration depends. We argue that the resilience of a CI asset can be determined by setting, for each relevant risk against the asset, the impact of the risk in relation to the preparedness against this risk. A metric that describes the resilience of an asset against all relevant risks can be obtained by summing up the risk-specific resilience metric according to the estimated likelihood of the risk. While preparedness and likelihood are assumed to be mostly qualitative measures that can be obtained in known ways in the context of traditional organizational risk analysis (e.g., expert interviews), the impact of a risk – having in mind interconnectedness of critical infrastructures – is a crucial value that heavily influences the accuracy of resilience estimation. We therefore propose a quantitative impact measure which is a simulation based and risk-specific impact estimation that takes into account the impact of critical dependencies in relevant risk scenarios. Eliciting these values is a matter of classical risk assessment and as such aided by the palette of existing standards in the area (like ISO and others, as mentioned in Sect. 2). Nonetheless, the information can partly be obtained from simulations, such as the likelihood of an incident to *have* an impact (not telling how big it would be) at all on a CI. Especially for the case of the likelihood parameter, such values are expectedly difficult for a person to quantify, so simulations can (and should) be invoked as auxiliary sources of information (e.g., [14,22] to mention only two examples). We stress that the simulation is a nonlinear model and distinct from the resilience model. The simulation is based on knowledge about the system dynamics. It provides input for the actual linear resilience model intended for resilience management. The two models are thus separate, and the simulation model can be replaced by other means of obtaining the respective parameters (if more relevant to a specific use case).

Preparedness is the entirety of the preparatory measures taken at asset A against a risk scenario s, e.g., an insurance. Formally, we quantify the preparedness by a number $P_{s,A}$ that reduces the impact accordingly (for example, by reducing the damage to a lower impact level through insurance recovery payments), and hence is measured on the same scale as the impact. In the following sections, we formalize our resilience metric, describe which qualitative parameters are required for this metric, and how the impact of an incident will later be simulated in order to facilitate the computation.

3.1   A Measure of Resilience

Intuitively, resilience can be understood as the ability to "resist" the consequences of an incident, at least to some extent. Inspired by the well known formula "Risk = Likelihood × Impact" we define the resilience of a CI A as

$$R(A) = \sum_{s=1}^{N} \omega_s \cdot (P_{s,A} - \mathsf{E}[I_{s,A}]), \tag{1}$$

where the sum is over all considered scenarios s, ω_s is the probability of scenario s to occur, $\mathsf{E}[I_{s,A}]$ denotes the expected impact for the CI A under scenario s and $P_{s,A}$ denotes the preparedness of the CI A in case s occurs. Note that ω_s, unlike the other parameters, is independent of the asset A, since the likelihood for a scenario to occur is the same for all assets, but each of them can suffer different impacts depending on their importance, structure and preparedness levels. To ease notation in the following, let us take the asset A as generically arbitrary but fixed, and omit the dependence of the impact and preparedness to ease the notation (the asset to which the values refer will be clear from the context) towards writing R, P_s and $\mathsf{E}[I_s]$ for the resilience, preparedness and expected impact (under scenario s).

We stress that for N different scenarios, the impact relates to failure, loss or other damage to an asset *conditional on the scenario to become reality*. That is, the expected impact would be obtained from simulations, where a specific scenario is assumed to happen (say, fire, earthquake, cyber attack, etc.) which causes some assets to fail which in turn affects asset A.

The result from Eq. (1) is a number that can be interpreted as follows. Large positive values of R indicate a high robustness, a value of zero indicates that on average the preparedness equals the expected damage and large negative values indicate that there is still some potential to improve protection of the infrastructure (at least for some scenarios s). More explicitly, for each risk scenario s the value $P_s - E[I_s]$ is positive if the CI A is "well prepared" against the risk scenario s, that is, the expected impact is smaller than the preparedness. Thus, if the weighted average over all scenarios is still positive (i.e., $R > 0$), we can think of the corresponding CI as being resilient. Similarly, if the average is negative the CI does not seem to be sufficiently prepared against the various risk scenarios. The definition in (1) also agrees with the intuition that a well prepared CI is more resilient, i.e., a high value of P_s increases the value of $P_s - E[I_s]$ and thus of

R. Finally, the structure of the formula accounts for the fact that preparedness has only an influence on the impact, but none on the likelihood: for example, a fire insurance reduces the impact of a fire, but leaves the (natural) chances of this to happen unchanged. This is not necessarily reflected in other related formulas in the area, such as the ISO heuristic [11] being ($likelihood \times impact$)/$status$. Herein, $status$ refers to the level of preparedness or degree of implementation of countermeasures against the respective risk. It is, however, obvious that the associativity of the multiplication would let the status hereby be treated as affecting either the impact (plausible) or the likelihood (implausible), or even both (also implausible). Contrary to this, the above convention (1) is designed to avoid this implausibility. The expected value $E[I_s]$ of the impact of a realization of risk scenario s can be estimated by the use of simulations, as described in more detail below.

Since CIs can choose their own interpretation of the scale describing its states, a competition between infrastructures in terms of maximizing resilience can be avoided because the values are not directly comparable.

3.2   Parameter Estimation

In order to obtain estimates for the parameters required for the proposed resilience metric, an analysis of the CI is necessary. While much of the required information and assessments may be derived from traditional risk assessment results, the aim of this section is to outline the steps to obtain the results specific to our approach. Our assessments are based on an identification of critical assets within CIs, and the internal and external dependencies between those assets that influence the availability to the asset. Thus, the first step in our analysis consists of representing the various CIs as a graph where each CI is represented as a node and each dependency is represented as a directed edge from the CI providing input to the dependent CI (sometimes called input provider). From this high-level representation of a CI network, each CI operator can substantiate the asset and dependency list for their own infrastructure based on their organizational set-up and on their individual understanding of the most important internal and external dependencies.

We assume that the various dependencies can be classified, i.e., we have a predefined set of "types" of dependencies (say, n different types) and to each edge exactly one type is assigned. Such classification has been used in earlier work on dependencies between critical infrastructures [24]. Example types include (but are not limited to) geographical dependencies (e.g., spatial proximity), logical dependency (e.g., a client-server relation), physical dependency (e.g., between the hardware and the software application that runs or otherwise depends on it) and social dependency (e.g., local inhabitants depending on an infrastructure and thus being affected by its outage). In our model we consider the classes "minor", "normal" and "critical" to characterize the dependencies between assets. Each class is then represented by a classical probability, i.e., a value between 0 and 1.

In the next step, the most relevant risk scenarios that influence the availability of an asset are identified, for example by assessing the relevance of specific risks from a risk catalog. This results in a list of, say, the N most important risks. This list is extended with the *likelihood of occurrence*, denoted by ω_s for risk scenario s with $s \in \{1, \ldots, N\}$. These values need to be estimated from historical data (where available) or from experts familiar with the CI. Similar to the likelihood, the *preparedness* P_s of a CI against risk scenario s can be estimated. The scale for this qualitative estimation needs to be a trade-off between giving an expert doing the assessment the option of fine-grained choice, and the practicality of an assessment. For our model, we have chosen a predefined qualitative scale from 1 (corresponding to smooth operation) to 5 (corresponding to total failure). The simulation based impact estimation, which will be described in the next section, also requires qualitative estimates. Unlike likelihood and preparedness, which both depend on the specific risk scenario, the parameters required for the impact only depend on the asset as it describes the consequences of a (partial) failure of another CI. Similarly as for the preparedness, we assume that the impact of each asset is described through a state between 1 and 5 with intermediate states indicating a certain degree of interruption of operation. For each dependency type, an assessment of the most likely state of an asset needs to be estimated, given the current state of its provider. This results in a state transition matrix for each dependency type, enabling the simulation-based impact estimation.

3.3   Impact Estimation

The dynamics of the consequences of an incident are described through a stochastic model as introduced in [14]. This model assumes that due to problems in a CI (i.e., the CI is in a state where it does not operate smoothly, which is represented by a state value larger than 1) the CI depending on it changes its state with a certain probability. In the case of a hospital, if the electricity provider faces some problems this should not affect the hospital too much due to the availability of an emergency power system. However, if this system fails (which happens with a very low probability), then the effect would be enormous, so there is a small chance that the state of the hospital is very bad (which is represented by a high value). These likelihoods of a state change in a CI due to a reduced availability of one of its input providers need to be assigned for every type of connection and every risk by experts familiar with the CI. This procedure can be simplified (and the quality of data improved) by allowing experts to only assess the values of that part of the CI they are familiar with. Furthermore, the framework can handle disagreeing (inconsistent) estimates [15] so experts are not forced to consent to a single value as representative for a heterogeneous opinion pool (thus avoiding the consensus problem). Based on this model, the propagation of an incident in a network of interdependent CIs can be simulated which allows estimating the impact of an incident (realized risk) on a specific critical infrastructure. More explicitly, it yields an empirical probability distribution over all possible impacts, as discussed next.

4 An Illustrative Example

Let us numerically demonstrate our approach by investigating a subnetwork of interconnected CIs consisting of a hospital that depends on an electricity provider, on a water provider, and on a transportation infrastructure. This example is for illustration only and based on a largely simplified case study conducted during a national research project concerned with critical infrastructure resilience. We consider the risk scenarios listed below that potentially affect the CIs providing input to the hospital.

s_1 Earthquake
s_2 Blackout
s_3 Water contamination

For our simulation, we assume that s_1 mostly influences the transportation system, i.e., its state changes from 1 to 3 which corresponds to serious problems (e.g., roads are blocked). Scenario s_2 on the other hand influences the electricity provider and causes it to change its state from 1 to 4 (that is, heavy damage but not complete failure). The water contamination scenario s_3 finally causes a problem for the water provider to some extent, so we assume it changes its state form 1 to 2 if this scenario becomes real (i.e., there are some problems with providing drinking water but other services such as cooling water should still be possible).

4.1 Parameter Estimation

As described in Sect. 3, the next step is to estimate the parameters needed to compute the resilience value (1).

Likelihood of Risk and Preparedness: As described in Sect. 3.2, the likelihood of a risk scenario as well as the preparedness against a risk of the asset "Hospital" need to be qualitatively estimated. Table 1 lists the estimates for this example, which are in a real case estimated by experts familiar with the system.

Table 1. Likelihood of risk scenario and preparedness level

Risk	Risk likelihood	Preparedness level
s_1 Earthquake	0.2	3
s_2 Blackout	0.3	4
s_3 Water contamination	0.2	3

For illustrative purposes only (and not claiming any accuracy of these values for reality), the parameters ω_s are here chosen based on available scientific considerations and reports on the respective scenarios that allows us an "educated guess". We let ω_1 (earthquake) be 0.2 (see [7] for more accurate data), ω_2

(blackout) be 0.3 (see [8] for a formal treatment of such likelihoods based on a given power supply system), and ω_3 (water contamination) be 0.2 (see [2,3] for systematic methods to get realistic figures for real scenarios). In any practical case, these likelihoods would be w.r.t. a fixed period of foresight (say, the probability of an earthquake to occur within the next 30 years). The values for the preparedness parameter can be seen as the amount of damage that can still be handled in the sense that due to the implemented counter measures operation is still possible up to a desired level. We chose values 3 and 4 to describe the situation where a CI is equipped against a medium (3) or high (4) damage. While it is often desirable to have a maximal protection, this also involves resources and monetary cost so that the actual level of protection also depends on the expected impact and on the likelihood of occurrence (i.e., no one is willing to invest a lot of effort to protect against a very unlikely risk that causes only limited damage).

State Transitions: As detailed in Sect. 3.2, we assume that the transmission matrices are characteristic to the CI (asset) we consider, but do not change with the concrete risk scenario we look at. This assumption is based on the observation that the main factor describing the impact of a (partial) failure of a provider is the condition of the CI. In particular, it depends on factors such as the geographical location of the CI or on the availability of substitutes and only to a very limited degree on the scenario that causes trouble for a provider.

To ease matters of modeling, we propose grouping dependencies into a few distinct classes, each of which can be represented by its own transition matrix. For example, a dependency of a CI X on another CI Y may be *minor*, if the outage of Y can be bridged (if temporarily) or substitutes are available to X (on a permanent loss of Y); thus we expect only negligible impact. Likewise, the dependency can be *normal*, if the outage of Y will have an impact on X that does not cause X itself to fail, but continue with limited services. Finally, a dependency can be *critical*, if X vitally depends on Y and an outage of Y with high likelihood implies the subsequent outage of X. The difference between these dependencies is then to some extent reflected in the setting of the transitions and transition matrices shown next as T_{minor}, T_{normal} and $T_{critical}$. For a minor dependency, say if there is an outage and thus Y is in state 5, there is only a small likelihood of 0.1 for X to fail upon this (as indicated by the last entry in the last row of the corresponding matrix). On the other hand, for a critical dependency, the same scenario bears a likelihood of 0.8 for X to fail if Y breaks down.

For our example, we choose the (artificial) values

$$
T_{\text{minor}} = \begin{pmatrix} 0.6 & 0.2 & 0.2 & 0.0 & 0.0 \\ 0.5 & 0.2 & 0.2 & 0.1 & 0.0 \\ 0.4 & 0.2 & 0.2 & 0.2 & 0.0 \\ 0.3 & 0.2 & 0.2 & 0.2 & 0.1 \\ 0.3 & 0.2 & 0.2 & 0.2 & 0.1 \end{pmatrix}, \quad T_{\text{normal}} = \begin{pmatrix} 0.4 & 0.2 & 0.2 & 0.2 & 0.0 \\ 0.4 & 0.2 & 0.1 & 0.3 & 0.0 \\ 0.3 & 0.2 & 0.2 & 0.2 & 0.1 \\ 0.2 & 0.2 & 0.2 & 0.3 & 0.1 \\ 0.2 & 0.2 & 0.1 & 0.3 & 0.2 \end{pmatrix},
$$

$$T_{\text{critical}} = \begin{pmatrix} 0.3 & 0.2 & 0.2 & 0.2 & 0.1 \\ 0.2 & 0.2 & 0.2 & 0.2 & 0.2 \\ 0.0 & 0.2 & 0.2 & 0.3 & 0.3 \\ 0.0 & 0.1 & 0.2 & 0.3 & 0.4 \\ 0.0 & 0.0 & 0.0 & 0.2 & 0.8 \end{pmatrix}.$$

For a real use case these values need to be estimated by experts familiar with the CI or can be based on historical data (where these are available).

4.2 Impact Estimation

In order to estimate the impact due to a risk scenario, we need to classify the connections between the CIs. Here, we classified input from the electricity provider as "minor" since the existence of an emergency power system is required by law. Input from a water provider as "critical" since substitution by bottled water is usually just possible for a limited period of time and water is also needed for cooling which is essential for the functionality of a hospital (water for firefighting is even harder to substitute). The transport connection is classified as "normal", since even if roads are temporarily blocked, aerial transportation should still be possible. However, it is worth pointing out that blocked roads may also prevent employees from coming to work and hamper food delivery, which might be a problem if the interruption lasts too long. The situation is illustrated in Fig. 1.

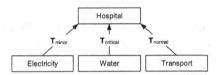

Fig. 1. Upstream CI dependencies in our hospital example

For each CI we consider five possible states where 1 represents smooth operation and 5 represents total failure (and intermediate states correspond to limited operation). For a specific risk scenario the dependency matrices $T_{minor/normal/critical} = (t_{ij})_{i,j=1}^{5}$ describe the dynamics of the system of interconnected CIs where the ij-th entry corresponds to the conditional likelihood $t_{ij} := \Pr(\text{CI gets into state } j \mid \text{provider is in state } i)$, i.e., this stochastic matrices describe the (random) consequences of the various states of a provider on the dependent CI. For a specific risk scenario s the impact of an incident on a CI can be empirically estimated as described in [14].

In Table 2, we give the empirical distribution of the impact on the CI "Hospital" due to risk scenario s_1, s_2 and s_3, respectively, based on $N = 1000$ repetitions of the simulation of the stochastic dependency.

Typically, each status corresponds to (or is characterized by) a certain impact to a CI. So, in computing the resilience, we assume a mapping from the CI status to a concrete impact value, from which we can compute $\mathsf{E}[I_{s,A}]$ in (1) by

Table 2. Simulated likelihoods (relative frequencies) for CI status under different risk scenarios

Risk scenario	CI status				
	1	2	3	4	5
s_1	0.052	0.152	0.277	0.311	0.208
s_2	0.035	0.115	0.228	0.443	0.179
s_3	0.048	0.150	0.281	0.314	0.207

weighting the impacts with the respective likelihoods. The results are shown in Table 3. For simplicity and transparency of the example calculations here, we let the impact be equal to the CI status.

Table 3. Expected impact for each considered risk scenario

Scenario	s_1	s_2	s_3
Expected Impact $E[I_{s,A}]$	3.471	3.616	3.482

4.3   Resilience

Based on the estimated impacts from Sect. 4.2 and the likelihoods and preparedness values from Table 1, we can now compute the resilience measure for a hospital depending on electricity, water and transportation facing the risks considered here. Plugging the numbers into Eq. (1) yields

$$R(A) = \sum_{s=1}^{N} \omega_s \cdot (P_{s,A} - \mathsf{E}[I_{s,A}]) = -0.0754,$$

i.e., to a slightly negative number. That is, the CI is on average not as resilient as it wants to be (represented by a non-negative value). However, if we manage to increase the preparedness against risk scenario s_1 from level 3 to level 4, we get

$$R(A) = \sum_{s=1}^{N} \omega_s \cdot (P_{s,A} - \mathsf{E}[I_{s,A}]) = 0.1246,$$

and would think of the corresponding CI of being resilient against the considered risks.

5   Conclusion and Future Work

Managing critical infrastructures is a matter that can benefit from mathematical models, but is ultimately too complex to be left to any simplified mathematical formula. Similarly as how risk measures serve as guiding benchmarks, resilience measures can play the role of pointers towards weak and strong parts of an infrastructure.

Likewise, risk can be taken as a "global" indication to *take action* against certain scenarios, whereas resilience can serve as a "local" indicator on *where* to take the action. A decision maker can thus first prioritize risks based on their magnitude, and then continue for each risk to rank CIs based on their resilience against a risk scenario so as to recognize where the demand for additional security is the most.

Simulation studies as carried out in the worked example may provide a valuable source of data for computing risk and resilience, since likelihood is often an abstract term whose mere magnitude already can create misinterpretations (the fact that people over-, resp. underestimate low and large likelihoods, as well as they differently weigh impacts is at the core of social choice theories like prospect theory and others). The measure proposed here is designed for "compatibility" with existing (standard) notions of risk, and can be generalized in various ways. The aforementioned psychological factors of over- and under-weighting of impacts and likelihoods can be integrated as nonlinear functions wrapped around the parameters in formula (1). The degree to which this is beneficial over the direct version of (1) is a matter of empirical studies and as such outside the scope of this work. Still, we emphasize it as a generally interesting aisle of future research.

Acknowledgment. This work was done in the context of the project "Cross Sectoral Risk Management for Object Protection of Critical Infrastructures (CERBERUS)", supported by the Austrian Research Promotion Agency under grant no. 854766.

References

1. Alberts, C., Dorofee, A.: Managing Information Security Risks: The OCTAVE Approach. Addison-Wesley Professional, Boston (2002)
2. Brown, J.A., Darby, W.P.: Predicting the probability of contamination at groundwater based public drinking supplies. Math. Comput. Model. **11**, 1077–1082 (1988). https://doi.org/10.1016/0895-7177(88)90659-0
3. Chaudhary, M., Mishra, S., Kumar, A.: Estimation of water pollution and probability of health risk due to imbalanced nutrients in river Ganga, India. Int. J. River Basin Manage. **15**(1), 53–60 (2016). https://doi.org/10.1080/15715124.2016.1205078
4. Creese, S., Goldsmith, M.H., Adetoye, A.O.: A logical high-level framework for critical infrastructure resilience and risk assessment. In: 2011 Third International Workshop on Cyberspace Safety and Security (CSS), pp. 7–14, September 2011. https://doi.org/10.1109/CSS.2011.6058564
5. Cuisong, Y., Hao, Z.: Resilience classification research of water resources system in a changing environment. In: 2008 2nd International Conference on Bioinformatics and Biomedical Engineering, pp. 3741–3744, May 2008. https://doi.org/10.1109/ICBBE.2008.437

6. D'Agostino, G., Cannata, R., Rosato, V.: On modelling of inter-dependent network infrastructures by extended Leontief models. In: Rome, E., Bloomfield, R. (eds.) CRITIS 2009. LNCS, vol. 6027, pp. 1–13. Springer, Heidelberg (2010). https://doi.org/10.1007/978-3-642-14379-3_1

7. Field, E.H.: Members of the 2014 WGCEP: UCERF3: a new earthquake forecast for California's complex fault system (2015). https://doi.org/10.3133/fs20153009

8. Gou, B., Zheng, H., Wu, W., Yu, X.: Probability distribution of power system blackouts. In: IEEE Power Engineering Society general meeting, vol. gou, pp. 1–8. IEEE Service Center, Piscataway (2007). https://doi.org/10.1109/PES.2007.385471

9. Gouglidis, A., Green, B., Busby, J., Rouncefield, M., Hutchison, D., Schauer, S.: Threat awareness for critical infrastructures resilience. In: 2016 8th International Workshop on Resilient Networks Design and Modeling (RNDM), pp. 196–202, September 2016. https://doi.org/10.1109/RNDM.2016.7608287

10. Gouglidis, A., Shirazi, S.N., Simpson, S., Smith, P., Hutchison, D.: A multi-level approach to resilience of critical infrastructures and services. In: 2016 23rd International Conference on Telecommunications (ICT), pp. 1–5, May 2016. https://doi.org/10.1109/ICT.2016.7500410

11. ISO/IEC 31000:2018: Risk management – Guidelines. Standard, ISO/IEC (2018). https://www.iso.org/iso-31000-risk-management.html

12. Kamalahmadi, M., Parast, M.M.: A review of the literature on the principles of enterprise and supply chain resilience: major findings and directions for future research. Int. J. Prod. Econ. **171**, 116–133 (2016). https://doi.org/10.1016/j.ijpe.2015.10.023

13. Karabacak, B., Sogukpinar, I.: Isram: information security risk analysis method. Comput. Secur. **24**(2), 147–159 (2005). http://www.sciencedirect.com/science/article/pii/S0167404804001890, https://doi.org/10.1016/j.cose.2004.07.004

14. König, S., Rass, S.: Stochastic dependencies between critical infrastructures. In: IARIA, SECURWARE 2017: The Eleventh International Conference on Emerging Security Information, Systems and Technologies, pp. 93–98 (2017)

15. König, S., Rass, S., Schauer, S., Beck, A.: Risk propagation analysis and visualization using percolation theory. Int. J. Adv. Comput. Sci. Appl. **7**(1) (2016). https://doi.org/10.14569/ijacsa.2016.070194

16. Leveson, N., Woods, D.D., Hollnagel, E.: Resilience Engineering: Concepts and Precepts. CRC Press, Boca Raton (2006)

17. Liu, M., Hutchison, D.: Towards resilient networks using situation awareness. In: 12th Annual Postgraduate Symposium on Convergence of Telecommunications, Networking and Broadcasting (2011)

18. Boumphrey, R., Bruno, M.: Foresight review of resilience engineering - designing for the expected and unexpected. Technical report, Lloyd's Register Foundation (2015). https://doi.org/10.13140/RG.2.1.5161.6729

19. Martin, H., Ludek, L.: The status and importance of robustness in the process of critical infrastructure resilience evaluation. In: 2013 IEEE International Conference on Technologies for Homeland Security (HST), pp. 589–594 (2013). https://doi.org/10.1109/THS.2013.6699070

20. Naderpajouh, N., Yu, D., Aldrich, D., Linkov, I.: Towards an operational paradigm for engineering resilience of interdependent infrastructure systems (2017)

21. National Institute of Standards and Technology: Framework for improving critical infrastructure cybersecurity - version 1.1. https://www.nist.gov/publications/framework-improving-critical-infrastructure-cybersecurity-version-11. Accessed June 2018

22. Nepomnyashchiy, V.A.: Electrical network reliability and system blackout development simulations. Thermal Eng. **62**(14), 993–1007 (2015). https://doi.org/10. 1134/S0040601515140104
23. Panteli, M., Mancarella, P., Trakas, D.N., Kyriakides, E., Hatziargyriou, N.D.: Metrics and quantification of operational and infrastructure resilience in power systems. IEEE Trans. Power Syst. **32**(6), 4732–4742 (2017). https://doi.org/10. 1109/tpwrs.2017.2664141
24. Rinaldi, S.M., Peerenboom, J.P., Kelly, T.K.: Identifying, understanding, and analyzing critical infrastructure interdependencies. IEEE Control Syst. **21**(6), 11–25 (2001). https://doi.org/10.1109/37.969131
25. Royal Academy of Engineering: Cyber safety and resilience - strengthening the digital systems that support the modern economy (2018). ISBN 978-1-909327-38-2
26. Schaberreiter, T., Bouvry, P., Röning, J., Khadraoui, D.: Support tool for a Bayesian network based critical infrastructure risk model. In: Schuetze, O., et al. (eds.) EVOLVE - A Bridge between Probability, Set Oriented Numerics, and Evolutionary Computation III. Studies in Computational Intelligence, vol. 500. Springer, Heidelberg (2014). https://doi.org/10.1007/978-3-319-01460-9_3
27. Setola, R., De Porcellinis, S., Sforna, M.: Critical infrastructure dependency assessment using the input-output inoperability model. Int. J. Crit. Infrastruct. Protection (IJCIP) **2**, 170–178 (2009)
28. Shen, L., Tang, L.: A resilience assessment framework for critical infrastructure systems. In: 2015 First International Conference on Reliability Systems Engineering (ICRSE), pp. 1–5 (2015). https://doi.org/10.1109/ICRSE.2015.7366435
29. Svendsen, N.K., Wolthusen, S.D.: Graph models of critical infrastructure interdependencies. In: Bandara, A.K., Burgess, M. (eds.) AIMS 2007. LNCS, vol. 4543, pp. 208–211. Springer, Heidelberg (2007). https://doi.org/10.1007/978-3-540-72986-0_27
30. The European Parliament and the Council of the European Union: Directive (eu) 2016/1148 of the European Parliament and of the council of 6 July 2016 concerning measures for a high common level of security of network and information systems across the union. Official Journal of the European Union L 194/1 (2016)
31. Theocharidou, M., Kotzanikolaou, P., Gritzalis, D.: Risk assessment methodology for interdependent critical infrastructures. Int. J. Risk Assess. Manage. **15**(2–3), 128–148 (2011). http://www.inderscienceonline.com/doi/abs/10.1504/IJRAM. 2011.042113. Accessed 20 Apr 2018
32. Tokgoz, B.E., Gheorghe, A.V.: Resilience quantification and its application to a residential building subject to hurricane winds. Int. J. Disaster Risk Sci. **4**(3), 105–114 (2013). https://doi.org/10.1007/s13753-013-0012-z
33. Trivedi, K.S., Kim, D.S., Ghosh, R.: Resilience in computer systems and networks. In: Proceedings of the 2009 International Conference on Computer-Aided Design. ACM Press (2009). https://doi.org/10.1145/1687399.1687415
34. UCL, ARUP: Infrastructure and digital systems resilience (2017). https://www. nic.org.uk/wp-content/uploads/CCCC17A21-Resilience-of-Digitally-Connected-Infrastructure-Systems-20171121.pdf
35. UCTE: Final report of the investigation committee on the 28 September 2003 blackout in Italy, April 2004
36. Yazar, Z.: A qualitative risk analysis and management tool-CRAMM (2003)

Earthquake Simulation on Urban Areas: Improving Contingency Plans by Damage Assessment

Gregorio D'Agostino[1], Antonio Di Pietro[1(✉)], Sonia Giovinazzi[2,3,4],
Luigi La Porta[1], Maurizio Pollino[1], Vittorio Rosato[1], and Alberto Tofani[1]

[1] ENEA Laboratory for the Analysis and Protection of Critical Infrastructures
(APIC), Rome, Italy
{gregorio.dagostino,antonio.dipietro,luigi.laporta,maurizio.pollino,
vittorio.rosato,alberto.tofani}@enea.it
[2] Sapienza University of Rome, Rome, Italy
[3] University of Canterbury, Christchurch, New Zealand
sonia.giovinazzi@canterbury.ac.nz
[4] INGV Istituto Nazionale di Geofisica e Vulcanologia, Rome, Italy

Abstract. Crisis produced by earthquake events are often dramatic for their severity and their impact on population. Damages may extend from buildings to Critical Infrastructures. Predicting the functionality of the latter after an event is relevant for the design of contingency plans, as availability of primary services empowers the action of first responders in the aftermath management. This work deploys a complex earthquake simulator (CIPCast-ES) which allows to explore a realistic earthquake event occurring in the city of Florence (Italy) by predicting disruptions on buildings and Critical Infrastructure and by designing a reliable scenario, accounting for roads obstruction due to building collapse, to be used to design an efficient contingency plan.

Keywords: Earthquake simulation · Collapsed buildings · Roads

1 Introduction

Earthquakes are relevant, endemic phenomena affecting a large portion of the globe. Italy is among the most seismic areas in the world, as being at the border between the African and the Indo-European tectonic plates [1]. This geological situation produced, in the course of the centuries, a large number of earthquakes (it has been estimated that over 15.000 earthquakes with moment magnitude $M_w > 3$ occurred in Italy in the last 1000 years [2]) which caused several victims, also due to the extreme vulnerability of the territory and of the urban settlements. The study described in the present paper was carried out to provide an estimate of the impact induced by the earthquakes on urban areas particularly with respect to buildings and road conditions after the event. Road obstruction,

© Springer Nature Switzerland AG 2019
E. Luiijf et al. (Eds.): CRITIS 2018, LNCS 11260, pp. 72–83, 2019.
https://doi.org/10.1007/978-3-030-05849-4_6

electricity outages and other primary resources could constitute severe limitations in the emergency phase and should be known in order to design reliable contingency plans. Our work attempts to provide a mean to support an informed planning for post-earthquake emergency management and improve urban development and transition toward "smartness" and security. The city of Florence was elected as a test-case due to the availability of extremely rich land data and the historical reports of several medium-intensity earthquakes occurred in the city area during the last century. The plan of the work is as follows: in the next section the model is shown with the input data used to perform seismic simulation. In the last section results are presented (for several quakes of different magnitudes occurring in the Florence city area) together with the illustration of the type of results that the CIPCast-ES system is able to produce, together with their use in the design of emergency plans.

2   Simulation Model

The earthquake simulation model referred to as CIPCast-ES, Critical Infrastructure Protection - Earthquake Simulator, described elsewhere [6–8], is a relevant component of the Decision Support System (DSS) CIPCast designed and realized within EU-FP7 Project CIPRNet and the Italian Project RoMA (funded by Italian Ministry of Research MIUR). The latest implementation of the CIPCast-ES is also related to the Italian National Program "Ricerca di Sistema Elettrico"? ("Research on Electric System"), carried-out in the framework of an agreement between the Italian Ministry of Economic Development and ENEA.

CIPCast-ES was developed to assess the earthquake-induced damage at single building level, and the relative expected consequences on the residents in term of casualties and population to be evacuated in the aftermath. CIPCast-ES works as a Decision Support System (DSS) on a deterministic base, simulating damage and impact scenarios for earthquake preliminary defined by the end-user in terms of location of the epicentre, magnitude, hypocentral depth. In this regard, CIPCast-ES can support preparedness planning and emergency management, allowing for testing alternative strategies and resource allocations. Furthermore, its results can be presented on a WebGIS interface, which was purposely developed to provide a geographical interface for complex results visualization. Basic information, maps and scenarios can be visualized and queried via web, by means of standard Internet browsers and, consequently, the main results can be easily accessible to the users and exploitable for further analyses.

The model is fed by the main earthquake data input, which can be either retrieved from the site of the National Earthquake Observatory [5] or defined by the user. The earthquake propagation model enables to simulate the dynamics of the shake waves along the terrain, which is represented in terms of a homogeneous bedrock, unless otherwise specified (in terms of amplification effects) upon seismic microzoning [13].

For this study, the CIPCast-ES deterministic approach was used to estimate, for the area of interest, the expected ground motion and related consequences, for a selected seismic event (e.g., the maximum historical event from a pertinent seismogenetic source, or the maximum earthquake compatible with the known tectonic framework). CIPCast-ES allows to evaluate the deterministic hazard in terms of macroseismic intensity I providing a qualitative description of the seismicity in relation to the damage observed on the built environment [13]. In this respect it can be easily communicated and understood by the end-user and easily handled for managing post-disaster emergencies [14]. The model allows the use of different Ground Motion Prediction Equations (GMPE) to describe the damping of the ground motion as a function of the distance from the fault rupture [13]. CIPCast-ES currently implements three GMPE, selected from a review available for the Italian territory [19,20]. For the sake of this study, the GMPE defined in [3], i.e. Eq. 1, was selected and used for the simulation for the reasons described in [13]:

$$I = 2.085 + 1.428 \cdot M_w - 1.042 \ln \sqrt{R^2 + h^2 + (2.042e^{(M_w-5)} - 0.209)^2} + S \quad (1)$$

where M_w is the moment magnitude of the earthquake, R (km) is the epicentral distance, h (km) is the hypocentral depth, S is a site topographic factor (not considered here). Equation 1 is validated for hypocentral distance less or equal to 50 km [3]. Macroseimic intensity I was given referring to Modified Mercalli scale [15]. The possibility to account for the seismic microzoning, included within CIPCast-ES, was used for the case study of Florence Municipality.

The damage that might affect a building stock, when subjected to a seismic event, can be predicted via different approaches: CIPCast-ES identifies the vulnerability functions (i.e., a function connecting the expected level of damage, expressed in some standard scale, with respect to the parameter measuring the local seismic intensity) for the structural elements [17].

For the sake of this study three detailed data-bases in GIS format were exploited, namely: Registry of Buildings (RB); Map of the Amplification Factor of the seismic wave (MAF), Road Network Map (RNM). In particular, the RB database provided information about building material, state of preservation, height, age of construction. CIPCast-ES elaborates a "Damage Scenario"?, correlating the intensity of the event with the vulnerability of the different elements in the affected area. Thus, the model allocates the level of damage to each building, according to the European Macroseismic Scale EMS-98 [9].

2.1   Road Vulnerability Assessment Due to Ground Failure

The CIPCast-ES methodology used to assess the road vulnerability to ground failure is based on the model of reference [4]. According to that work, a functionality level of a road after an earthquake can be estimated by evaluating the possible invasion of the debris of collapsed buildings on the road itself with the subsequent reduction of its available width. The method correlates the building geometry and shape with the resulting debris volume and shape.

To apply such a methodology, CIPCast-ES makes use of the following data layers provided by the Florence municipality, by the Italian National Institute of Statistics(ISTAT) and by the Italian National Corp of Fire Fighters (CNVVF):

- $\mathbf{T_i}$: building material (i.e., reinforced concrete, masonry);
- $\mathbf{H_i}$: average height of the building;
- $\mathbf{W_i}$: width of the building;
- $\mathbf{W_r}$: width of the nearby road pavement;
- $\mathbf{W_{br}}$: distance between the building facade and the nearby road;
- $\mathbf{k_v}$: average building volume reduction after collapse;

A Gaussian distribution is used to estimate the variation of the debris width W_d (Fig. 1) based on two parameters: the mean value $E[W_d]$ and the standard deviation σ_{W_d}, which can be both calculated given the angle of collapse ϕ and the building volume reduction k_v according to [12]:

$$W_d = \sqrt{W^2 + \frac{2 \cdot k_v \cdot W \cdot H}{\tan \phi}} - W \qquad (2)$$

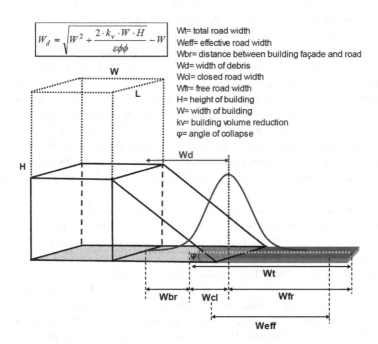

Fig. 1. Estimation of debris width and road closure [4].

Based on the earthquake simulation described in [7], the CIPCast-ES platform produces a physical damage assessment for the buildings that is characterized by the following data:

- **damage level**: for each building, a damage level according to the European Macroseismic Scale EMS-98 [9] (ranging from D1 to D5, plus the absence of damage D0);

- $\mathbf{W_d}$: the width of the debris heap resulting from the collapse of the building (with D5 damage level);
- $\mathbf{W_{fr}}$: the width of the road that remains clear after the debris fall.

In order to evaluate the road blockage due to collapsed buildings (Fig. 1), a functionality level FL, based on three thresholds FL_0, FL_1 and FL_2, was defined for each building i, assuming a necessary minimum width of 3.5 m for (ordinary, not tracked) emergency vehicles to go through:

- FL_0, when $W_{d,i} \leq W_{br}$: the road is open;
- FL_1, when $W_{br} \leq W_{d,i} \leq W_{br} + W_r - 3.5$: the road is only open for emergency;
- FL_2, when $W_{d,i} \geq W_{br} + W_r - 3.5$: the road is closed.

It should be noted that the simulations carried out by this approach were performed under the assumption of a worst case scenario, i.e. when a generic building collapses, it spreads its debris ONLY in the direction of the road (corresponding to the facade overlooking the road itself).

The information on the usability state of buildings is extremely relevant on its own: one may estimate the number of people injured or trapped in the rubbles and the number of people needing to be displaced and to whom a shelter should be provided. This helps the emergency and the rescue team to plan their intervention and immediate post-event strategies. In other words the knowledge of the state of all buildings allows to infer the damages on the population and the possible losses in the Emergency Preparedness Resources (EPR). Providing the communications are granted during the emergency, the decision maker in charge to coordinate the operations (i.e. the Mayor or the Prefect depending on the size of the event) will be provided with a list of needs and available means to deal with.

Dealing with the emergency requires moving people from inoperable houses to the gathering points and first aid centers or hospitals, goods (water, food, drugs, dresses etc.) from their storage sites to the centers of first lodging, the rescue teams from their houses to the operational and directional centers while possibly receiving further help from the external areas not affected by the earthquake. To these purposes, the road viability plays a central role. A relevant information thus consists in assessing which areas in the city remain connected, which parts are still reachable from outside and which resources are directly available in the connected areas. From the direct roads disruption and from the identification of their blockage by building disruptions, we can infer the viability of each road. In order to assess the *reachability* of the different areas, some further analysis is required (see [10] for the definition of the parameters related to the nodes reachability in a network).

In the present work, road networks are modeled in a *primal* representation [11] i.e. the nodes are the road junctions and the links are the roads themselves. A node can thus be defined "reachable" from an other when there is set of "contiguous" roads that connect them (i.e., when a car or an ordinary vehicle can move from one point to an other). In this calculation, far from crises or contingencies, one-ways were appropriately considered; however, in emergency situations, roads directionality could be reasonably omitted as, under those situations, authorities will usually remove circulation constraints to improve reachability of all city's areas.

When a group of junctions and roads is mutually reachable, but not reachable from the others, we will say that the former group represents an "island" and we will name "islanding" the spontaneous formation of such regions upon roads unavailability produced by the event.

Based on the operability of each single road, which in turn results from the stability model of buildings, an appropriate CIPCast-ES module helps identifying the resulting islands (if any) after the event and analyzing their extent and their internal situation (in term of casualties, available resources etc.). A special attention is devoted to the identification of directional centers (emergency, shelter etc.) contained in the islands, as they would be unavailable for the global emergency while remaining available to support local emergency activities.

The analysis of the islands allows also to predict which part of the city may require the support of excavators or other vehicles to remove debris and restore reachability. The percentage of inoperable buildings represents a useful indicator of damage (loss of lodging), whereas the percentage of houses in the connected component may provide a complementary index to evaluate the extension of first aid actions.

2.2   Input Data

Several simulated earthquakes were designed for the urban area of the city of Florence (Italy). This area was chosen for different reasons:

- the city of Florence is surrounded by territories (in the north-east and north-west parts of Tuscany) which are seismically active which, up to the last century, generated several earthquakes of sizeable magnitudes. This study analyses the damage scenarios generated by two historical events with epicentre location one in the Florentine area (Impruneta) and the other in the Mugello area, respectively: (i) 18 May 1895, estimated magnitude $M_w = 5.50$ (epicentre located only few km outside the municipal boundaries: 43.7N - 11.267E); 29 June 1919, estimated magnitude $M_w = 6.38$ (epicentre: 43.95N - 11.483E).
- the city of Florence has an accurate and updated (2015) building database (RB), allowing an appropriate estimate of the building vulnerability at the level of single buildings
- due to its seismic propensity and the presence of an invaluable cultural heritage, the urban territory of the city was subjected to a seismic zoning which allowed to produce an accurate map of the amplification factor (MAF)
- there were several (moderate) earthquakes during 1900 whose damages were accurately reported; this allowed us to perform a realistic data assimilation which allowed to appropriately fix model parameters.

The scheme of the simulation experiment was as follows:

- seismic data are inserted into the model: epicentre coordinates (Lat, Long), magnitude, hypocentral depth, GMPE (Eq. 1) and amplification factor;
- the simulation model estimates the diffusion dynamic of the shake wave and determines the Macroseismic Intensity I in the different areas affected by the quake, also accounting for site amplification effects;
- the model produces a Damage Map of the different infrastructures (buildings, roads, electrical network, water and gas pipelines based on vulnerability functions of the different assets [7, 16–18]);
- building collapse is produced and the volume of debris able to clutter the streets was estimated

3   Results and Discussion

In this work we limited our investigation to building disruption and its role in producing roads obstruction due to debris. The analysis thus produced a map of road unavailability (due to debris obstruction) and the consequent redesign of the contingency road-map to be used to reach the buildings identified as public shelters foreseen in the Emergency Plan.

The implementation within CIPCast-ES of the Florence case-study allowed estimating of the expected physical damage both to buildings and to the urban road network. Simulations were carried out to reproduce the effects of two recent historical earthquakes in the Florece area (Impruneta 1895 with $M_w = 5.5$ and Mugello 1919 with $M_w = 6.3$). In order to make predictions for other possible situations (i.e. different magnitude of the quakes) simulation of further (simulated) events of smaller and larger magnitudes were also performed. Thus, for each event, 4 different simulations were carried out with $M_w = 4.4, 5.5, 6.3, 7.3$. Results of major quakes are pictorially reported in Figs. 2 and 3, while a summary of the obtained results reported in Table 1 and explained in the following.

Table 1. Nr. of connected, isolated and interrupted roads after seismic event. Results obtained after different simulations for the two historical events considered (Impruneta 1895 and Mugello 1919). Asterisk* indicates magnitudes actually occurred

Epicentre	Impruneta				Mugello			
Magnitude	4.4	5.5*	6.3	7.3	4.4	5.5	6.3*	7.3
Connected	100%	100%	97.0%	86.5%	100%	100%	100%	98.1%
Isolated	0%	0%	0.6%	3.7%	0%	0%	0%	0.5%
Interrupted	0%	0%	2.4%	9.8%	0%	0%	0%	1.4%

For each of the designed test-cases, we estimated the fraction of roads that were kept operable and connected to the largest operable area. This index provides a first quantitative estimate of the connectivity of the city. As reported in

Table 2. Nr. of still reachable EPRs after seismic event. Results obtained after different simulations for the two historical events considered (Impruneta 1895 and Mugello 1919). Asterisk* indicates magnitudes actually occurred

Epicentre	Impruneta				Mugello			
Magnitude	4.4	5.5*	6.3	7.3	4.4	5.5	6.3*	7.3
Prefecture (1)	1	1	**0**	**0**	1	1	1	**0**
City Hall (1)	1	1	1	1	1	1	1	1
Fire Station (3)	3	3	3	**2**	3	3	3	3
Hospital (12)	12	12	12	**10**	12	12	12	12
Police Station (11)	11	11	**9**	**9**	11	11	11	**10**
Assistance Center (27)	27	27	**26**	**26**	27	27	27	**26**
Assistance Area (15)	15	15	15	15	15	15	15	15
Waiting Area (19)	19	19	19	**18**	19	19	19	19
Storage Area (3)	3	3	3	3	3	3	3	3

Table 1 the seismic events effectively occurred in the past (marked by asterisks) did not lead to loss of road viability (in Florence), while synthetic (stronger) seismic events are expected to lead to some 13.5% loss of connectivity. The total unreachable area results from the contribution of interrupted roads and isolated ones, that is some 3.7% of roads are not covered by debris and yet disconnected. It is worth stressing that islands are also isolated from the main roads incoming into the city. The simulations also provide a (minimal) list of roads that need to clear from the rubble in order to reconnect islands to the main operable area. This information can be used by the rescue team in order to optimise their efforts. Present simulations are deterministic, assuming an average level of debris to fall in the closest road thus representing the worst-case scenario (the real phenomenon is rather stochastic and the exact prediction of the resulting islands cannot be easily performed).

CIPCast-ES would also allow to estimate the level of damage of other infrastructures: damages to electrical wires and substations, telecommunication cables and water pipelines can be also predicted and the consequent level of service reduction estimated. In the present work, however, the focus has been given to buildings collapse only and to the consequent reduction of road functionality due to the current lack of data on Critical Infrastructure. CIPCast-ES has been tested on Critical Infrastructure damages in the area of the city of Roma where a large dataset on critical infrastructure is available.

As already mentioned, apart from the extension of the damage and reachable area, an other important information is related to the location of the EPR (Fig. 4). Table 2 reports the number of reachable EPR as a function of the seismic intensity. The number of each EPR is reported in parentheses in the first column. When, upon the quake, the number of reachable EPR is not equal to the total number of that EPR, the value is reported in bold character in the

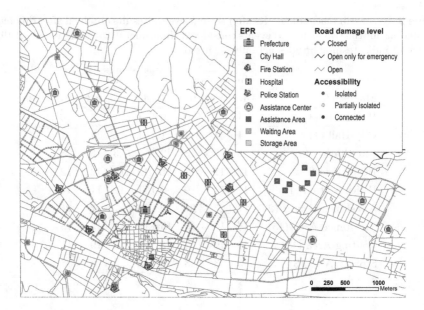

Fig. 2. Simulation result (1919 event, M = 7.3): EPRs and road functionality. The location of different EPR (symbols in the inset) can be identified and compared with the emergence of islands. The Prefecture is located in the disconnected area and it is thus flagged with a red spot. (Color figure online)

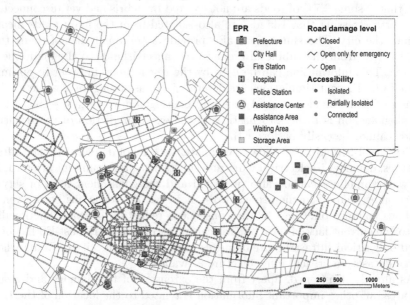

Fig. 3. Simulation result (1895 event, M = 7.3): EPRs and road functionality. As in Fig. 2 for the other event. This event produces a larger disconnected area containing several EPR (symbols with red spots inside). Also in this case, the Prefecture is located in one (the larger) disconnected area. (Color figure online)

Table. The prediction of the map of operable EPR allows to design appropriate contingency plans according to the seismic intensity. While results show that for low-moderate intensities the EPR availability is still granted, in case of stronger events (Mw>6.3) their possible unavailability and/or unreachability should be appropriately considered. Beside the contingency planning these information may also support the urban development and maintenance plans. It is worth stressing that, the Prefecture and the City Hall, which are supposed to host the headquarters for emergency management, were left operable in the real events, but they were not reachable in the simulations. This result is significant and implies to redesign contingency plans. Strictly speaking those two buildings, with great historical and architecture value, should be allocated to other less critical activities, not hosting potential centres for emergency coordination. The buildings themselves are solid and they could support also strong seisms, however they are surrounded by other buildings that may isolate them. This may significantly undermine management capabilities upon severe events.

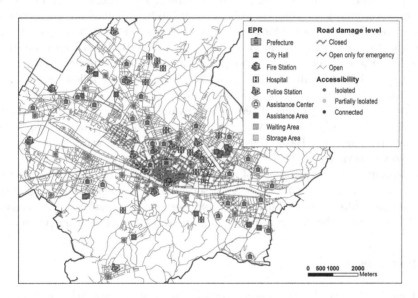

Fig. 4. Simulation results (1895 event, M = 7.3): EPRs and accessibility. Same as Fig. 3 with a larger view on the city. The event seems capable to produce a number of islands in the city center where the most of historical heritages is located. The outer parts of the city seem to be unaffected by road unavailability; this is a result which could be carefully exploited in the design of the emergency plan.

4   Conclusions

We presented novel results achieved by the CIPcast-ES simulator and a methodology to improve the management of seismic-induced crisis in urban areas. Most of the results refers to the city of Florence, imagining seismic events similar or close to the historical ones occurred in the last century; however the approach can be extended to any urban area, providing the structural data and the topology of the city are known. A deterministic model for building stability and the fall of debris on the road allows to infer operability of buildings and roads' practicability. Predicting the damages of human edifices and infrastructures allows to foresee seisms impact and plan the resources for mitigation. The present approach allows also to predict the "islanding" phenomenon where areas are still operable on their own although being not reachable from the other areas of the city. The combination of the CIPCast-ES capabilities with an accurate road network analysis upon building disruptions has allowed to produce a realistic map of the level of connectivity of the city and the reachability level of the most relevant EPR in a city after a seismic event of a given magnitude. Data assimilation with recent historical events in the area of Florence has allowed to fix appropriate models parameters (in particular for the choice of the seismic waves propagation law), producing a model setting able to provide reliable results. As an example on how the simulation results could be appropriately exploited, the prediction of a large islanding in Florence for large quakes scenarios (Figs. 2, 3 and 4) with the subsequent disconnection of major EPRs such as City Hall and Prefecture from the rest of the city should be necessarily considered in the specific contingency plan, to avoid its difficult revision in the hours immediately following the event (as it has been the case in other recent seismic events). The availability of other city data such as the graphs of technical networks (electrical and water distribution, telecommunication network etc.) and the location of their major active elements (transformer, Basic Telecommunication Stations, water pumping stations and reservoirs) might be further analysed; the expected damage of such infrastructures and the presence of a behavioral model (i.e. a model connecting their physical integrity with the level of service they are able to deliver) would be a further information which could compose a much reacher crisis scenario which could drive the design of more accurate and effective contingency plans.

References

1. Palano, M.: On the present-day crustal stress, strain-rate fields and mantle anisotropy pattern of Italy. Geophys. J. Int. **200**(2), 969–985 (2015). https://doi.org/10.1093/gji/ggu451
2. Rovida, A., Locati, M., Camassi, R., Lolli, B., Gasperini, P. (eds.) CPTI15, The 2015 Version of the Parametric Catalogue of Italian Earthquakes. Istituto Nazionale di Geofisica e Vulcanologia (2016). https://doi.org/10.6092/INGV.IT-CPTI15
3. Allen, T.I., Wald, D.J., Worden, C.B.: Intensity attenuation for active crustal regions. J. Seismol. **16**, 409–433 (2012)
4. Argyroudis, S., Selva, J., Gehl, P., Pitilakis, K.: Systemic seismic risk assessment of road networks considering interactions with the built environment. Comput. Aided Civ. Infrastruct. Eng. **30**, 524–540 (2015)
5. INGV National Earthquake Centre. http://cnt.rm.ingv.it/

6. Di Pietro, A., Lavalle, L., La Porta, L., Pollino, M., Tofani, A., Rosato, V.: Design of DSS for supporting preparedness to and management of anomalous situations in complex scenarios. In: Setola, R., Rosato, V., Kyriakides, E., Rome, E. (eds.) Managing the Complexity of Critical Infrastructures. SSDC, vol. 90, pp. 195–232. Springer, Cham (2016). https://doi.org/10.1007/978-3-319-51043-9_9
7. Giovinazzi, S., Di Pietro, A., Mei, M., Pollino, M., Rosato, V.: Protection of critical infrastructure in the event of earthquakes: CIPCast-ES. In: L'Ingegneria sismica in Italia - ANIDIS 2017 - XVII Convegno (2017)
8. Giovinazzi, S., et al.: Towards a decision support tool for assessing, managing and mitigating seismic risk of electric power networks. In: Gervasi, O., et al. (eds.) ICCSA 2017. LNCS, vol. 10406, pp. 399–414. Springer, Cham (2017). https://doi.org/10.1007/978-3-319-62398-6_28
9. Grunthal, G.: European Macroseismic Scale 1998 (EMS-98). Centre Européen de Géodynamique et de Séismologie, Luxembourg. (Cahiers du Centre Européen de Géodynamique et de Séismologie n. 15)
10. Lammer, S., Gehlsen, B., Helbing, D.: Scaling laws in the spatial structure of urban road networks. Phys. A Stat. Mech. Appl. 363(1), 89–95 (2006). https://doi.org/10.1016/j.physa.2006.01.051. ISSN 0378–4371
11. Porta, S., Crucitti, P., Latora, V.: The network analysis of urban streets: a dual approach. Phys. A Stat. Mech. Appl. 369(2), 853–866 (2006). https://doi.org/10.1016/j.physa.2005.12.063. ISSN 0378–4371
12. Harr, M.E.: Reliability-Based Design in Civil Engineering. McGraw-Hill, New York (1987)
13. Matassoni, L., Giovinazzi, S., Pollino, M., Fiaschi, A., La Porta, L., Rosato, V.: A geospatial decision support tool for seismic risk management: florence (Italy) case study. In: Gervasi, O., et al. (eds.) ICCSA 2017. LNCS, vol. 10405, pp. 278–293. Springer, Cham (2017). https://doi.org/10.1007/978-3-319-62395-5_20
14. McGuire, R.K.: Deterministic vs. probabilistic earthquake hazards and risks. Soil Dyn. Earthq. Eng. 21, 377–384 (2001)
15. Musson, R., Grunthal, G., Stucchi, M.: The comparison of macroseismic intensity scales. J. Seism. 14(2), 413–428 (2010). https://doi.org/10.1007/s10950-009-9172-0
16. Pitilakis, K., Crowley, H., Kaynia, A.M. (eds.): SYNER-G: Typology Definition and Fragility Functions for Physical Elements at Seismic Risk. GGEE, vol. 27. Springer, Dordrecht (2014). https://doi.org/10.1007/978-94-007-7872-6. ISBN 978-94-007-7872-6
17. Pitilakis, K., Franchin, P., Khazai, B., Wenzel, H. (eds.): SYNER-G: Systemic Seismic Vulnerability and Risk Assessment of Complex Urban, Utility, Lifeline Systems and Critical Facilities. GGEE, vol. 31. Springer, Dordrecht (2014). https://doi.org/10.1007/978-94-017-8835-9. ISBN 978-94-017-8834-2
18. Kongar, I., Giovinazzi, S.: Damage to infrastructure: modeling. In: Beer, M., Kougioumtzoglou, I.A., Patelli, E., Au, I.S.K. (eds.) Encyclopedia of Earthquake Engineering, pp. 1–14. Springer, Heidelberg (2014). https://doi.org/10.1007/978-3-642-36197-5
19. Mak, S., Clements, R.A., Schorlemmer, D.: Validating intensity prediction equations for Italy by observations. Bull. Seism. Soc. Am. 105, 2942–2954 (2015)
20. Mak, S., Schorlemmer, D.: Erratum to validating intensity prediction equations for Italy by observations. Bull. Seism. Soc. Am. 106, 823 (2016)

IVAVIA: Impact and Vulnerability Analysis of Vital Infrastructures and Built-Up Areas

Erich Rome[✉], Oliver Ullrich, Daniel Lückerath, Rainer Worst,
Jingquan Xie, and Manfred Bogen

Fraunhofer-Institut für Intelligente Analyse- und Informationssysteme,
Schloss Birlinghoven, 53757 Sankt Augustin, Germany
erich.rome@iais.fraunhofer.de

Abstract. This paper presents "Impact and Vulnerability Analysis of Vital Infrastructures and Built-up Areas – IVAVIA", a standardized process for the assessment of climate change-related risks and vulnerabilities in cities and urban environments. IVAVIA consists of seven modules aimed at supporting practitioners and end-users through the risk-based vulnerability assessment process, beginning with a systematic selection of hazards and drivers in their local context, and ending with a standardized presentation of the resulting outcomes to decision makers and stakeholders. IVAVIA offers a set of web-based software tools developed to support end-users executing the IVAVIA process. The paper includes a short summary of a risk-based vulnerability analysis undertaken in the context of the city of Bilbao, Spain.

Keywords: Risk analysis · Vulnerability assessment · Climate change
Critical infrastructure protection

1 Introduction

Climate change-related extreme events, including coastal, fluvial and pluvial flooding, flash floods caused by heavy precipitation, rockslides and landslides, temperature extremes, thunderstorms and tornados, winter storms, and rising sea levels [1], are severe threats to urban population centers and their critical infrastructure systems [2]. The increasingly complex dependencies of these infrastructure components combined with the ongoing trend towards further urbanization – in 2050 over 80% of Europeans are projected to live in cities [3] – make it necessary for local authorities to develop proactive crisis management strategies against climate change-related extreme weather events. One of the prerequisites for designing effective management and adaptation strategies is a comprehensive understanding of the specific risks and vulnerabilities in the local or regional context. However, not many standardized methods and toolsets exist today that enable municipal decision makers to consider, analyze, and evaluate risks and vulnerabilities under specific extreme weather events and climate change-related scenarios. A standardized approach to vulnerability assessment would enable comparison and benchmarking between cities with similar make-ups, ensure interoperability between methods and tools, enable the establishment of data standards, and ease monitoring and reassessment.

© Springer Nature Switzerland AG 2019
E. Luiijf et al. (Eds.): CRITIS 2018, LNCS 11260, pp. 84–97, 2019.
https://doi.org/10.1007/978-3-030-05849-4_7

This paper presents "Impact and Vulnerability Analysis of Vital Infrastructures and Built-up Areas – IVAVIA", a standardized process for the assessment of climate change-related risks and vulnerabilities in cities and urban environments, based on the well-established approach by the German Federal Ministry for Economic Cooperation and Development [4]. Seven interconnected modules guide practitioners and end-users through the risk-based vulnerability assessment process, beginning with a systematic selection of hazards and drivers in their local context, and ending with a standardized presentation of the resulting outcomes to decision makers and stakeholders [5].

The Intergovernmental Panel on Climate Change (IPCC) provides a scientific reference view on climate change, including a conceptual framing of climate change adaptation, in their periodic assessment reports. Since their most recent fifth assessment report (AR5), published in 2014 [7], the IPCC shifted their assessment paradigm from a vulnerability-oriented to a risk-based scheme, with the intention to facilitate synergetic collaboration between the disaster risk management and the climate change adaptation communities. They left it to the scientific communities to operationalize and apply risk-based vulnerability assessment. To this end, IVAVIA has been developed as part of the EU project "Climate Resilient Cities and Infrastructures – RESIN" [6], one of the first large-scale research projects based on the conceptual approaches of the IPCC AR5. One aim of the RESIN project in general and this paper in particular is to foster the mutual exchange and understanding of concepts between the disaster risk management, critical infrastructure protection and the climate change adaptation communities.

The RESIN project develops practical and applicable methods and tools to support municipalities in designing and implementing adaptation and mitigation strategies for their local contexts and in a participatory way. Other interdisciplinary, practice-based research projects investigate climate change-oriented resilience in European cities too: The recently concluded project "Reconciling Adaptation, Mitigation and Sustainable Development for Cities – RAMSES" [8] developed methods and tools to quantify the impacts of climate change and the costs and benefits of adaptation measures to cities. The ongoing project "Smart Mature Resilience – SMR" [9] aims at developing a resilience management guideline to support city decision-makers in developing and implementing resilience measures.

IVAVIA has been developed by means of co-creation with local domain experts from four cities: Bilbao (Spain), Greater Manchester (United Kingdom), Paris (France), and Bratislava (Slovakia). This process allows close feedback from municipal stake-holders during IVAVIA's development. Instead of the usual waterfall-model process of eliciting requirements for a new tool or method, creating a specification, realizing and implementing the tool/method and evaluating it, co-creation comprises several cycles of lean versions of this process as well as iterative development and test of the tools/methods in close cooperation with the end-users. In total, co-creation takes longer, but partial results are available earlier and the final results can be more mature.

This paper continues with introducing the background of risk-based vulnerability analysis (Sect. 2), and then goes on to describe the IVAVIA process (Sect. 3). It presents insights from two applications of the methodology in the Cities of Greater Manchester and Bilbao (Sect. 4), and concludes with a short summary of the lessons learned and an outlook on further research steps (Sect. 5).

2 Background and State of the Art

2.1 Background and Basic Definitions for IVAVIA

The overall aim of an IVAVIA risk-based vulnerability assessment is to facilitate the understanding of the effects of climate change in a local context, to identify geographical hotspots of vulnerability and risk, and to assess what impact on people, economy, built-up area, and critical infrastructure under study can be expected now and for the future due to the changing climate. This allows identifying entry points for adaptation measures and areas calling for priority actions. Also, the risk-based vulnerability assessment is able to provide qualitative and quantitative assessment results for substantiating the findings.

A risk-based vulnerability assessment utilizes a number of concepts (Fig. 1) to derive overall risk estimations: drivers, hazard, exposure, effective exposure, stressors, sensitivity, coping capacity, vulnerability, and impacts are the elements contributing to risk. Figure 1 shows the scheme that resulted from development, application, and test of IVAVIA in several city case studies. Quantitative data of suitable indicators for the aforementioned risk elements are weighted and aggregated along the black arrows. A detailed explanation of the technical methods used for normalizing, weighting (factor analysis and principal component analysis) and aggregating indicator values (weighted geometric and arithmetic weighted means) please find in [5].

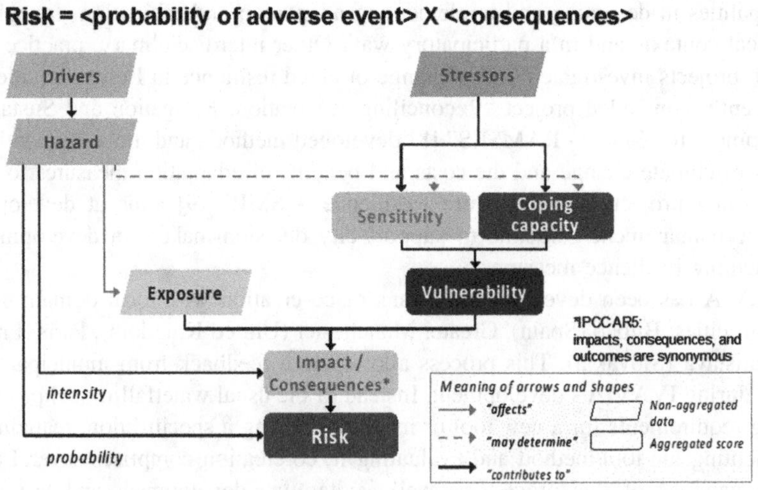

Fig. 1. A risk-adapted vulnerability assessment schema. Source: [5]

Here, a *hazard* is defined as "...the potential occurrence of a natural or human-induced physical event or trend, or physical impact that may cause loss of life, injury, or other health impacts, as well as damage and loss to property, infrastructure, livelihoods, service provision, and environmental resources" [10]. A climate-related hazard is a special case that is (at least partially) caused by climatic *drivers*. Examples for climate-related hazards include flooding, heatwave, and drought, while examples for related climatic drivers include sea-level rise, increased temperatures, and lack of precipitation.

Exposure refers to the objects or systems that might potentially be exposed: The presence of people, livelihoods, species or ecosystems, environmental services and resources, infrastructure, or economic, social, or cultural assets in specific places that could be adversely affected. In contrast, *effective exposure* describes the portion of the exposed assets that is actually affected by a specific hazard scenario, e.g. residential buildings in flood prone areas for a 100 year flood.

Non-climatic trends and events, which are called *stressors*, can have an important effect on an exposed system. Examples are population growth or change of land-use; a larger percentage of sealed surface will in general increase the susceptibility to flooding events and thus the vulnerability of all exposed objects.

Different objects are more or less sensitive to a hazard. This is captured by the concept of *sensitivity*, defined as the degree to which an exposed object, species or system could be affected by the considered hazard. As such, sensitivity towards a hazard can be perceived as a property of an exposed object in regard to a specific hazard. Examples for sensitivity include the degrees of surface sealing, age and density of a population, household-income, or elevation and density of buildings.

Coping capacity is defined as "the ability of people, institutions, organizations, and systems, using available skills, values, beliefs, resources, and opportunities, to address, manage, and overcome adverse conditions in the short to medium term" [10]. Examples include the draining capacity of sewer systems, a dike's height, education and awareness of the population, and availability of early warning systems.

Vulnerability is derived from the interplay of stressors, sensitivity, and coping capacity. It contributes directly to the impact or consequences that a hazard causes to the exposed objects.

Risk is classically computed by multiplying the probability of an adverse event with the magnitude of the expected consequences [10]. A risk assessment considers the characteristics and intensity of the considered hazard scenario, as well as the set of objects exposed to it. The probability of a hazard affecting the set of objects may be estimated from extrapolating historical data or simulation results concerning the frequency of the hazard and the development of the objects.

2.2   State of the Art

Several methods and tools for risk analysis exist. The Words into Action Guidelines for National Disaster Risk Assessment from the United Nations Office for Disaster Risk Reduction gives a comprehensive overview for the most frequently employed approaches [11].

The German Federal Ministry for Economic Cooperation and Development, together with Adelphi and EURAC, developed the Vulnerability Sourcebook [4], based on the Fourth Assessment Report of the IPCC, and the associated Risk Supplement to the Vulnerability Sourcebook [12], based on the changes promoted in the Fifth Assessment Report of the IPCC to provide guidance for indicator-based vulnerability and risk assessments. In this method, the usually massive amount of information and data about hazards, exposure, vulnerability, and other risk components is simplified by aggregating it to index scores (i.e. a number out of a full score), which are subsequently combined (e.g. using weighted arithmetic/geometric mean) to present risk levels with a single score.

In contrast, the German Federal Office of Civil Protection and Disaster Assistance (BBK) employs a multi-criteria impact and likelihood analysis based on risk matrices, an instrument that is also promoted as an ISO standard [13]. In this approach, impacts and probabilities of hazard scenarios are estimated (e.g. based on historical data or simulation models) and classified by defining threshold values for the different impact/probability classes, i.e. in which value range do potential impacts/probabilities have to lie to be classified in a certain way. Typically, risk matrices have four to seven impact classes and a similar number of probability classes. For any combination of impact and probability, a risk level or class (BBK: very high, high, intermediate, low) is determined. Both determining the thresholds and assigning risk levels requires political decisions that have to be taken with extreme care. It requires deciding when a certain number of fatalities is regarded as 'moderate' or 'significant' and which risk level requires which type of reaction, or, more simply put, which risk level is acceptable and which is not. This may constitute one of the most problematic steps of the risk analysis process.

If no (or not enough) information or means for carrying out an indicator-based multi-criteria analysis is available, expert elicitation approaches might be employed. Here, individuals with a good understanding of the various components of disaster risk components of the area under study conduct a qualitative analysis using their expert judgements. The Risk Systemicity Questionnaire developed during the Smart Mature Resilience project [14] and the UNISDR Disaster Resilience Scorecard for Cities [15] are recently developed expert elicitation approaches. Both employ spreadsheet- and/or web-based questionnaires to elicit knowledge from experts and combine the gathered information into comprehensive overviews, e.g. by assigning scores to predefined answers and visualizing them using spider charts.

The IVAVIA risk-based vulnerability assessment methodology is based on the indicator-based method from the original Vulnerability Sourcebook and combines this approach with the multi-criteria impact and likelihood analysis by the BBK.

3   A Process for Impact and Vulnerability Analysis of Vital Infrastructures and Built-Up Areas

The IVAVIA process consists of seven modules in three stages (Fig. 2): the qualitative stage, the quantitative stage, and the presentation of the outcome. Each module consists of three to six individual steps. These modules and their steps establish a structure for the whole process and make it more manageable for end-users. Following the whole sequence of seven modules is not mandatory. If an end-user is an expert in vulnerability assessments or already has available material from a previous assessment, lacks resources to conduct a complete assessment, or wants to use different approaches to specific steps, they may opt for customizing IVAVIA and its modules to their needs.

	Which hazards and drivers are relevant to my city?	M0	Systematically selecting hazards, drivers, and stressors
	How do I start the assessment process?	M1	Preparing for the vulnerability assessment
Qualitative stage	What are the cause-effect relationships relevant to my city?	M2	Developing impact chains
Quantitative stage	How do I want to measure and what data do I have available?	M3	Identifying indicators and data acquisition
	How to I want to calculate?	M4	Normalisation, weighting, and aggregation of indicators
	How do I assess vulnerability/risk?	M5	Aggregating vulnerability components to risk
Presentation	How do I present the results?	M6	Presenting the outcome of IVAVIA

Fig. 2. Steps of the risk-based vulnerability assessment process IVAVIA

Each step of the module descriptions contains information about input needed and output to be created. For a full qualitative and quantitative assessment, an end user should execute the modules in the given sequence, as each module generates input for the following ones. For a qualitative assessment only, the process has only to be run up to Module 2. In general, the amount of resources necessary for the assessment process varies widely, depending on the size of the studied area and the requested depth and scope of the evaluation.

The modules and steps are described in detail in the IVAVIA Guideline document [16] addressed to local decision makers, with the more technical details of the process and reference information being covered by the IVAVIA Guideline Appendix.

3.1   Qualitative Stage

Module M0, "Systematically selecting hazards, drivers, and stressors", starts off the process with a systematic analysis and selection of hazards, drivers, and stressors relevant to the region or urban area under examination. This serves as a base for the detailed planning of the assessment and ensures that the limited resources and budgets are spent on the most pressing current and future hazards, and that no threats or possible dependencies between different hazards are overlooked. In addition, a thorough documentation of the rationale for selecting hazards, drivers, and stressors ensures that future (re-)assessments can follow the same methodology, thus enabling result comparison. Module M0 consists of the following steps: (0.1) Identify the hazards considered potentially relevant; (0.2) Gather information on the identified hazards; (0.3) Identify generally relevant drivers and stressors; and (0.4) Kick-off meeting and management decisions.

As part of **Module M1**, "Preparing for the vulnerability assessment", a common taxonomy is defined and communicated, and the overall objectives, scopes, participants and their roles and responsibilities, as well as the target audiences have to be defined in agreement and, ideally, in cooperation with the relevant stakeholders. M1 also serves to identify and gather relevant information to form a detailed implementation plan. The information needed for this step includes a list of relevant stakeholders including both institutions and individuals, measures and strategies that are already in place or to be considered (e.g. sector strategies, community or national development plans, and ongoing adaptation measures), climatic, socio-economic, and sectoral information to be included, and a list of climate and city development scenarios to be examined. Module M1 consists of the following steps: (1.1) Understand the context of the risk-based vulnerability assessment; (1.2) Identify the objectives and expected outcomes; (1.3) Determine the scope of the assessment; (1.4) Develop the scenario settings; and (1.5) Prepare a work plan.

Based on this foundation for the vulnerability assessment, impact chains (Fig. 3) are developed as part of **Module M2**, "Developing impact chains" (for a more detailed description see [17]). These impact chains describe cause-effect-relationships between the elements that contribute to the consequences of a given combination of hazard and the exposed objects. Each element of an impact chain is to be described in a qualitative way by specifying attributes. Usually, impact chain diagrams are developed during collaborative workshops with domain experts. As a result, impact chains are not exhaustive, but describe the common understanding of these experts. An important rule of thumb is: keep it simple! Typically, the assessment starts with selecting a combination of hazard and exposed object, like hazard "pluvial flooding" and exposure "road transport". The more of such relevant combinations are assessed, the more

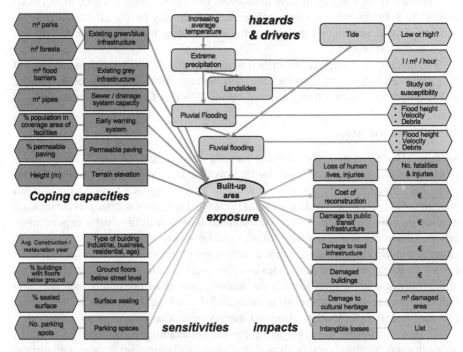

Fig. 3. Impact chain sample for the hazard-exposure combination "flooding on built-up area" in the city of Bilbao. Hazards & drivers in blue, exposed object in grey, coping capacity in green-blue, sensitivity in green, and impacts in orange. Hexagons: indicator dimensions (Source: [5]) (Color figure online)

comprehensive the assessment. Module M2 consists of five individual steps: (2.1) Determine exposure and hazard combinations; (2.2) Identify specific drivers and stressors; (2.3) Determine sensitivity; (2.4) Determine coping capacity; and (2.5) Identify potential impact.

3.2 Quantitative Stage

Module M3, "Identifying indicators and data acquisition", describes the identification and definition of measurable indicators for identified elements of the generated impact chains. The indicator identification and data collection steps are highly dependent on each other. The availability of data is of critical importance for the quantitative stage: Without a feasible way for data acquisition, the best indicator would be inoperable. To this end, it is important to include domain experts with extensive knowledge about data availability. To ease the indicator selection process, established directories of standard indicators should be employed, for example, the annex of the Vulnerability Sourcebook ([4], pp. 14–17) or the annex of the Covenant of Mayors for Climate and Energy Reporting Guidelines ([18], pp. 61–67). Module M3 consists of six operational steps: (3.1) Select indicators; (3.2) Check if the selected indicators are suitable; (3.3) Gather data; (3.4) Check data quality; (3.5) Manage data; and (3.6) Calculate indicator values.

Communicating a multitude of complex, multi-dimensional indicators in a comprehensive way is extremely complicated. Therefore, the calculated indicator values should be normalized (e.g. via min-max normalization [19]), weighted, and aggregated (e.g. using weighted arithmetic mean [19]) to composite scores for different risk components. These issues are addressed in the course of **Module M4**, "Normalization, weighting, and aggregation of indicators". The calculated indicator values often employ different measurement units and scales, and thus cannot be aggregated into composite scores without being normalized. The selected indicators may not necessarily have equal influence on their corresponding risk component, which should be reflected by assigning weights to them when combining them into composite scores. Module M4 consists of four steps: (4.1) Determine the scale of measurement; (4.2) Normalize coping capacity and sensitivity indicator values; (4.3) Weight coping capacity and sensitivity indicators; and (4.4) Aggregate coping capacity and sensitivity indicators.

Module M5, "Aggregating vulnerability components to risk", covers the actual risk assessment, which is based on the well-established risk analysis process by the German Federal Office of Civil Protection and Disaster Assistance [13], assuring organizational, legal, and political interoperability. In this approach, impacts and probabilities are classified using discrete, ordinal classes (e.g. "insignificant", "minor", or "disastrous" for impacts and "very unlikely", "likely", and "very likely" for probabilities). The resulting impacts and probability pairs, i.e. the risk scores, are then assigned to discrete, ordinal risk classes using a risk matrix. This matrix has one axis for the impact classes and one axis for the probability classes, and thus defines risk classes for every combination of the two. Module M5 consists of six steps: (5.1) Calculate vulnerability scores; (5.2) Define classification scheme; (5.3) Estimate hazard intensity and probability; (5.4) Determine coping capacity; (5.5) Estimate impacts and consequences; and (5.6) Validate results.

3.3 Presentation

The last **Module M6**, "Presenting the outcome of IVAVIA", concerns the systematic presentation of outcomes to all relevant stakeholders and funding bodies, including external risk analysis experts to assure external result validation. Best practices are shared, and supporting material, i.e. report and presentation templates are being provided, as well as graphs exported by the developed software tools. M6 consists of three steps: (6.1) Plan your report; (6.2) Describe the undertaken assessment process; and (6.3) Illustrate the findings. With the successful conclusion of Module M6 the risk-based vulnerability analysis process is complete. Building on this base the municipal stakeholders can now go on to systematically plan, and then finally implement, adaptation measures.

3.4 Climate Change-Related Risk to Critical Infrastructures

(Critical) Infrastructure (CI) can be addressed with IVAVIA in the following ways: As practiced in several RESIN city case studies, CI can be the exposed object (exposure), that is, it is the immediate subject of the analysis. IVAVIA then results in an overall risk and vulnerability of the investigated CI with regard to consequences of climate change. This result can also be used in more comprehensive risk analyses in the areas of Critical Infrastructure Protection and Resilience (CIP/CIR).

Impacts of consequences of climate change on CI may also be addressed in the investigation of impacts as element of impact chains. Here, primary impacts and secondary impacts can be analyzed by methods developed in the CIPRNet project [20]. Secondary impacts may include cascading effects on other, dependent CI and socio-economic impacts as identified in the European Directive on CIP [21].

Semi-quantitative methods for analyzing climate change-related risk, which are not part of IVAVIA, may yield additional information on climate change-related risk to CI. For instance, an overlay of a flood risk map and a map of a transport network (road, railway, public transport) may identify risk hot spots of climate change-related risk to spatially constrained parts of the transport network.

In the case studies to be presented in the next section, thirteen assessments using IVAVIA have been performed, covering the hazards fluvial and pluvial flooding, heat waves, and drought. Three assessments investigated resulting risk for health and the quality of life of citizens, three other assessments investigated resulting risk for green infrastructure and built infrastructure, and two assessments investigated resulting risk for high rise buildings and their users. A total of five assessments investigated resulting risk for critical infrastructure. In these cases, the exposed CI included city traffic infrastructure, a major arterial road in one city, the Paris metro, blackout caused by fluvial flooding on high rise buildings in general and more specifically on sensitive buildings (governmental buildings, embassies, jails, banks, museums etc.).

4 Analyzing Risks and Vulnerabilities Regarding Climate Change for Two Cities

4.1 Risk Assessment for the City of Greater Manchester, UK

The assessment for the City of Greater Manchester had the goal to develop impact chains for two different infrastructures and thus comprised only the qualitative part of the IVAVIA process. Local stakeholders, who worked on climate resilience and relevant critical infrastructure as well as RESIN research partners developed these impact chains during two workshops in Greater Manchester.

The first impact chain focused on the effects of an extended period of hot dry weather on green infrastructure, while the second impact chain focused on the effects of fluvial flooding on a major arterial road.

Figure 4 shows the second impact chain and illustrates how cascading effects from failure of a critical infrastructure component can be modeled via cascading impacts. Here, the road closure due to flooding results in impacts to network managers, infrastructure, road users, and the city as a whole, e.g. in form of impacts to maintenance procedures, a shift in transport mode choice, the necessity of emergency services,

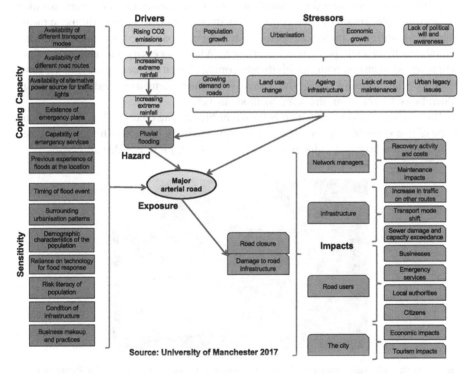

Fig. 4. Impact chain sample for the hazard-exposure combination "pluvial flooding on a major arterial road" in the City of Greater Manchester. Hazards & drivers in blue, exposed object in grey, coping capacity in green-blue, sensitivity in green, and impacts in orange. Both stressors and impacts included cascading effects (Source: University of Manchester/RESIN) (Color figure online)

and overall economic impacts. Based on the identification of these factors, the city and its local research partners conducted a semi-quantitative and quantitative risk assessments, which did not follow the IVAVIA approach.

4.2   Risk Assessment for the City of Bilbao, Spain

For the City of Bilbao three impact chains were developed during a workshop with relevant stakeholders and RESIN research partners. These impact chains covered the effects of heatwaves on public health, extreme precipitation on road traffic infrastructure, and flooding on built-up infrastructure (see Fig. 3).

To conduct the assessments for these impact chains, the Bilbao City council provided city wide spatial data for all sensitivity and coping capacity indicators and, where possible, also historic data related to the defined impacts. The spatial data included, for example, the distribution of parks and forests across the city, building location, construction/restauration year, and number of floors, as well as position, length, and diameter of sewer pipes. Where necessary the provided data was further processed (e.g. lengths and diameters of pipes where used to calculate volume) before being further processed to calculate indicator values. Subsequently, the indicator values where normalized to a scale from 0 ('optimal') to 1 ('critical') using min-max normalization and aggregated to sensitivity and coping capacity scores via weighted arithmetic mean. Weights for different indicators were chosen by the partners from the Bilbao city council based on their perceived importance. Where necessary the indicator values were reversed to ensure both sensitivity and coping capacity scores increase in the same direction. The resulting composite scores were then normalized and aggregated to vulnerability scores using the same methods as before.

The resulting vulnerability map is shown in Fig. 5. The colors in Fig. 5 correspond to one of five vulnerability levels (very low, low, medium, high, very high), determined by dividing the potential vulnerability range ('0' to '1') into equidistant classes.

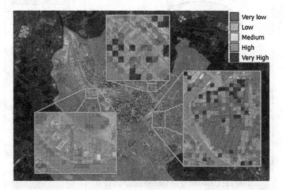

Fig. 5. Left: Vulnerability map of Bilbao for flooding in built-up areas. (Color figure online)

Based on these results, risks were calculated for a 500 year flood. To this end, the Bilbao City council provided flood maps, with information about flooded area, flood velocity, and flood depth. This information was used to identify exposed built-up infrastructure and estimate expected worst-case impacts for all impact categories defined in the impact chain using flood depth-damage functions (see [22] and [23]). These functions combine flood depth and velocity to derive damage values (e.g. residential building damage per m^2), which were combined with the actual exposed objects (e.g. the surface area of residential buildings situated in flooded areas) and multiplied by the vulnerability scores to arrive at expected impacts for every cell.

Finally, the expected impacts as well as the local flood probability for all cells were classified using discrete classes and combined into risk levels according to the risk analysis approach by the BBK [13]. Figure 6 shows the resulting risk levels for material impacts in Bilbao. The colors in Fig. 6 correspond to one of the four different risk levels defined by the BBK approach. In order to not equate losses of human lives and (monetary) material damages, the categorization differentiated between material impacts (e.g. residential, commercial, and industrial building damages) and human impacts (e.g. fatalities and injuries).

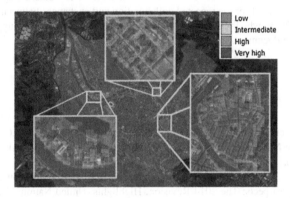

Fig. 6. Right: Material risk map of Bilbao for flooding in built-up areas (Color figure online)

5   Conclusion

This paper presented "Impact and Vulnerability Analysis of Vital Infrastructures and Built-up Areas – IVAVIA", a standardized process for the assessment of climate change related risks and vulnerabilities in cities and urban environments. It shared some background on the concepts behind risk-based vulnerability assessments. Notably, IVAVIA realizes the paradigm shift in the IPCC Assessment Report 5 [7] towards risk-based assessment, proposed as to get more in line with concepts in the Disaster Risk Reduction (and CIP) communities. The paper described the seven interconnected modules constituting the IVAVIA process, presented the set of software tools developed to support end-users in the course of the IVAVIA process, and shared some experiences gained while executing a risk-based vulnerability analysis for the city of Bilbao, Spain. As demonstrated by applying IVAVIA on the municipalities Bilbao,

Greater Manchester, Paris, and Bratislava, the process is a feasible means to analyze risks and vulnerabilities regarding the impact of climate change in local urban contexts. While supporting its end-users with practical guidance, IVAVIA is flexible enough to be applicable to urban areas of different size and organization, and suffering from different combinations of hazards. In further steps, the case studies will be completed, enabling further validation of the process and tool set, and helping to ensure applicability for end-users.

Acknowledgments. The authors thank their partners in the RESIN consortium for their valuable contributions during the development and test process. This paper is based in part upon work in the framework of the project "RESIN – Climate Resilient Cities and Infrastructures". This project has received funding from the European Union's Horizon 2020 research and innovation program under grant agreement no. 653522. The sole responsibility for the content of this publication lies with the authors. It does not necessarily represent the opinion of the European Union. Neither the EASME nor the European Commission are responsible for any use that may be made of the information contained therein.

We would like to thank Till Below (GIZ) and Stefan Schneiderbauer (Eurac) as representatives of the colleagues in their organizations who have created the "The Vulnerability Sourcebook" in 2014. We are also grateful for the repeated collaboration and exchanges between GIZ, Eurac and Fraunhofer since 2016, which contributed to shaping both the Sourcebook supplement and the IVAVIA Guideline document.

References

1. Rossetti, M.A.: Potential impacts of climate change on railroads. In: Workshop on the Potential Impacts of Climate Change on Transportation, Washington, D.C. (2002)
2. Coletti, A., De Nicola, A., Villani, M.L.: Building climate change into risk assessment. Nat. Hazards **84**(2), 1307–1325 (2016)
3. United Nations, Department of Economic and Social Affairs, Population Division: World Urbanization Prospects: The 2014 Revision, Highlights. United Nations, New York (2014)
4. German Federal Ministry for Economic Cooperation and Development: The Vulnerability Sourcebook. Concept and guidelines for standardised vulnerability assessments. Deutsche Gesellschaft für Internationale Zusammenarbeit, Bonn and Eschborn, Germany (2014)
5. Rome, E., et al.: IVAVIA guideline, annex to deliverable D2.3 realisation and implementation of IVAVIA. EU H2020 Project RESIN, Sankt Augustin, Germany (2017)
6. RESIN – Climate Resilient Cities and Infrastructures. http://www.resin-cities.eu/. Accessed 11 Nov 2017
7. Intergovernmental Panel on Climate Change (IPCC): Summary for Policymakers. In: Climate Change 2014. Part A: Global and Sectoral Aspects, pp. 1–32. Cambridge University Press, Cambridge, United Kingdom, and New York, NY, USA (2014)
8. RAMSES – Reconciling adaptation, mitigation and sustainable development for cities. http://www.ramses-cities.eu/. Accessed 05 Dec 2017
9. SMR – Smart Mature Resilience. http://smr-project.eu. Accessed 05 Dec 2017
10. IPCC. Annex II: Glossary, in: Climate Change: Synthesis Report. IPCC, Geneva, Switzerland, pp. 117–130 (2014)
11. United Nations Office for Disaster Risk Reduction: "National Disaster Risk Assessment", Words into Action Guidelines, UNISDR (2017)

12. German Federal Ministry for Economic Cooperation and Development: "Risk Supplement to the Vulnerability Sourcebook. Guidance on how to apply the Vulnerability Sourcebook's approach with the new IPCC AR5 concept of climate risk", Deutsche Gesellschaft für Internationale Zusammenarbeit, Bonn, Germany (2017)
13. German Federal Office of Civil Protection and Disaster Assistance: "Method of Risk Analysis for Civil Protection". Wissenschaftsforum 8 (2011)
14. Pyrko, I., Howick, S., Eden, C.: Risk systemicity and city resilience. In: EURAM 2017. University of Strathclyde, 21–24 June 2017
15. United Nations Office for Disaster Risk Reduction: "Disaster Resilience Scorecard for Cities", UNISDR (2017)
16. Rome, E., et al.: IVAVIA Guideline – Impact and Vulnerability Analysis of Vital Infrastructures and built-up Areas (plus Appendix). EU H2020 Project RESIN publication, Fraunhofer, Sankt Augustin, Germany, Revision 3.0, 15 June 2018
17. Lückerath, D., et al.: The RESIN climate change adaptation project and its simple modeling approach for risk-oriented vulnerability assessment. In: Proceedings of ASIM-Workshop STS/GMMS 2018, ARGESIM Report 54, ARGESIM/ASIM Pub., Vienna, Austria, pp. 21–26 (2018)
18. Neves, A., et al.: The Covenant of Mayors for Climate and Energy Reporting Guidelines, EUR 28160 EN (2016). https://doi.org/10.2790/586693
19. Organisation for Economic Co-operation and Development (OECD): Handbook on constructing composite indicators: methodology and user guide. Technical Report, OECD Publishing, Paris (2008)
20. Rome, E., Doll, T., Rilling, S., Sojeva, B., Voß, N., Xie, J.: The use of what-if analysis to improve the management of crisis situations. In: Setola, R., Rosato, V., Kyriakides, E., Rome, E. (eds.) Managing the Complexity of Critical Infrastructures. SSDC, vol. 90, pp. 233–277. Springer, Cham (2016). https://doi.org/10.1007/978-3-319-51043-9_10
21. European Council: Council Directive 2008/114/EC of 8 December 2008: Identification and designation of European critical infrastructures and the assessment of the need to improve their protection. Technical report, Official Journal of the European Union, (L 345/75) (2008)
22. Huizinga, J., de Moel, H., Szewczyk, W.: Global flood depth-damage functions. Methodology and the database with guidelines. EUR 28552 EN (2017). https://doi.org/10.2760/16510
23. Kok, M., Huizinga, H.J., Vrouwenvelder, A.C.W.M., Barendregt, A.: Standard method 2004. Damage and casualties caused by flooding. Highway and Hydraulic Engineering Department (2004)

Securing Internet of Things and Industrial Control Systems

SMuF: State Machine Based Mutational Fuzzing Framework for Internet of Things

Neeraj Karamchandani[1], Vinay Sachidananda[2], Suhas Setikere[2(✉)],
Jianying Zhou[2], and Yuval Elovici[2]

[1] Pennsylvania State University, State College 16801, USA
njk5270@cse.psu.edu
[2] iTrust, Singapore University of Technology and Design, Singapore, Singapore
{sachidananda,suhas_setikere,jianying_zhou,yuval_elovici}@sutd.edu.sg

Abstract. The Internet of Things (IoT) exposes vulnerabilities at various levels. In this paper, we propose a mutation-based fuzzing framework called SMuF in order to find various vulnerabilities in IoT devices. We harness the power of state machine to generate distinct states of a protocol. In addition, we also generate legitimate packets as levels and sub-levels to intelligently mutate the data fields in the packet. Our mutation technique lies in mutation based on location, context and time. We propose a probability score for selecting the inputs for fuzzing based on payload length. We implemented and evaluated the proposed framework in our IoT security testbed. Using SMuF, we have discovered various vulnerabilities such as Denial of Service (DoS), Buffer Overflow, Session Hijacking etc.

Keywords: IoT security · Mutational fuzzing · Vulnerability discovery

1 Introduction

Internet of things (IoT) is an exponentially growing field. Accordingly, IoT is experiencing huge security and privacy challenges [26]. From the recent study conducted in 2017, more than 57% of the companies have adopted IoT technology and 84% have already experienced an IoT related security breach [13]. A study by HP [12] in 2015 found out that most of IoT devices had one or more significant vulnerabilities.

In this regard, we perform security analysis by choosing fuzzing as our technique. Fuzzing is an age-old concept, first used to detect vulnerabilities in UNIX utilities [3]. Fuzzing is an automated software testing technique in which invalid, unexpected or random data is provided as an input to a target system/program so as to get a crash or an exception which can potentially lead to a vulnerability. Although fuzzing technique is random and straightforward, its benefit-cost ratio is very high. Thus, it is more efficient than other standard techniques and is often used with other proven debugging and testing methods like black-box

© Springer Nature Switzerland AG 2019
E. Luiijf et al. (Eds.): CRITIS 2018, LNCS 11260, pp. 101–112, 2019.
https://doi.org/10.1007/978-3-030-05849-4_8

testing, beta-testing, etc. Fuzzing can be done in random, mutational or generational fashion. In our work, we adapt mutation fuzzing method. Mutation-based fuzzers are very effective when dealing with unstructured inputs [15].

In the current state-of-the-art, there are several fuzzers such as American Fuzzy Lop [23], Peach [20], Sulley [2], Radamsa [16], etc. Most of the current works focus on the type of inputs rather than the sequence. One of the challenging tasks of developing an IoT protocol fuzzer involves generation of inputs for IoT-related protocols.

In most of the cases, the target rejects inputs due to various factors such as semantics, data-types, illegal sequences, protocol fields, etc., since it does not adhere to the target's input specifications. The current mutation techniques related to fuzzing lack consideration for location, context and time [20]. Most of the fuzzers mutate blindly and often lack a mutation strategy that is usually random or based just on the structure. The assumption that every mutation has a higher probability of generating a crash does not hold true and leads to inefficient fuzzing.

In order to fill this gap, our goal is to propose a framework called SMuF (**S**tate Machine based **Mu**tational **F**uzzing Framework for Internet of Things) for fuzzing IoT protocols. Our design focuses on input mutation which remains orthogonal to the traditional mutation based fuzzer. Based on our goal, first, in our work, we use state machine to understand and generate various states and paths of a protocol. Our technique makes sure that the state machine of the protocol can fuzz all the possible protocol paths. Next, we determine the various fields of the protocol and generate legitimate protocol packets.

Second, we propose a mutation technique which focuses on mutating certain locations of the input, context of the data being carried and mutating based on time. This makes our fuzzing method more efficient. Location-based mutation will be able to mutate particular fields which will still be legitimate enough to be able to reach the target. For example, we will not mutate fields like a checksum or target IP addresses. Moreover, mutating the context will help us in identifying privacy leakage when an IoT device is not able to distinguish between two different types of data carrying different context. Mutating based on time will involve mutating time-related factors including the rate of sending packets, TTL of the packet and so on. This will be helpful in detecting race time-related vulnerabilities. Next, just not limiting on approach of mutation, we also focus on how to mutate or which mutation operator to use for mutation. For example, we use various mutation techniques such as bit-flipping, bit-shifting, etc., and also various crossover techniques inspired from genetic algorithms [10].

Third, We have also proposed a probability score to differentiate between different mutated inputs in terms of diversity. Probability score ensures that we are testing the protocol implementation with unusual packets or paths. A mutation-based fuzzer can also use the probability score as a fitness function. After we have generated new inputs by mutation, we use probability score to select those inputs whose characteristics are comparatively uncommon in the normal input for the IoT device.

Finally, we have implemented and evaluated our fuzzing framework in our IoT security testbed. We fuzzed more than 30 IoT devices and found various known vulnerabilities such as Denial of Service (DoS), Buffer Overflow, Session Hijacking, etc.

This work makes the following main contributions:

- We propose a mutational fuzzing framework called SMuF for IoT protocols that takes the help of directed graph of the state machine of the protocol. Also, we consider various levels and sub-levels of the IoT protocol packet.
- We propose a mutational fuzzing technique based on location, context and time.
- We propose a method to select the most uncommon input generated based on probability score.
- We have implemented and evaluated our framework in our IoT security testbed on various IoT devices and found various vulnerabilities.

The rest of the paper is structured as follows: In Sect. 2, we provide the overview of our fuzzing framework and in Sect. 3, we give the details of our approach used in our work. In Sect. 4, we jot down the experimental setup, experimentation and provide results. In Sect. 5, we provide the related work and conclude in Sect. 6.

2 Framework Overview

We have designed and developed mutational fuzzing framework called SMuF that targets various IoT devices and their respective protocols. Our design is generic and any existing fuzzers can be used as a plugin.

To develop an efficient mutational fuzzing framework, we have set the following goals. The first goal is to ensure that the mutated inputs generated are valid as per the specification and will not be rejected before communicating with the IoT device. The second goal is to ensure that we explore all possibilities using state machine representation and packet mutation for generating valid and legal inputs. Also, we ensure that we explore as many possible varieties of inputs. The third goal is to design an effective mutation strategy for ensuring diversity of inputs. The fourth goal is to make sure that from the generated inputs we select the most uncommon or the most diverse input in order to cause the crash of the target. Keeping our goals in mind, we design our framework. The modules of SMuF are: *Protocol Identifier, Protocol State Machine, Packet Generator, Mutation by Location, Context and Time, Mutated Input and Probability Score* as shown in Fig. 1.

First, SMuF is initiated by scanning the network and identifying the protocol which could be IP, BLE, Zigbee, etc., from our *Protocol Identifier* module. Next, from *Protocol State Machine* module we create various states of the identified protocol. Simultaneously, the *Protocol State Machine* module creates a directed graph representation along with the transition. From the directed graph, we use Depth First Search (DFS) to find all possible paths in the graph and then

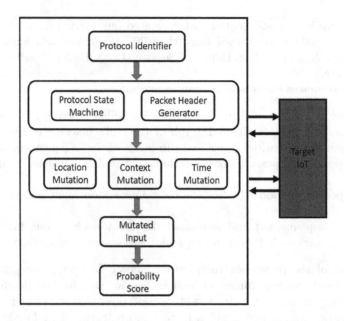

Fig. 1. Overview of IoT protocol fuzzing framework (SMuF)

leverage the shortest path from the start state to the final state. Each of the paths represent a valid sequence of input packets. The *Packet Header Generator* module then generates a legitimate packet based on the protocol. Every field in the packet represents the corresponding level with regard to their hierarchy.

Next, our mutation strategy is used for location, in our case fields in a packet, context and time along with standard mutation operators such as bit-flipping, bit-shifting, etc. Using *Mutation based on location*, we mutate certain fields of a protocol packet. In *Mutation based on context*, we change the context of one packet to create a new input with a different context thus changing the context of the original input. For example, the context we consider are based on the different payloads of the packets and also the authentication process between different states of a protocol. In *Mutation based on time*, we change the time-related factors like the rate at which the packets are transmitting or time-related fields like TTL.

After the mutation, we are left with a set of *Mutated inputs* which can be used for fuzzing. However, as we want to choose the inputs with higher probability of causing a crash, we use a *Probability score* to find and select the types of inputs that are not commonly encountered by the target IoT device. We select those inputs whose characteristics are comparatively uncommon in the normal input for the IoT device.

3   Approach

In this section, we elaborate on our approach used in each of the module of SMuF. In our framework, before initiating other modules, we will capture the information of the protocols from our **Protocol Identifier Module**.

3.1   Protocol State Machine

We take the help of the state machine diagram of a protocol to cover all the possibilities while at the same time generating valid inputs [8,11,14]. Here, we can either manually create the state machine using specifications or automate this by inferring state machine from real-world network traces in case of some protocols [32]. We create a directed graph from the state machine to represent all the possible states a protocol goes through as shown in Fig. 2. One complete path from one of the start states to one of the final states represents one valid communication path. Our mutation starts by picking one of the possible paths. For example, **Start state → State A → Final state** is one path. We modify DFS to find all possible paths between start and end states.

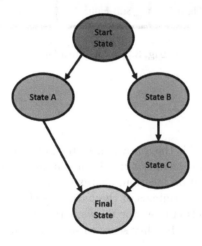

Fig. 2. Example of a state machine directed graph

We simultaneously begin from one of the start states and keep track of visited states. When we reach one of the end states, we take all the states from our visited state data structure and store them as a path. We make sure that we do not end up in an infinite loop by marking the current state as visited state. To keep it simple, we can start with one of the shortest paths, if there is a tie, we break it randomly. In the chosen path, we select one of the packets that causes a transition and apply the mutation to that transition. Once we have fuzzed one particular path, we move on to the other paths. Thus, eventually covering all possible paths in the end.

3.2   Packet Representation

In the previous section, we applied state machine approach for covering all the states for a protocol. Now, we narrow down by focusing on packet structure. After selecting a path which we want to fuzz, we select the packets involved in the transitions. From there, we identify a packet and represent a packet in various levels and sub-levels as shown in Fig. 3. This gives flexibility with respect to the fields we would like to mutate with all fields under our scope.

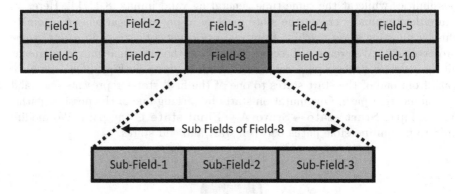

Fig. 3. Protocol header

3.3   Mutation

The whole crux of SMuF is the mutation. Instead of just mutating traditionally, i.e., using standard mutation operators like bit-flipping, byte-flipping, etc., mutation is carried out based on location, context and time as a factor. We mutate terminals as well as non-terminals of the packet levels depending on the packet structure and the mutation operator we want to use. After we have generated mutated inputs, we use probability score to select the most uncommon inputs.

Mutation Based on Location. For mutation based on location, instead of blindly fuzzing all the fields of packet or packets of all the state, we mutate those fields and states which have a higher probability of either creating a vulnerability or creating a more diversified input. We can choose to apply different strategies to identify which field or state to mutate first. The strategies can be derived using manual analysis, static analysis, etc., based on previously recorded crashes/vulnerabilities or a combination, etc. One example of manual analysis is that we prohibit our fuzzer to mutate field of checksum in a packet as in almost all of the cases if the checksum is not right, the packet is going to get dropped.

Mutation Based on Context. For mutation based on the context, we identify a packet to be processed in one particular context or a field in the packet with a certain context attached to it. We then mutate the context based on the different contexts possible. We mutate two different packets which are to be processed in two different contexts say Packet1 in context A and Packet2 in context B. We then apply a simple crossover algorithm to generate a new packet which is an offspring of Packet1 and Packet2. This packet will have properties of Packet1 but the context of Packet2. We do this at the payload level for devices in which we can distinguish between different contexts. Such mutations help in identifying privacy bugs [31]. On the other hand, we take into consideration the acknowledgement exchanged between the sender and the receiver states to determine the context in which the fuzzing activity needs to be performed. The context here refers to swapping of payload context and authentication processes between each state of the protocol.

Mutation Based on Time. Mutation-based on time is done in two ways. One is by mutating time-related factors like the rate of sending packets. Second, is to mutate time-related/sensitive fields like time-to-live (TTL) in TCP or Leap indicator, precision in NTP and manipulate the packet accordingly. This would help in uncovering vulnerabilities caused due to insufficient rate-limiting protection, deadlocks or the ones that easily result in DoS [19,21,29].

3.4   Probability Score

Once we have generated different inputs based on different mutation strategies, we now will have to play those inputs to the target system. The fuzzing activity is a time-sensitive operation, i.e., one cannot send all the inputs at once to process. From the inputs we have generated, we have to send our most efficient inputs first in an ideal scenario. For this, we use the probability score of a packet which is nothing but a probability that the target has previously encountered the input for causing crash. We use a classifier to group packets based on certain properties and then decide the common and uncommon groups. We prefer to send those set of inputs which have a low probability score and a diverse structure. This makes our approach more efficient.

We now calculate probability score based on the set of observed packets. Let S be the set of observed packets which we can further divide into different groups based on their length and S_i be a subset of S having collection packets whose max length is i. Let P be one of the packets generated after mutation. Then the probability score of that packet P is:

$$P_p = \frac{|S_i|}{|S|} \tag{1}$$

4   Experimentation and Evaluation

In this section, we look at the experimental setup of our framework in a state-of-the-art IoT testbed [28] and evaluate the same.

4.1   Experimental Setup

Figure 4 shows the various IoT devices in the IoT testbed. We chose many IoT devices such as TP-Link Cam, D-Link Cam, Netatmo Cam, ARD Cam, Philips Hue Lights, BLE Fitbits, Samsung Smart Things Hub, etc., for our experiment. All the IoT devices were connected to a dedicated access point through a wifi connection. We monitored the communication of the IoT devices through Wireshark [9] on a workstation and collected the network traffic for a total time period of 24 h. The total collected network traffic was around 2 GB. We used some Philips Hue Lights in the experimental setup to simulate a real-world environment of day and night. Every six hours, the lights of the testbed were turned off/on completely. The reason behind creating such a simulation with regard to lights is to ensure the IP cameras switch to *Night/Day* mode depending on the state of the Philips Hue Lights. Also, we issued commands for controlling the various features such as orientation, streaming, etc., of the IP cameras via their respective Android applications and local web servers.

Fig. 4. IoT security testbed with IoT devices

We analyzed the network traffic to understand the communication of IP cameras throughout the experimentation time period. We were able to obtain information such as session identifiers, tokens, and values for several features. The IP cameras use TCP protocol for the streaming operation and HTTP protocol to communicate commands for feature changes. We analyzed each of the TCP packet responsible for a feature change.

We implemented fuzzing framework in Python. It makes use of Scapy [24] module to interact with the IoT devices. The fuzzing framework was set up on a workstation running Kali Linux (2017.1) [18]. We connected the workstation to the same access point as that of the other IoT devices.

4.2   Experimentation

Based on the observed states and various packet levels, we performed the fuzzing operation on all the IoT devices. We mutated the packet using various mutation techniques such as random mutation, byte-flipping, integer mutation, known dictionary and arithmetic flips. We mutate specific packets responsible for a feature change. The reason for mutating only the packets responsible for feature change is to maximize the impact of fuzzing that we can see in the IoT devices. We see the impact in the form of session hijacking, DoS etc. Also, we mutate specific fields like source/destination ports to make sure the IoT devices do not reject the packets. We analyzed each field in the HTTP packet and found out that source/destination ports, payload and flags can be fuzzed while still being accepted by the IoT devices. After intense experimentation, we were able to identify the mutation factor for the various fields at which the fuzzing framework successfully fuzzes the IoT devices at the quickest rates.

Table 1. Probability score

Size of the packets (in bytes)	Probability score
Less than 10	0.2011
Between 10 to 60	0.047
Between 60 to 100	0.226
Between 100 to 300	0.1032
Between 300 to 500	0.3168
Between 500 to 1000	0.0785
Greather than 1000	0.0274

We collected the normal traffic from the IoT devices and used it to assign the probability score on the basis of payload length. Based on the size of the payloads, we were able to arrive at the probability score for the packets. The probability score for packets whose payload length is less than 10 bytes is 0.2011, greater than 10 but less than 60 bytes is 0.047 etc. Based on the count of packets of different size we gave the probability score as shown in Table 1.

We mutate based on few mutation factors which we have chosen for each field manually. We chose mutation factor to be 0 for checksum field, 0.8 for payload, 0.5 for ports and 0.4 for flags. We tried our experiment with different values but got the fastest result in this configuration. Instead of randomly mutating we mutate it based on location, context and time. We place a high priority on mutating fields like source/destination port and HTTP payload and low priority on fields like a checksum. For the time-based mutation, we mutated rate of packet sending based on TTL.

4.3   Results and Analysis

When we mutated based on location (payload data with feature change), we were able to force the IoT device to start rejecting packets eventually due to TCP buffer being full. As a result, we were able to carry out TCP buffer overflow on most of the IoT devices.

With regard to context, we chose to take over the session with the help of session IDs. After analyzing the network traffic, we fuzzed the *payload* of the feature change packets with session IDs that previously existed. We were able to change the video streaming rates and the modes of the IP cameras based on the previous session IDs. We were able to perform session hijacking as a result of fuzzing of payload. Also, we were able to bypass the authentication process by fuzzing the IP Cameras such as TP-Link and D-Link during the handshake. We analyzed the tokens captured during the network traffic analysis stage and then used the same to subsequently bypass BLE Fitbit authentication.

In regard to mutation by time, we first noticed that when the *TTL* field was considered for fuzzing, IoT devices experienced DoS. When feature change packets were used to fuzz IoT devices with valid TTL values (Integer Fuzzing - Only integer values were considered for TTL field), the IoT devices accepted the packets and changed the features. The packets contained toggling features such as day/night mode, audio streaming set to True/False, etc., for IP cameras. Since the features were toggled, the IP cameras after a while, stopped toggling the features even though we were sending valid packets from the fuzzing framework, local web server, and the Android applications. This resulted in DoS on IP cameras. Next, we were able to perform DoS for the video and audio streaming for the camera by sending just one packet. When we fuzzed the port numbers of the HTTP packet through our framework, the cameras went down. The cameras were inaccessible via the android applications and the local web servers.

We found various vulnerabilities such as Buffer Overflow, DoS, Session Hijacking, By-pass authentication, etc., across the IoT devices through our fuzzing framework.

5   Related Work

Skyfire [17] is a seed generation technique for a fuzzer that leverages the power of the probabilistic context-sensitive grammar (PCSG). Its design is for programs whose inputs are highly structured files which are guarded by syntax and semantic rules. The end goal is to generate good, diverse, uncommon and valid seeds that a fuzzer can start with. Thus, can easily be used with other fuzzing tools. The output of Skyfire will be the input of a fuzzer. Skyfire lacks to work on IoT and also does not cover various states based on location, context and time. Shastry et al. [4] have proposed fuzzing using an input dictionary to help with the mutation. Their method is applicable only if you have the source code available and not tailored for IoT. Veggalam et al. [27] proposed a fuzzing framework for interpreters using a genetic algorithm. This method is limited only to interpreters and depends on the quality of test samples provided and lacks to work on IoT.

Ruiter et al. [14] describe a state machine learning technique to extract the state machines from protocol implementations of TLS and then doing a manual analysis to look for vulnerabilities. Lahmadi et al. [1] method is rule-based, and its accuracy depends on how good a scenario-based model can be created. This can be quite challenging for some of the protocols.

Peach [20] is one of the most widely used commercial fuzzer which can work as a generation based as well as mutation based fuzzer. Sulley [2] is open source block based fuzzer. It takes all the values which are in the form of blocks that are often used for stateful network protocol fuzzing. Radamsa [16] is a mutation based fuzzer which contains multiple mutation algorithms. However, all the above-mentioned work still lacks to cover the large search space of the target IoT.

6 Conclusion and Future Work

We have introduced a mutation-based fuzzing framework called SMuF which incorporates various modules such as protocol identifier, protocol state machine, packet generator, mutation, and probability score. SMuF incorporates not only works with all the current fuzzing operators but also introduced three more strategies to mutate: mutation based on location, mutation based on context and mutation based on time. We implemented and evaluated our framework in our IoT security testbed. We have discovered various known vulnerabilities such as DoS, Buffer Overflow, Session Hijacking, etc. In future, we will expand the framework with more modules that can evaluate various IoT devices and discover large scale known and unknown vulnerabilities.

Acknowledgments. The first author's work was done during his internship in SUTD supported by the SUTD start-up research grant SRG-ISTD-2017-124.

References

1. Lahmadi, A., Brandin, C., Festor, O.: A testing framework for discovering vulnerabilities in 6LoWPAN Networks. In: DCOSS, pp. 335–340 (2012)
2. Amini, P., Portnoy, A.: Sulley fuzzing framework. https://github.com/OpenRCE/sulley
3. Miller, B.P., Fredriksen, L., So, B.: An empirical study of the reliability of UNIX utilities. Commun. ACM **33**(12), 32–44 (1990)
4. Shastry, B., et al.: Static program analysis as a fuzzing aid. In: International Symposium on Research in Attacks, Intrusions, and Defenses, pp. 26–47 (2017)
5. Miller, C., Peterson, Z.N.: Analysis of mutation and generation based fuzzing, independent security evaluators. Baltimore, Maryland. Technical report (2007)
6. Babic, D., Martignoni, L., McCamant, S., Song, D.: Statically-directed dynamic automated test generation. In: ISSTA, pp. 12–22 (2011)
7. Denial of service. https://www.owasp.org
8. Banks, G., Cova, M., Felmetsger, V., Almeroth, K., Kemmerer, R., Vigna, G.: SNOOZE: toward a Stateful network protocol fuzzer. In: 9th Information Security Conference (ISC) (2006)

9. Combs, G.: Wireshark. http://www.wireshark.org/
10. Liu, G.H., Wu, G., Tao, Z., Shuai, J.M., Tang, Z.C.: Vulnerability analysis for x86 executables using genetic algorithm and fuzzing. In: Third International Conference on Convergence and Hybrid Information Technology, ICCIT 2008, vol. 2, pp. 491–497. IEEE, November 2008
11. Abdelnur, H.J., Festor, O.: KiF: a stateful SIP fuzzer. In: Proceedings of the 1st International Conference on Principles, Systems and Applications of IP Telecommunications (2007)
12. Hewlett Packard: Internet of things Research Study, Available via HP Enterprise (2015). http://www8.hp.com/
13. Hewlett Packard Enterprise. The Internet of Things: Today and Tomorrow, HPE report (2017). http://www.arubanetworks.com
14. De Ruiter, J., Poll, E.: Protocol state fuzzing of TLS implementations. In: USENIX Security Symposium 2008, 193–206 (2008)
15. DeMott, J.: The evolving art of fuzzing. In: DEF CON 14 (2006)
16. Viide, J., et al.: Experiences with model inference assisted fuzzing. In: USENIX Security (2008)
17. Wang, J., Chen, B., Wei, L., Liu, Y.: Skyfire: data-driven seed generation for fuzzing. In: IEEE S&P (2017)
18. Kali Linux: Penetration Testing and Ethical Hacking Linux Distribution (2017). https://www.kali.org/news/kali-linux-20171-release/
19. Leap Second. https://gtacknowledge.extremenetworks.com/articles/Vulnerability
20. Eddington, M.: Peach fuzzer. https://www.peach.tech
21. Mimoso, M.: Exploit code released for NTP vulnerablity. https://threatpost.com/exploit-code-released-for-ntp-vulnerability/122104/
22. Rajpal, M., Blum, W., Singh, R.: Not all bytes are equal: neural byte sieve for fuzzing, arXiv preprint arXiv:1711.04596 (2017)
23. Zalewski, M.: American fuzzy lop. http://lcamtuf.coredump.cx/afl/
24. Biondi, P.: Scapy. http://www.secdev.org/projects/scapy/
25. Godefroid, P., Levin, M.Y., Molnar, D.: Sage: whitebox fuzzing for security testing. Commun. ACM **55**(3), 40–44 (2012)
26. Roman, R., Zhou, J., Lopez, J.: On the features and challenges of security and privacy in distributed internet of things. Comput. Networks **57**(10), 2266–2279 (2013)
27. Veggalam, S., Rawat, S., Haller, I., Bos, H.: Ifuzzer: an evolutionary interpreter fuzzer using genetic programming. In: ESORICS, pp. 581–601 (2016)
28. Sachidananda, V., Siboni, S., Shabtai, A., Toh, J., Bhairav, S., Elovici, Y.: Let the cat out of the bag: a holistic approach towards security analysis of the internet of things. In: Proceedings of the 3rd ACM International Workshop on IoT Privacy, Trust, and Security, pp. 3–10. ACM, April 2017
29. Vlajic, N., Andrade, M., Nguyen, U.T.: The role of DNS TTL values in potential DDoS attacks: what do the major banks know about it? Procedia Comput. Sci. **10**, 466–473 (2012)
30. WFuzzing/Fuzz testing. http://en.wikipedia.org/wiki/Fuzzing
31. Jia, Y.J., et al.: ContexIoT: towards providing contextual integrity to appified IoT platforms. In: NDSS (2017)
32. Wang, Y., Zhang, Z., Yao, D., Qu, B., Guo, L.: Inferring protocol state machine from network traces: a probabilistic approach. In: Proceedings of the 9th International Conference Applied Cryptography and Network Security (ACNS) (2011)

Leveraging Semantics for Actionable Intrusion Detection in Building Automation Systems

Davide Fauri[1(✉)], Michail Kapsalakis[2], Daniel Ricardo dos Santos[1],
Elisa Costante[2], Jerry den Hartog[1], and Sandro Etalle[1,2]

[1] Eindhoven University of Technology, Eindhoven, Netherlands
d.fauri@tue.nl
[2] SecurityMatters, Eindhoven, Netherlands

Abstract. In smart buildings, physical components (e.g., controllers, sensors, and actuators) are interconnected and communicate with each other using network protocols such as BACnet. Many smart building networks are now connected to the Internet, enabling attackers to exploit vulnerabilities in critical buildings. Network monitoring is crucial to detect such attacks and allow building operators to react accordingly. In this paper, we propose an intrusion detection system for building automation networks that detects known and unknown attacks, as well as anomalous behavior. It does so by leveraging protocol knowledge and specific BACnet semantics: by using this information, the alerts raised by our system are *meaningful* and *actionable*. To validate our approach, we use a real-world dataset coming from the building network of a Dutch university, as well as a simulated dataset generated in our lab facilities.

1 Introduction

Building Automation Systems (BAS) are control systems that manage core physical components of buildings such as elevators, heating and ventilation, access control, and video surveillance [4,12]. Besides residential and commercial buildings, BAS also control critical facilities such as hospitals, airports, and data centers. Within a BAS, devices communicate with each other using network protocols such as BACnet, KNX, and Zigbee [8].

With the introduction of the Internet of Things (IoT), BAS may even be connected to the Internet. Hence, attackers can exploit vulnerabilities of protocols and devices to launch attacks on a building, which can lead to economic loss or harm building occupants [9,15]. Attacks on smart buildings can, e.g., cause blackouts by damaging power systems, grant access to restricted areas by tampering with physical access control, or damage data centers by stopping air

Partially funded by EU-H2020-CITADEL (nr 700665), ITEA3-APPSTACLE (nr 15017), NWO-IDEA-ICS (nr 628.001.023) and NWO-SotJ (nr 628.013.001).

conditioning. Reported attacks[1] include the 2016 attack that turned off the heating systems in two buildings in Finland and the 2017 attack that locked hotel guests in their rooms in Austria.

Intrusion Detection Systems (IDS) can monitor network activity to detect attacks. IDS are typically categorized into *knowledge-based* (when detection rules are specified from attack signatures; also known as misuse-based) and *behavior-based* (when the IDS relies on a model of legitimate behavior). Behavior-based approaches, in turn, are subdivided in *anomaly-based* (when a model of legitimate behavior is *learned*) and *specification-based* (when the model is *specified*) [6]. Applying knowledge-based approaches to BAS is challenging because attack signatures may be device-dependent, which limits their scope and makes them hard to obtain. Anomaly-based approaches [11,17,21] tend to adopt "black-box" machine learning techniques (e.g., artificial neural networks), which do not provide meaningful information to help understand the cause of an anomaly [19] (e.g., whether the anomaly is the result of an attack, or an irregular yet legitimate change). Specification-based approaches are based on vendor-provided documents [2,5], which is problematic when the documents are not available or not easily parsable.

Smart buildings are different from IT systems and even Industrial Control Systems. On one hand, they are dynamic environments where network traffic is a combination of multiple streams belonging to different categories—e.g., periodic time-driven patterns or unstructured human-driven activity [24]—which requires the use of fine-tuned anomaly-based detection that can raise meaningful alerts. On the other hand, the kind of devices hosted by BAS are relatively well-standardized and their protocols are expressive [2], allowing us to more easily derive knowledge-based detection rules. To achieve interpretable and actionable alerts, we leverage BACnet's rich protocol semantics and a semantics-aware detection model.

In this paper, we propose an IDS to monitor building automation networks based on one of the most widely used protocols for BAS; BACnet. The proposed IDS uses knowledge about the semantics of BACnet and the BAS to improve both white-box anomaly detection [3] techniques (for unknown threats), and knowledge-based techniques (for known attacks). To the best of our knowledge, the use of protocol semantics for securing building automation networks has never been proposed. Our approach has two important benefits when compared to related work. First, the white-box intrusion detection approach learns models that are understandable by users, and provides semantically rich alerts that clearly indicate the reasons of an anomaly. The alerts are thus easier to interpret for network operators, which improves actionability [7]. Second, our approach does not depend on vendor-specific descriptions of each device. Instead, we exploit the structure imposed by the BACnet standard to elevate the knowledge-based part from signatures to more general knowledge about attack patterns.

---

[1] See, e.g., https://securityledger.com/2016/11/lets-get-cyberphysical-ddos-attack-halts-heating-in-finland/ and https://www.nytimes.com/2017/01/30/world/europe/hotel-austria-bitcoin-ransom.html.

Note that, although we focus on BACnet, similar methods and techniques may be used for other building automation protocols, provided that they are as expressive as BACnet.

The rest of this paper is organized as follows. Section 2 provides background on the BACnet protocol and attacks in this scenario. Section 3 details our combined IDS approach. Sections 4 and 5, respectively, discuss implementation and experiments using a real dataset from the network of a Dutch university, and a simulated dataset generated in our lab facilities. Section 6 concludes the paper.

2   Background

BACnet [1] is one of the most widely used protocols for building automation. It is based on four layers: Physical, Data Link, Network, and Application. There are several BACnet variants. The Network and Application layers are the same for all variants, but there are seven possible combinations of Physical and Data Link layers, which are chosen according to requirements such as cost and speed.

A BACnet subnetwork is a connection of devices with the same Physical and Data Link layers that can directly exchange unicast, multicast or broadcast messages. A BACnet network consists of multiple subnetworks connected by BACnet Broadcast Management Devices used to broadcast messages from one subnetwork to another. If the interconnected subnetworks use different Physical and Data Link layers, they must also be connected by a BACnet Router.

BACnet defines a standard set of *Objects*, each with a standard set of *Properties* that together describe a device and its current status. *Services* are used by one BACnet device to obtain information from another device or command another device to perform an action. Each service request and service acknowledgment transmits properties of objects using a message packet sent over the network.

Every BACnet device must have a `Device` object, whose properties describe the device to the network. The choice of which other objects, properties, and services are present in a device is determined by its function and capabilities (e.g., an `AnalogInput` object is used to represent an analog sensor input). Some properties, such as `Description` and `DeviceType`, are set during installation; others, such as `PresentValue`, provide status information (e.g., the sensor input represented by the `AnalogInput` object). The `ReadProperty` service is implemented by every device to inform its properties to another device.

BACnet Security. The BACnet standard specifies some security features to provide, e.g., data confidentiality and integrity, but their implementation is optional. This means that, in most smart buildings, BACnet data is exchanged without any kind of authentication, and BACnet devices are programmed to process every received message, opening them to exploitation by internal and external attackers [23]. There are several examples of attacks on BACnet devices and networks in the literature (see, e.g., [9,13,17]). We classify these attacks in the following four categories:

Network Reconnaissance (or Snooping) aims at gaining knowledge of network topology and information about objects, properties, and services. This knowledge can be used to plan the next actions of an attack or to organize a break-in by determining if people are present in the building (see, e.g., [14]).

Device Writing Access (or Tampering) can be used to isolate devices, compromise them to operate abnormally, or remotely control devices such as doors and elevators.

Traffic Redirection (or Spoofing) impersonates a device or a BACnet Router so that messages intended for a certain device never reach their destination.

Denial of Service (DoS) disables the communication between devices or makes a whole subnetwork unavailable. DoS attacks can isolate critical systems of a building, such as fire detectors.

Related Work. Pan et al. [17] use a rule learner to detect abnormal BACnet traffic and to classify it according to attack types. They also propose an action handler to discard malicious packets. Johnstone et al. [11] used an Artificial Neural Network to detect specific timing attacks, e.g., values that are changed in quick succession, in BACnet. Tonejc et al. [21] introduced a framework that allows the characterization of BACnet network traffic using unsupervised machine learning algorithms, such as clustering, random forests, one-class support vector machines and support vector classifiers, after a pre-processing step that includes principal components analysis for dimensionality reduction. They consider packet headers, which reflect the network structure, but not the actual application data.

A major disadvantage of the machine learning methods above is that they are "black-box" models, in the sense that they are hard to understand and modify and their alerts have a wide semantic gap, i.e. they do not provide enough semantic information to help understand the cause of an anomaly and to fix it [19].

Zheng and Reddy [24] observe that BACnet traffic is a combination of multiple flow-service streams that belong to "THE-driven" categories: Time-driven, Human-driven, and Event-driven. The authors then developed different intrusion detection systems based on traffic classification and different anomaly-detection models: interarrival-based for time-driven traffic, safe range-based for human-driven traffic, and volume-based for event-driven traffic. The authors do not consider knowledge or specification-based detection in their system.

Caselli et al. [2] presented a specification-based BACnet IDS. In their implementation, when model names and vendor IDs are discovered, the system looks for documentation related to each device in the Internet. From these documents (e.g., PICSs) and system configuration files, the IDS automatically generates detection rules, e.g., permissible services, objects, and properties of each device. The IDS then monitors the network with the extracted rules, raising an alert when a packet violates any of them. Their approach suffers the already mentioned disadvantages of depending on the availability and readability of specification documents. More specifically, it requires documents to have a specific format and unambiguous notation. To overcome these limitations, the approach of [5] generalizes the interpretation of different PICS formats using network traffic to solve the incompleteness and ambiguity problems.

Some works aim to not only detect but also prevent attacks in BACnet. Examples include firewalls [10] and intrusion prevent systems [13] that drop non-conforming packets, as well as traffic normalizers [20] that actively modify malicious BACnet traffic. All such tools can have serious consequences in building automation networks when dropping or modifying legal messages, thus delaying or ignoring critical actions. Another disadvantage is that they are unable to detect or prevent unknown attacks.

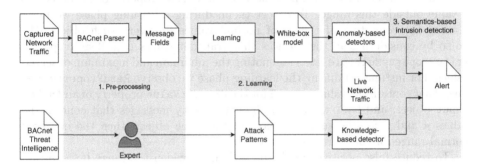

Fig. 1. Overview of our proposed solution

3 Intrusion Detection

Figure 1 shows an overview of the IDS divided in three phases. The *Preprocessing* phase analyzes two sources of knowledge. The first is the BAS *Network Traffic* capture, which is processed by a *BACnet Parser* to extract the relevant *Message Fields* from each message. The second is a collection of *BACnet Threat Intelligence* resources, which are interpreted by a human domain *Expert* and manually refined into *Attack Patterns*.

In the *Learning* phase, a white-box model of legitimate (normal) behavior is learned from the parsed Message Fields.

The *Intrusion detection* phase is divided in two modules, one for *Knowledge-based* and one for *Anomaly-based* detection. Both modules continuously take Message Fields as input and can raise alerts for malicious behavior detected in the network, but they are complementary. The knowledge-based module compares a black-list of well-known Attack Patterns with the activity in the network traffic: the false positives rate is usually very low, but the obvious shortcoming is that unknown attacks are not detected. The anomaly-based module detects previously unseen attacks: it raises an alert whenever a device sends an anomalous number of messages, or when the content of the observed messages is abnormal.

The modular system described above supports different detection approaches, where modules are knowledge-based or anomaly-based detectors that are executed in parallel. Below, we describe the concrete detectors used in our implementation: the anomaly-based detection engine is composed by two detectors that are triggered by messages, or time passing; while the knowledge-based detection engine is composed by a detector triggered by messages.

3.1 Semantics-Based Anomaly Detectors

Value Range. BACnet objects assuming different values, such as an `AnalogInput` representing temperature, will have their values stay within a bounded range during normal behavior. Tampering attacks can be detected, and an alert raised, when an attacker tries to change the `PresentValue` property of an object to a value outside this range. To detect them, during a learning phase we build a white-list consisting of ranges of normal values for every such object. We do so by considering all the services that transmit values (e.g. `ReadProperty`, `WritePropertyMultiple`, etc.) and noting the minimum and maximum observed values. For instance, if during the learning phase we observe `ReadProperty` messages that contain the values 2 and 5 for the `PresentValue` property of an `Analog Input` object; and later we observe `WriteProperty` messages that contain the values 4 and 6 for the same property of the same object; then the observed normal range for that property is [2,6].

To reduce false positives in the detection, we widen the range by a certain tolerance t: in the example above, $t = 5\%$ would expand the normal range to [1.9, 6.3]. The BACnet protocol specification distinguishes between `Output` objects, usually sensor measurements, and `Input` objects, usually setpoints sent to actuators. This semantic distinction allows us to set two values for t: a stricter tolerance for setpoints, which have typically a low variance, and a more lenient one for noisy sensor readings. The tolerance value may also depend on the criticality of the object being monitored: for instance, a temperature setpoint of a server room should have a strict tolerance, while a hot water setpoint in a house could be much more lenient.

Number of Messages. During normal behavior, we expect the frequency of messages having similar sources and types to fall within a normal range of values. If a device is compromised or an attack occurs (e.g. reconnaissance, denial of service), it may lead to an abnormal number of messages sent for a specific service. We thus raise an alert whenever we observe an anomalous frequency of messages sent for a service (either in general or by a specific device). We focus on computing the frequency per-service instead of per-device because due to how messages are propagated among BACnet subnetworks, knowledge of the initiated service is crucial in diagnosing the reason of excessive traffic [16].

To learn this normal frequency feature, we first divide the learning period $\mathcal{L} = \{I_0, ..., I_n\}$ in a sequence of consecutive time intervals $I = [t, t + T)$ with equal duration T. For each time interval, we gather a sample set $\mathcal{O}$ consisting of all the messages observed over that interval. We then define, for each given source device s and service k, a feature that counts the total number of messages sent by s that refer to k in an interval: $f(I) = \#\{m \in \mathcal{O} \mid m.source = s \wedge m.service = k\}$.

We similarly compute the average count of messages referring to the service k, normalized on the number of devices that have ever been observed initiating that service: $g(I) = \#\{m \in \mathcal{O} \mid m.service = k\}/\#\{s \in D \mid s \text{ is active for } k\}$, where D is the set of all monitored network devices, and a device s is active for a service k if we observed s initiating k at least once during the learning period.

In learning an interval NV of normal values for the feature f (equivalently for g), we apply a metric over the set F of features computed over all time intervals, $F = \{f(I_0), \ldots, f(I_n)\}$. We considered three possible choices of metric: min-max, distance from mean, or deviation from median. We already used the min-max metric above; the interval runs from the minimum to the maximum value seen in F, extended with a tolerance t; i.e. $NV = [(1-t) \cdot \min_{f \in F} f, (1+t) \cdot \max_{f \in F} f]$. Similarly, the distance from mean starts from the mean frequency μ_f and is extended to $NV = [(1-t) \cdot \mu_f, (1+t) \cdot \mu_f]$. Deviation from median m_f uses a tolerance based on Median Absolute Deviation (MAD) rather than a fixed percentage: $NV = [(1 - c \cdot MAD) \cdot m_f, (1 + c \cdot MAD) \cdot m_f]$, where $MAD = median_{f \in F}(|f - m_f|)$ and c is a constant (called cutoff) given by the user.

In the detection phase, messages are filtered by source s and service k, and are sampled with time intervals of the same length T as above. The feature f is calculated over each of these intervals as they come. An alert is raised if the observed number of messages is outside the learned normal range for f and g. When s is a new device on the network, a normal range of values is not available as it has not been learned yet. Instead, we compare the value of the feature f with only the normal range for the average service frequency, that is g. Because our method tries to detect anomalies that can harm the system, we concentrate on message frequencies that are more than the upper bound of NV; as a consequence, devices that send less messages than the lower bound will not trigger any alert.

3.2   Knowledge-Based Detector

This detector uses a black-list of known attack patterns expressed in terms of the BACnet and BAS semantics. An expert can specify stateless detection rules, checking for known malicious values in a combination of one or more message fields. For example, a rule may raise an alert if the source address of observed messages is set to a broadcast address, either in the IP layer or in the BACnet Network Layer, as this is indicative of a DoS attack. We also consider stateful rules; for example, observed messages having the same BACnetAddress but different DeviceID are indicative of device spoofing; similarly, network number spoofing may be detected by looking for different NetworkNumbers for the same Router. In this case, the state comprises the pairs (BACnetAddress,DeviceID) and (Router,NetworkNumber) observed so far.

```
Device does not conform to device and service normal number of messages for service
ReadPropertyMultiple. Details:
BACnet device 100 sent 3643 messages during a 30 minutes interval.
Normal number of messages for this device for this service: [0, 703].
Normal number of messages for this service: [3593, 3641].
```

Fig. 2. Example alert

4 Implementation

We implemented the intrusion detection modules on top of SilentDefense[2], an IDS for industrial control systems developed by SecurityMatters. We used Wireshark's BACnet dissector[3] to represent BACnet packets in a readable format and developed a custom parser using binpac [18]. The parser provides the extracted fields to the Deep Protocol Behavior Inspection engine of SilentDefense, which allows a security operator to see all BACnet message details. The intrusion detection scripts were implemented in Lua.

Figure 2 shows an example alert raised by the IDS when a device does not conform to its normal behavior for service ReadPropertyMultiple. Notice how this alert is informative and enables a security operator to quickly assess the situation. In case the operator realizes this is a false positive, the upper limit in the valid range can be easily changed to an appropriate value (i.e. there is no need to learn the model again).

BACnet Testbed. To run attacks and test our intrusion detection approach, we developed a testbed modeling a lighting and temperature control system in a small building, and containing the following real devices:

- two sensors (motion & temperature) and two actuators (fan & LED bulb);
- one digital I/O and two analog I/O devices connected via serial cable to the sensors and actuators, and communicating via BACnet MS/TP;
- a BACnet Router that connects one MS/TP network with one IP network;
- a BACnet/IP Controller that implements the logic of the system by reading and writing inputs and outputs of the I/O modules;
- a BACnet/IP Workstation used to configure devices in the network;
- a BACnet/IP Workstation that monitors the testbed and lets users modify setpoints;
- a Raspberry Pi used to run attacking scripts from the IP network.

The testbed implements two automated functions. First, when the motion sensor state goes from 0 to 1, the controller sends a command to the I/O module to switch on the LED by changing the state of one of its outputs. Second, the I/O module continuously reads the temperature values sent by the sensor and informs the controller. The controller activates the fan when the sensed value is greater than a setpoint set by the operator.

---

[2] https://www.secmatters.com/product.
[3] https://wiki.wireshark.org/Protocols/bacnet.

Attacks. We implemented the following synthetic attacks in Python, using the bacpypes[4] library to exchange BACnet messages between the Raspberry Pi and the rest of the testbed network. All the attacks are successful, because the BACnet devices in the testbed do not implement any authorization check and accept all the messages that come from any device. This is typical for building automation systems [23].

Snooping. We broadcast `Who-Is` messages to retrieve the address and instance number of all devices in the network, and then send `ReadProperty` services to these devices to read their model name, vendor ID, and the objects and services supported by them.

Tampering1. We send a `WriteProperty` request to the digital I/O controller and toggle the state of the LED bulb or of the cooler fan. In this attack, we send a single message to change the state of an output only once.

Tampering2. We send a `ReadProperty` request to the main controller to extract the current (analog) temperature setpoint value; we then send a `WriteProperty` request to the same controller to increase this value by five degrees. As a result, the fan stops working and the temperature increases in the room.

Spoofing1. We listen to BACnet messages until receiving an `I-Am` unconfirmed request with device instance number equal to that of the digital I/O controller. We then immediately send a new `I-Am` message with the same details, except for a malicious IP address. As a result, the connection between the other BACnet devices in the network and the legitimate device is broken and the attacker is able to read and change their contents.

Spoofing2. Similar to the previous attack, but in this case we impersonate a BACnet Router by sending fake `I-Am-Router-To-Network` messages including the network number of another legitimate BACnet Router. The goal of this attack is twofold: (i) traffic redirection, since all BACnet/IP devices that want to communicate with non-BACnet/IP devices nested behind this router send messages to the attacker machine; (ii) denial of service, since the nested devices cannot receive messages from BACnet/IP devices. However, BACnet/IP devices reconfigure their routing tables when a nested device sends any kind of message, because the network number is included in BACnet Network Layer and the message is sent by the legitimate BACnet Router.

Reflected DDoS. We broadcast 1000 `Who-Is` requests in a few seconds, without a device range. As a result, a total of 6000 `I-Am` messages are broadcasted by the 6 BACnet devices in the testbed. The BACnet Router is overloaded and starts rejecting all the messages that it receives: as a result, the BACnet/IP devices cannot communicate with BACnet MS/TP devices.

5 Experiments

The goal of the experiments was to validate the attack detection capabilities of our IDS, and to measure how many false positive alerts (FP) it raised on

---

[4] https://github.com/JoelBender/bacpypes.

legitimate traffic. To achieve those goals, we used a real and a synthetic dataset. We split each of them into 70% for learning the white-box model, and 30% for validating the false alerts. We considered these datasets to be attack-free: therefore, we regarded any alert raised from the validation data as a false alert.

Dataset 1 comes from a real BACnet network of a Dutch University. We analyzed nine days of traffic, totalling 106 GB of data and 20 million BACnet messages. We could not use the infrastructure of the university to perform attacks, but Dataset 1 helped us to evaluate the number of false alerts that our IDS might raise when deployed in a real scenario. We extracted two partial datasets from Dataset 1 to examine whether the duration of the learning period affected the accuracy of our IDS. The first partial dataset (D1.1) includes approximately 4 days of network traffic, split in 50 h of training and 47 h of testing. The second partial dataset (D1.2) includes the whole 9 days of traffic, split in 172 h of training and the same 47 h of testing as in D1.1.

Dataset 2 comes from our BACnet testbed presented in Sect. 4. We captured 10 min of traffic with no attacks: due to the small size of our testbed, this short time span is still sufficiently representative of the normal behavior on the network. After measuring the number of false alerts from the validation data, we then re-used the same white-box model learned from the training data to test the detection capabilities of our IDS. To do so, we launched the attacks described in Sect. 4 and evaluated if the IDS raised a corresponding alert.

Table 1. False positive alerts raised by the anomaly detectors

	D1.1	D1.2
$t = 5\%$	6144	1531
$t = 20\%$	2510	3

(a) Value range detector

Interval	D1.1		D1.2		D2	
	30m	60m	30m	60m	30s	60s
min-max	204	141	54	8	1	1
mean	1058	506	1151	528	6	5
$median_{c=1}$	676	521	763	563	4	4
$median_{c=3}$	505	398	511	444	1	1
$median_{c=5}$	456	379	418	400	0	0

(b) Number of messages detector

Results. Our IDS managed to raise alerts for 5 out of 6 attacks: all of the *Snooping*, *Spoofing* and *Reflected DDoS* attacks were detected by either the number of messages anomaly detector, or the knowledge-based detector. Among the *Tampering* set of attacks, the IDS could only detect the *Tampering2* attack, through the value range anomaly detector; the other attack took place unnoticed. This is not surprising: the *Tampering1* attack was expected to be undetectable by our approach, as it is just an isolated command that simply toggles the binary value of a switch from on to off. During the learning phase we observed both of these values, which were then included in the range of normal data. From the point of view of the IDS, the attack was thus indistinguishable from the action of a legitimate user. It is important to note that no single detector could catch all types of attacks; we conclude that we need a combination of anomaly-based and behavior-based detectors to detect different kinds of attacks.

To evaluate the usability of our IDS, we followed the work of [22] and computed both the total number of FP and the average rate of FP per hour which were raised on our datasets. We limit this analysis on the two semantics-based anomaly detectors, as we reasonably expect that the specified detection rules used in the knowledge-based detector are precise enough to not generate many FP.

Table 1a presents the evaluation results for the value range anomaly detector, with two possible settings for the interval tolerance parameter t. The training interval in D1.1 is clearly too short to learn the full range of behaviour leading to many false positives. The longer training period in D1.2 which spans a whole week leads to fewer FP. Buildings are live, dynamical systems with many time-driven and human-driven regularities [24]: seven days is a manageable period of time in which we expect to observe the full range of normal values. We still need to adjust t to balance the tradeoff between detection and FP rate, taking into account the criticality of the monitored value. Assuming a tolerance of 20% is acceptable throughout all the monitored buildings in the network, and using the longer training period (D1.2) results in around 0.06 FP/h.

Table 1b shows the results for the number of messages anomaly detector. We tested different settings during the learning phase. When computing the frequency values, we used two different interval durations: $T = 30$ and 60 min for Dataset 1, and $T = 30$ and 60 s for the considerably shorter Dataset 2. When computing the range of normal values, we used the following metrics and parameters: min-max with tolerance $t = 5\%$; deviation from the median with cutoff values $c = 1$, 3 and 5; and distance from mean with tolerance $t = 5\%$. The min-max metric provides the least false alerts, since by construction it does not regard any value from the training data as anomalous. However, outliers during training could lead to overly large intervals, hindering detection. Mean and especially median are more robust to outliers during training. The tighter resulting intervals do cause more FP. We also see that training on both work and weekend days (D1.2) skews the intervals for measures of central tendency such as mean and median, leading to slightly more FP. As behaviour differs between work and weekend days adding profiling [3] would likely improve results.

Furthermore, Table 1b indicates that both the duration of the intervals and the size of the dataset can have an effect on the number of false alerts. We observe that using longer time intervals reduces the number of FP. This reduction happens because, in both training and detection, we compute the frequency of messages over a longer time T. This increases the chance of 'averaging out' the effect of short, possibly anomalous bursts of intense traffic: frequencies computed during detection will tend to be closer to the learned normal values, unless the bursts last for a significant portion of the time interval defined by T. The parameter T should then be tuned with care to balance FP rate, duration of the attacks that can be detected, and the timeliness of the raised alerts.

6   Conclusion

We proposed an IDS approach for BACnet networks that leverages the semantic information provided by the communication protocol. It exploits known attack patterns and normal network behavior of BACnet devices to detect a significant number of attacks. Once an attack is detected, the system generates enriched alerts that include semantic information helpful to the operators.

The IDS provided good results to detect the implemented BACnet attacks, while raising a satisfactory number of false alerts. The tolerance levels for the anomaly-based modules depend on the operation and criticality of each building. In general, we suggest thresholds and cutoffs that are able to balance false alerts and detection rates. As future work, we intend to test whether other BAS protocols, such as KNX and ZigBee, offer enough semantics information to allow for a similarly made IDS.

References

1. ASHRAE: BACnet - a data communication protocol for building automation and control networks. Standard (2016)
2. Caselli, M., Zambon, E., Amann, J., Sommer, R., Kargl, F.: Specification mining for intrusion detection in networked control systems. In: Proceedings of USENIX Security (2016)
3. Costante, E., den Hartog, J., Petković, M., Etalle, S., Pechenizkiy, M.: A white-box anomaly-based framework for database leakage detection. JISA **32**, 27–46 (2017)
4. Domingues, P., Carreira, P., Vieira, R., Kastner, W.: Building automation systems: concepts and technology review. Comput. Stand. Interfaces **45**(Suppl. C), 1–12 (2016)
5. Esquivel-Vargas, H., Caselli, M., Peter, A.: Automatic deployment of specification-based intrusion detection in the BACnet protocol. In: Proceedings of CPS-SPC (2017)
6. Etalle, S.: From intrusion detection to software design. In: Foley, S.N., Gollmann, D., Snekkenes, E. (eds.) ESORICS 2017, Part I. LNCS, vol. 10492, pp. 1–10. Springer, Cham (2017). https://doi.org/10.1007/978-3-319-66402-6_1
7. Fauri, D., dos Santos, D., Costante, E., den Hartog, J., Etalle, S., Tonetta, S.: From system specification to anomaly detection (and back). In: CPS-SPC (2017)
8. Hersent, O., Boswarthick, D., Elloumi, O.: The Internet of Things: Key Applications and Protocols. John Wiley & Sons, Chichester (2011)
9. Holmberg, D.: BACnet wide area network security threat assessment. Technical report, NIST (2003)
10. Holmberg, D.: Using the BACnet firewall router. ASHRAE J. **48**(11), B10–B14 (2006)
11. Johnstone, M., Peacock, M., den Hartog, J.: Timing attack detection on BACnet via a machine learning approach. In: Proceedings of AISM (2015)

12. Kastner, W., Neugschwandtner, G., Soucek, S., Newman, H.M.: Communication systems for building automation and control. Proc. IEEE **93**(6), 1178–1203 (2005)
13. Kaur, J., Tonejc, J., Wendzel, S., Meier, M.: Securing BACnet's pitfalls. In: Federrath, H., Gollmann, D. (eds.) SEC 2015. IFIP AICT, vol. 455, pp. 616–629. Springer, Cham (2015). https://doi.org/10.1007/978-3-319-18467-8_41
14. Möllers, F., Sorge, C.: Deducing user presence from inter-message intervals in home automation systems. In: Hoepman, J.-H., Katzenbeisser, S. (eds.) SEC 2016. IAICT, vol. 471, pp. 369–383. Springer, Cham (2016). https://doi.org/10.1007/978-3-319-33630-5_25
15. Mundt, T., Wickboldt, P.: Security in building automation systems - a first analysis. In: Proceedings of Cyber Security (2016)
16. Newman, H.: Broadcasting BACnet®. ASHRAE J. **52**, B8–B12 (2010)
17. Pan, Z., Hariri, S., Al-Nashif, Y.: Anomaly based intrusion detection for building automation and control networks. In: Proceedings of AICCSA (2014)
18. Pang, R., Paxson, V., Sommer, R., Peterson, L.: Binpac: a yacc for writing application protocol parsers. In: Proceedings of IMC (2006)
19. Sommer, R., Paxson, V.: Outside the closed world: on using machine learning for network intrusion detection. In: Proceedings of IEEE S&P (2010)
20. Szlósarczyk, S., Wendzel, S., Kaur, J., Schubert, F.: Towards suppressing attacks on and improving resilience of building automation systems - an approach exemplified using BACnet. In: GI Sicherheit (2014)
21. Tonejc, J., Guttes, S., Kobekova, A., Kaur, J.: Machine learning methods for anomaly detection in BACnet networks. JUCS **22**(9), 1203–1224 (2016)
22. Urbina, D., et al.: Limiting the impact of stealthy attacks on industrial control systems. In: Proceedings of ACM SIGSAC CCS (2016)
23. Wendzel, S., Tonejc, J., Kaur, J., Kobekova, A.: Cyber security of smart buildings (2017)
24. Zheng, Z., Reddy, A.: Safeguarding building automation networks: THE-driven anomaly detector based on traffic analysis. In: Proceedings of ICCCN (2017)

Need and Tool Sets for Industrial Control System Security

Cybersecurity Self-assessment Tools: Evaluating the Importance for Securing Industrial Control Systems in Critical Infrastructures

Georgia Lykou, Argiro Anagnostopoulou, George Stergiopoulos, and Dimitris Gritzalis[✉]

Information Security and Critical Infrastructure Protection (INFOSEC) Laboratory, Department of Informatics, Athens University of Economics and Business, 76 Patission Ave., 10434 Athens, Greece
{lykoug, anagnostopouloua, geostergiop, dgrit}@aueb.gr

Abstract. Periodically assessing the security status of Industrial Control Systems (ICS) is essential to enable cybersecurity compliance and performance evaluation against an organization's risk appetite. Ensuring appropriate security level is especially important in Critical Infrastructures (CI). Existing cybersecurity risk management methodologies provide frameworks through which CI stakeholders can enhance security and better protect their assets, against cybersecurity risks. Following traditional risk assessment procedures, a self-assessment tool can support an organization to build up on knowledge and security awareness, check implemented cybersecurity practices and responsibilities. Such methods and tools, when systematically implemented, can identify security weaknesses, establish cybersecurity targets and improve resilience. This paper aims to provide a review and analysis of available cybersecurity Self-Assessment tools, which can be used by ICS owners and CI operators. We also focus on questionnaire content analysis, used in these self-assessment tools, with the purpose to create a classification of questions content, according to core functions of NIST Cybersecurity Framework.

Keywords: Cyber security · Self-assessment tools
Industrial control systems security · Critical infrastructure protection

1 Introduction

Adequate security of information in Industrial Control Systems (ICS) and supporting Critical Infrastructures (CI) is a fundamental management responsibility. ICS employees and supervisors must be constantly aware of the status of their information security controls, in order to make informed judgments and investments that appropriately mitigate risks to an acceptable level. Cybersecurity self-assessment tools realize risk assessment and risk management procedures, provide automated solutions for CI operators and owners to determine the current status of their information security programs and, where necessary, pinpoint specific targets for improvement. Self-

© Springer Nature Switzerland AG 2019
E. Luiijf et al. (Eds.): CRITIS 2018, LNCS 11260, pp. 129–142, 2019.
https://doi.org/10.1007/978-3-030-05849-4_10

assessment tools utilize extensive and structured questionnaires containing specific control objectives and security measures against which any ICS or group of inter-connected ICS systems can be tested and evaluated [1].

1.1 Motivation and Contribution

This paper aims to provide a review and analysis of available cybersecurity Self-Assessment tools, which can be used by ICS owners and CI operators. These tools support organizational risk management and enforce cybersecurity by identifying operating weaknesses, employee's security awareness and by evaluating implementa-tion of effective control practices to protect ICS against realistic threats and associated risks. In addition, we deepen our research into questionnaire content analysis, which is used by the examined self-assessment tools, with the purpose to create a classification on questions content, according to the Core Functions presented by the newly pub-lished "Cybersecurity Framework" (v.1.1) of National Institute of Standards and Technology (NIST), which promotes the protection and resilience of critical infras-tructures [2].

1.2 Outline/Structure

The structure of this paper after the introductory part is as following: Sect. 2 presents Security Challenges for ICS and related work on ICS Cybersecurity Risk Assessment and Management. Section 3 presents four developed self-assessment tools and pro-vides a comprehensive comparison. In Sect. 4, the analysis is extended to questionnaire content analysis and classification. Finally, Sect. 5 extracts main conclusions and importance evaluation of using Cybersecurity Self-Assessment Tools for risk man-agement purposes.

2 Cybersecurity Challenges for Industrial Control Systems

ICS is a general term describing cyber-physical and automation systems responsible for data acquisition, visualization and control of processes found in industrial sectors and supporting CIs. They play a critical role, not only in maintaining the business automation, but also in ensuring functional and technical safety, preventing large industrial accidents and environmental disasters [4]. In the past, ICS had little resemblance to the traditional information technology (IT) systems, since they were isolated systems, running proprietary control protocols and using specialized hardware & software [1]. Widely available, low-cost Internet Protocol devices are now replacing proprietary solutions, which increase their functionality and interoperability, along with the possibility of cyber security vulnerabilities and incidents. Moreover, the goals of safety and efficiency sometimes conflict with security in the design and operation, as ICS have unique execution criticality and reliability requirements (24 × 365) and change management can jeopardize their integrity and performance [3].

The trend towards integrating ICS systems with IT networks provides significantly less isolation from the outside world, creating a greater need to secure these systems from remote, external risks. Threats to both ICS and IT systems can come from numerous sources, including malicious intruders, terrorist groups, disgruntled employees, accidents and others [4]. Therefore, ICS have greater security challenges to confront, since they have not achieved yet the same level of cybersecurity maturity as other cyber or IT resources.

2.1   Related Work on ICS Security Management

Over the last decade, a number of standards and directives dealing with cybersecurity of ICS systems have emerged. In 2004, NIST published the System Protection Profile for Industrial Control Systems, which covered the risks of ICS systems [5]. In 2007, the US President's Critical Infrastructure Protection Board and the Department of Energy outlined the steps an organization must undertake to improve the security of ICS networks by introducing 21 Steps to Improve Cyber Security of SCADA Networks [6]. In 2008, the UK Centre for Protection of National Infrastructure (CPNI) produced a Good Practice Guide for Process Control and SCADA Security encapsulating best security practices [7]. In 2013, the European Union Agency for Network and Information Security (ENISA) released the recommendations for Europe on ICS security [8] and three years later published security good practices for ICS/SCADA Systems [9]. In 2014, North American Electric Reliability Corporation (NERC) introduced the development of a wide range of standards covering ICS cyber security [10]. NIST has released a comprehensive guidance on wide range of security issues, and technical, operational and management security controls, last updated in 2015 [1]. Finally, in 2018 the ISA99 committee published ISA/IEC 62443 security standard, which suggests the adoption of a flexible framework in order CI to address and mitigate current and future security vulnerabilities in industrial automation and control systems [11]. Over and above to these guidance work, scientific research has developed various CIP tools, able to model CI characteristics, their interdependencies and the impact of potential failures in their systems. In previous work [12], a review of sixty-eight available in literature tools, frameworks and methodologies for CI protection were analyzed and classified. However, these tools do not focus only on ICS systems; instead, they examine CIs entities as a whole.

Risk assessment is generally understood as the process of identifying, estimating and prioritizing risks to the organizational assets and operations [1]. This is an essential activity within security management as it provides the foundation for risk identification and treatment with the adoption of effective cybersecurity measures. Although several methods and tools are available in literature for conducting risk assessments, the particularities of SCADA often prevent the straight forward application and adjustment is required to fit the context of SCADA systems. Therefore, focused on ICS systems, a detailed overview of 24 risk assessment methods developed for SCADA systems was presented by Cherdantseva et al. [13]. This work pinpointed that there was no software prototype or automated tool for the vast majority of the methods examined for ICS, in order to support their implementation. Instead, in several methods the development of software prototype was outlined as a subject for future work. Our literature research revealed that despite exhaustive work on ICS cybersecurity protection guidance, risk assessment and management tools, no research has been presented related to self-assessment tools analysis and their complementary effect on ICS cybersecurity and efficient risk management.

Self-assessments usually provide an additional tool for organizations to determine current status of their information security programs, improve staff security awareness, prepare organization before security audits and establish new targets for improvement [3]. Most self-assessment methods utilize an extensive questionnaire survey, containing specific audit objectives, for testing and evaluating control systems or group of inter-connected systems. These questionnaires do not establish new security requirements. Instead, their control objectives and techniques are abstracted directly from long-standing requirements and established standards, as found in statute, policy, and guidance on security. For a self-assessment to be effective, a complementary risk assessment should be conducted by security experts in parallel or in advance. There-fore, a self-assessment does not eliminate the need for a risk assessment within the organization Risk Management Program.

Since 2003, NIST has introduced the first Automated Security Self-Evaluation Tool to automate the process of completing a system self-assessment, contained in NIST Special Publication 800-26, which was later retired and replaced by NIST SP 800-53A [3]. Since then several security self-assessment tools have been developed, evolved and enhanced with functionalities which are presented, analyzed and compared in Sect. 3. As part of its efforts to increase awareness, understanding and reducing cyber risks to critical infrastructures, NIST has also developed a voluntary framework, based on existing standards, guidelines and practices [2]. NIST Cybersecurity Framework cre-ates a solid basis for managing cybersecurity risks related to critical infrastructure. The framework provides a risk-based approach for cybersecurity through five core func-tions: (i) identify, (ii) protect, (iii) detect, (iv) respond, and (v) recover. These core functions represent the 5 primary pillars for a successful and holistic cybersecurity program. They aid organizations in easily expressing their management of cyberse-curity risk at a high level and enabling risk management decisions. A short description of each function follows:

(1) *The Identify Function* assists in developing an organizational understanding to managing cybersecurity risk to systems, people, assets, data and capabilities.
(2) *The Protect Function* outlines appropriate safeguards to ensure delivery of critical infrastructure services.
(3) *The Detect Function* defines the appropriate activities to identify the occurrence of a cybersecurity event. It enables timely discovery of cybersecurity events.
(4) *The Respond Function* includes appropriate activities towards a detected security incident, by enhancing the ability to contain impact of any cybersecurity incident.
(5) *The Recover Function* identifies appropriate activities to maintain plans for resi-lience and to restore any capabilities or services that were impaired due to a cybersecurity incident, by supporting timely recovery to normal operations.

3 ICS Cyber Security Self-assessment Tools

In this section we briefly present four self-assessment tools that have been developed with the scope to support cybersecurity management in critical CIs and provide specific analysis, or a dedicated section for ICS & SCADA evaluation.

(i) **Control System Cyber Security Self-Assessment Tool (CS^{2}SAT):** A desktop software tool that gathers information about the facility of ICS, guides users through a step-by-step process to collect specific control system information and makes appropriate recommendations for improving system's cyber-security. The purpose of CS^{2}SAT is to provide organizations that use ICS to control any physical process with a self-assessment tool for evaluating the programmatic and certain aspects of security [14]. It is designed as a self-contained tool to assist individuals in identifying cyber security vulnerabilities and then it provides a comprehensive evaluation of implemented security programs and comparison to existing industry standards and regulations. The CS^{2}SAT also provides recommendations from a database of industry available cyber-security practices. Each recommendation is linked to a set of actions that can be applied to remediate specific security vulnerabilities [14].

(ii) **Cyber Security Evaluation Tool (CSET):** A desktop software tool, which helps through a step-by-step process, owners to assess information and operational systems cybersecurity practices, by asking a series of detailed questions about system components and architectures, as well as operational policies and procedures [15]. These questions are derived from accepted industry cybersecurity standards. CSET includes a dedicated section to support ICS and SCADA security analysis for a tailored assessment of cyber vulnerabilities. Once ICS standards have been selected and the resulting questionnaire is answered, CSET creates a compliance summary, compiles variance statistics, ranks top areas of concern, and generates security recommendations.

(iii) **SCADA Security Assessment Tool (SSAT):** A tool developed by UK Centre for the Protection of National Infrastructure (CPNI) for SCADA utilities and CIs. According to CPNI, it provides a high-level snap-shot of the information assurance of an organization's ICS that are deemed to constitute the UK critical national infrastructure [16]. Moreover, it contains 99 questions divided into various categories for physical, personnel and electronic evaluation performance, based upon CPNI Good Practice Guidance and international good practices. SSAT output result is a performance scoring, aggregating users answering on specific targeted questions and providing high level understanding of SCADA/ICS security status [17]. Finally, SSAT is not a standalone self-assessment tool, so it is less robust tool than the previous examined ones.

(iv) **Cyber Resilience Review Self-Assessment Package (CRR):** An interview-based assessment able to evaluate a CIs organization's cybersecurity practices and operational resilience. It has a dedicated section for control management and can be either conducted as a self-assessment or as on-site assessment facilitated by cybersecurity professionals [18]. CRR focuses on key areas that typically contribute to the overall cyber resilience and measures essential cybersecurity capabilities to provide indicators of an organization's operational resilience during normal operations and during times of operational stress. CRR can evaluate cyber resilience capabilities of a wide range of organizations both in terms of different critical services or CI sectors and in terms of organizational size and maturity [19].

3.1 Cybersecurity Self-assessment Tools Comparison

In this subsection, we compare the above presented tools, based on standards compliance, usability and functionalities offering to their users. Analysis has revealed many commonalities in their design and principal characteristics, as summarized in Table 1. Three out of four examined tools have been developed in the US and comply with the majority of cybersecurity guidance, standards and regulatory requirements for Critical Infrastructures, such as NIST, NERC, DHS, CIP, etc. Also, since it is quite important for organizations to certify compliance with specific standards both CSET and CS^2SAT provide compliance check functionality, while SSAT and CRR do not; CRR is focused on resilience capabilities and contingency plans and reflects best practices from industry for managing operational resilience across the disciplines of security management. All tools provide a list of recommendations, while only CSET and CS^2SAT can relate each recommendation with included database of industry cybersecurity practices. In addition, CSET and SSAT can provide a sector average scoring result, which can assist operators to evaluate their performance related to industry average.

From graphical facilities, CSET and SSAT contain a graphical user interface that allows users to diagram network topology and identify the "criticality" of the network components. Moreover, in CSET user can import a pre-built template diagram or import an MS Visio diagram. One main difference occurs in the presentation of the results, where CSET gives a full report of evaluation performance with compliance analysis according to selected standards. Less detailed report is produced by CS^2SAT, while CCR report focus more on resilience and contingency reporting analysis and recommendations. Finally, the SSAT provides a simple scoring result with limited technical analysis and recommendations. Overall the CSET is the most technical complete tool, which covers all particular issues of ICS control and adjusts to users' needs for every standard compliance. In addition, it can be characterized as the most user-friendly, although sometimes, its detailed analysis can be time consuming for users.

Last but not least, one common functionality of all the above presented tools is that they base they evaluation on a well-structured and specific targeted questionnaire to assess the security programs and organization risk management effectives. Therefore, in the following section we will further investigate questionnaire functionalities, design and characteristics.

Table 1. Cybersecurity self-assessment tools comparison

Tool description	CS²SAT	CSET	SSAT	CRR
Type	Desktop software application tool	Desktop software application tool	Questionnaire XLS assisted Tool	Questionnaire PDF assisted Tool
Developer	Department of Energy National Laboratories	ICS-CERT/DHS	CPNI	US-CERT/DHS Carnegie Mellon University
Origin	USA	USA	UK	USA
Description	Self-contained tool step-by-step process	Self-contained tool step-by-step process	SSAT Questionnaire which links directly to the CPNI SCADA security good practice	Self-contained tool
Step Process	6	5	1	1
Survey Method	Structured Questionnaire	Structured Questionnaire	Structured Questionnaire	Structured Questionnaire
Security Expertise Needed	YES	NO	YES	NO
Standards Compliance	NERC CIP, NIST SSP-CIPCS, NIST SSP-ICS, NIST SP 800-53, DoD 8500.2 ISO/IEC 15408	DHS Cat. of CS NERC CIP 002-009 NIST SP 800-82 NIST SP 800-53 NRC Reg. Guide 5.7 CNSSI 1253 INGAA Control Security Guidelines NISTIR 7628 Guide	CPNI Good Practices NIST SPP-CIPCS NIST SPP-ICS ISO/IEC 15408 NERC CIP 002-009 NIST SP 800-53 DoD IA	NIST SP 800-18 NIST SP 800-30 NERC CIP FISCAM Clinger-Cohen law GISRA law FIPS 102 OMB Circul. A-130
Checks ICS Compliance with Security Standard	YES	YES	NO	NO
Database of industry available cyber-security practices	YES	YES	NO	NO
Sector average score	NO	YES	YES	NO
Recommendation List	YES	YES	YES	YES
Type of Result	Full Performance Evaluation	Full Performance Evaluation & Compliance of Selected Std	Scoring Result	Full Performance Evaluation

4   Questionnaire Content Analysis

As described in Table 1, for every Self-Assessment tool a structured questionnaire is used as a survey method for collecting valuable information for self-evaluation purposes. This is a common technique for collecting information and completing an internal assessment of the security controls designed, applied and performed. These questionnaires can serve for many purposes. First, they can be used by management team and experts who know their agency's systems and security controls to gain a general understanding of security assurance and make informed decisions about the agency improvement needs. Second, they can be used as a guide for thoroughly evaluating the status of security for a system. Third, they can enhance and support employees' security awareness. Finally, the results of such thorough reviews provide a much more reliable measure of security effectiveness and may be used to (1) fulfill reporting requirements; (2) prepare for audits; and (3) identify resource needs. Therefore, the completed self-assessment questionnaires are a useful resource for compiling agency reports, such as: security program management and security planned activities [15].

In this section we analyze and compare the questionnaires used is the above described tools used for assessing ICS security, which are namely: (i) NIST Security Self-Assessment Questionnaire which is used in the first three examined tools; (ii) CSET Scada Self-Assessment Questionnaire when not using NIST Cybersecurity Framework; and (iii) CRR Self-Assessment Questionnaire used by the CRR tool.

4.1   Overview of SCADA Self-assessment Questionnaires

NIST Security Self-assessment Questionnaire: NIST developed this questionnaire to assess the status of security controls of IT systems. There are 260 questions, which are separated into three major control areas, i.e., operational, management and technical controls. Figure 1 depicts the topics of each area included in the questionnaire.

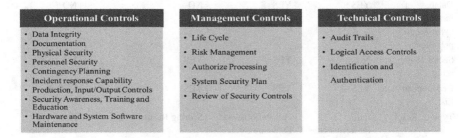

Fig. 1. NIST topic areas of questions

Moreover, instead of positive or negative answering for each question posed, a progressive scale of effective implementation has been developed to measure and evaluate 5 compliance levels, which are: (i) Level_1: Documented policies; (ii) L_2: Procedures for implementing the control; (iii) L_3: Control implemented; (iv) L_4: Control Tested; and (v) L_5: Controls are integrated in agency's organizational culture, so procedures and controls are fully integrated into a robust security program [3]. In Fig. 2 a screenshot of NIST questionnaire completing form is presented.

Specific Control Objectives and Techniques	L.1 Policy	L.2 Procedures	L.3 Implemented	L.4 Tested	L.5 Integrated	Risk Based Decision Made	Comments	Initials
Risk Management *OMB Circular A-130, III*								
1.1 Critical Element: **Is risk periodically assessed?**								
1.1.1 Is the current system configuration documented, including links to other systems? *NIST SP 800-18*								
1.1.2 Are risk assessments performed and documented on a regular basis or whenever the system, facilities, or other conditions change? *FISCAM SP-1*								

Fig. 2. NIST questionnaire screenshot

CSET SCADA Self-assessment Questionnaire: Assess security of information and operational systems cybersecurity practices by asking a series of detailed questions about system components and architectures, as well as operational policies and procedures. CSET provides a variety of questionnaires structures derived from selected by user industry cybersecurity standards. Specifically, CSET questionnaire starts survey by requesting information about the critical sector, the industry, the gross value of the assets that the organization wants to protect and time expected to be spent for the assessment effort. Moreover, users are able to choose whether privacy is a significant concern for their assets, their procurement supply chain assessment needs and the use of ICS systems. So, after completing this interactive section, next step is to specify Security Assurance Level and the appropriate standards. Depending on the above selections up to 1030 questions reposed to responders, which can be separated into three major areas, i.e., management, operational and technical controls. Figure 3 depicts the topics of each of the above areas that are included in the questionnaire.

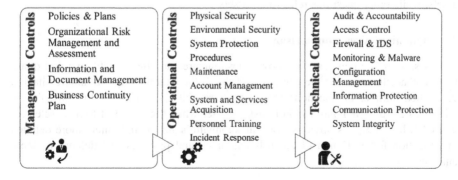

Fig. 3. CSET topic areas of questions

CRR Self-assessment Questionnaire: A resilience-focused questionnaire created by DHS for the purpose of evaluating the cybersecurity and service continuity practices of critical infrastructure owners and operators. The CRR consists of 365 questions, to elicit answers from the critical infrastructure organization's personnel in cybersecurity and operations. The CRR is derived from the CERT Resilience Management Model (CERT-RMM), which was developed by Carnegie Mellon University and reflects best practices from industry and government for managing operational resilience, business continuity management, and information technology operations management. As shown in Table 2, the number of goals and practice questions varies by domain and there are ten questionnaire domains examined.

Table 2. CRR questionnaire domain composition

CRR questionnaire domain	Goals	Goal practices	Questions
Asset Management (AM)	7	29	78
Controls Management (CM)	4	16	38
Configuration and Change Management (CCM)	3	23	37
Vulnerability Management (VM)	4	15	47
Incident Management (IM)	5	23	36
Service Continuity Management (SCM)	4	15	31
Risk Management (RM)	5	13	26
External Dependencies Management (EDM)	5	14	27
Training and Awareness (TA)	2	11	24
Situational Awareness (SA)	3	8	21
TOTAL	42	167	365

Each domain is composed of a purpose statement, a set of specific goals and associated practice questions unique to the domain, and a standard set of maturity indicator level questions. The MIL scale uses six maturity levels, which are: (i) Incomplete, (ii) Performed, (iii) Planned, (iv) Managed, (v) Measured, and (vi) Defined. The CRR divides assets into four categories: People, Information, Technology, and Facilities. Some questions require a separate answer for each of the four assets, while other questions refer to all assets.

4.2 Questionnaires Comparison

In this section, we compare the above questionnaires and their qualitative and quantitative characteristics. As we can see in Table 3 the examined questionnaires have a diversified number of questions (q), to perform self-assessment evaluations, that is NIST has 258q; CSET has 1030q to ask the user when high level of SAL is selected, and CRR has 365q. As obvious from questionnaire's size, CSET offers more detailed investigation for each area of controls examined and provides real defense-in-depth analysis.

Table 3. Questionnaire analysis

Questionnaire analysis	NIST	CSET	CRR
Number of Available Questions	258	1030	365
Question Type	Close Ended, Scaled Answering (L1-L5)	Open & Close Ended, YES/NO Answering	Open & Close Ended, YES/NO Answering
Link to supplementary information or explicatory info provided	No	Yes	Yes
Additional Comments Allowed	Yes	Yes	Yes
Complementary data requested based on user's answering allowed	No	Yes	No
Static/Dynamic security flow analysis	Static Flow	Dynamic Flow	Static Flow

NIST has a static flow of questioning structure for analyzing the 17 topic areas presented in Fig. 1, while question type permits a scaled answering with 5 implementation levels. CSET is the most detailed and advanced questionnaire with a dynamic flow of questions, and interaction based on user's selection. It can accept additional information either in the form of comments, data, files, graphs, diagrams and other material, while the user can override any question he considers as irrelevant. CRR uses both close and open-ended questions from ten thematic domains and can provide additional information to respondents to assist and facilitate their assessment.

Furthermore, by using the 5 Core Functions of NIST Cybersecurity Framework, as described in Sect. 3, we have analysed all questionnaires and classified according to their content. Each question was classified to a specify core function. Analysis result is depicted in Fig. 4. Although the examined questionnaires have a diversified number of questions, to perform self-assessment evaluations, when percentage analysis is performed, the majority of questions with percentage range from 54–61% belong to Protect Core Function. This reveals the importance given to technical measures and safeguards to ensure cybersecurity performance.

Questions related to the Identify Function vary from 16% or 41q in NIST Questionnaire, 19% or 194q in CSET and 32% or 116q in CRR, which indicates that organizational understanding to cybersecurity management is more trivial to assess. On the other hand, the questions dealing with Response and Recovery Function keep a low as a percentage, despite resilience and contingency necessity in ICS and CI facilities.

The greatest gravity of self-assessment questionnaires is given to protective measures and controls, related to less importance given on managerial and operational practices as included in the identify function. We can also realize that response and recovery investigation functions are significantly less examined, despite being an essential function for organization's resilience. This area should be further enriched in the future with additional content to assess specific areas to self-assessment questionnaires and related tools.

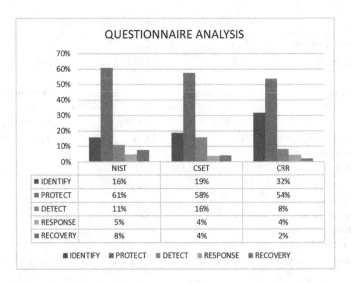

Fig. 4. Questionnaire analysis based on NIST cybersecurity framework

5 Conclusions

Adequate security of information in ICS supporting CIs is a fundamental management responsibility. ICS employees must be constantly aware of the status of their information security controls, in order to make informed judgments and appropriately mitigate risks to an acceptable level. There are several methods and tools for agency officials to help determine the current status of their security programs relative to existing policy. Ideally many of these methods and tools would be implemented on an ongoing basis to systematically identify weaknesses and where necessary, establish targets for continuing improvement.

Self-assessment tools provide a tailored assessment for CI operators and owners for assessing cyber vulnerabilities. Based on a selectable array of cybersecurity standards, these tools provide structured questionnaires to build organizational knowledge and create a cybersecurity compliance report with compiled statistics and security recommendations. Since self-assessment tools do not generate a complex risk assessment, they will not provide a detailed architectural analysis of the network or detailed hardware/software configuration review. Therefore, periodic onsite reviews and inspections must still be conducted using a holistic approach including facility inspection, interviews, and examination of facility practices and penetration testing.

From Self-Assessment Tools Comparison, commonalities and differences have been exhibited along with main tools' functionalities. In conclusion, the CSET is the most technical complete tool, which covers all particular issues of ICS control and adjusts to users' needs for every standard compliance. In addition, it is characterized as the most user-friendly, although sometimes its detailed analysis can be time consuming for users.

It is important to note that self-assessment tool is not intended to provide an all-inclusive list of control objectives and related techniques. Accordingly, it should be used in conjunction with the more detailed guidance listed in cybersecurity standards and government/legal mandates. In addition, specific technical controls, such as those related to individual technologies or vendors, are not specifically provided due to their volume and dynamic nature.

On the other side, while comparing Cybersecurity self-assessment questionnaires, we have found a diversified number of available questions, however the majority of them focuses on protection measures and technical safeguards to ensure cybersecurity performance. Response and recovery investigation are less examined, despite being an essential function for organization's resilience, so this area should be further enriched in the future with additional content to assess specific areas to self-assessment questionnaires and related tools.

After all, self-assessment questionnaires are only one component of the overall cyber security assessment and should be complemented with a robust cyber security evaluation program within the organization. A self-assessment cannot reveal all types of security weaknesses and should not be the sole means of determining an organization's security posture. It should also be noted that an agency might have additional laws, regulations, or policies that establish specific requirements for confidentiality, integrity, or availability. Each agency should decide if additional security controls should be added to the questionnaire and, if so, customize the questionnaire appropriately.

References

1. NIST: Guide to Industrial Control Systems (ICS) Security, Special Publication 800-82 (2015)
2. NIST: The Five Functions 2018 (2018). https://www.nist.gov/cyberframework/online-learning/five-functions. Accessed 2 May 2018
3. Swanson, M., Lennon, E.: Security Self-Assessment Guide for Information Technology Systems. NIST (2001). https://www.nist.gov/publications/security-self-assessment-guide-information-technology-systems-0. Accessed 12 Apr 2018
4. ENISA: Analysis of ICS-SCADA Cyber Security Maturity Levels in Critical Sectors (2015)
5. NIST: System protection profile – industrial control systems (ver. 1.0) (2004)
6. US Department of Energy: Infrastructure Security and Energy: 21 steps to improve cyber security of SCADA networks (2007)
7. CPNI: Good practice guide – Process control and SCADA security (2017)
8. ENISA: Window of exposure a real problem for SCADA systems? Recommendations for Europe on SCADA patching (2013)
9. ENISA: Communication network dependencies for ICS/SCADA Systems (2016)
10. NERG: Project 2014-02 Critical Infrastructure Protection Standards (ver. 5) (2014). www.nerc.com/pa/stand/pages/project-2014-xx-critical-infrastructure-protection-version-5-revisions.aspx
11. Piggin, R.S.H.: Development of Industrial Cyber Security Standards: IEC 62443 for SCADA and ICS Security (2018)

12. Stergiopoulos, G., Vasilellis, E., Lykou, G., Kotzanikolaou, P., Gritzalis, D.: Critical infrastructure protection tools: classification and comparison. In: Proceedings of the 10th International Conference on Critical Infrastructure Protection, USA, March 2016
13. Cherdantseva, Y., et al.: A review of cyber security risk assessment methods for SCADA systems. Comput. Secur. **56**, 1–27 (2016)
14. Lee, K.: CS2SAT: The Control Systems Cyber Security Self-Assessment Tool. No. INL/CON-07-12810. Idaho National Laboratory (INL) (2008)
15. ICS-CERT: Cyber Security Evaluation Tools (2018). https://ics-cert.us-cert.gov/sites/default/files/FactSheets/ICS-CERT_FactSheet_CSET_S508C.pdf. Accessed 12 Apr 2018
16. SANS: SCADA SAT (SSAT) (2018). https://www.sans.org/summit-archives/file/summit-archive-1493741491.pdf. Accessed 12 Apr 2018
17. NIST: Guide for Conducting Risk Assessments, SP-800-30 (Rev. 1) (2012)
18. DHS: Cyber Resilience Review (CRR): Self-Assessment Package (2016)
19. US-CERT (2016) Cyber Resilience Review (CRR). https://www.us-cert.gov/ccubedvp/assessments. Accessed 2 May 2018

Gathering Intelligence Through Realistic Industrial Control System Honeypots

A Real-World Industrial Experience Report

Óscar Navarro, Servilio Alonso Joan Balbastre, and Stefan Beyer[(✉)]

S2 Grupo, Valencia, Spain
{oscar.navarro, servilio.alonso, joan.balbastre,
stefan.beyer}@s2grupo.es

Abstract. Industrial control systems and critical infrastructures have become an important target for cyber-crime, cyber-terrorism and industrial espionage. In order to protect these systems from cyber-attacks it is important to obtain accurate and up-to-date intelligence on cyber security threats. Honeypots are simulated systems, deliberately exposed on the Internet to attract the attention of cyber criminals, in order to observe attacks and gain intelligence. Whilst honeypots can be a very effective way of gathering intelligence, it is not trivial to simulate a realistic industrial control system, without raising the attacker's suspicion. In this experience report, we describe the development of a honeypot, representing a water treatment plant, from the point of view of a cyber security service provider charged with the protection of critical infrastructure. The system has been continuously exposed and has provided intelligence for more than two years, feeding intelligence used in our monitoring toolchain and managed security services. (This work was partially supported by the Spanish Ministry for Industry, Energy and Tourism under grant number TSI-100200-2014-19 and the European Horizon 2020 Programme under grant agreement number 740477).

1 Introduction

Cyber security has become one of the most pressing concerns for critical infrastructures. As recent attacks, such as the 2016 attack on the Ukrainian power supply [1] and the 2017 world wide WannaCry [2] attack have shown, cyber security incidents can have a large scale impact on IT systems, critical infrastructure and society as a whole. At the same time as the number of incidents and the cost associated has increased, changes have taken place in the threat landscape, in that attacks are becoming more and more sophisticated and harder to detect by traditional means. So called Advance Persistent Threats (APT) are planned multimodal attacks, targeted at a specific organization or infrastructure. As advanced attacks are targeted at a specific organization, they are typically very stealthy and hard to detect. Traditional automated signature based malware detection falls short when it comes to detecting these attacks and thus, APTs have to be detected by different means, such as threat hunting strategies, in which the network is proactively scanned for anomalies and suspicious traffic. Threat intelligence is vital in this process, as information on ongoing malicious activities and

© Springer Nature Switzerland AG 2019
E. Luiijf et al. (Eds.): CRITIS 2018, LNCS 11260, pp. 143–153, 2019.
https://doi.org/10.1007/978-3-030-05849-4_11

sources of threats can provide important clues on where to center threat hunting and on the legitimacy of the traffic observed.

One very efficient way gaining intelligence on malicious activity is the creation of honeypots. Honeypots are systems which are deliberately exposed on the Internet, in order to attract cyber-attacks, which are monitored and studied. Apart from serving as educational tools and providing an insight into the current cyber-attack landscape, honeypots can provide important input to cyber security monitoring toolchains, such as signatures for intrusion detection systems (IDS), malicious source IPs for blacklists and other means by which attacks may be detected.

However, whilst it may be relatively trivial to create a honeypot simulating a basic IT system, such as a web server, it is difficult to design realistic honeypots simulating industrial control systems and critical infrastructures. In what remains of this paper we describe the design and development of our own honeypot which simulates a water treatment plant, the observations made during the two year exposure of the system and the role the system plays in our daily business of providing managed cyber security services through our industrial Security Operations Center (iSOC).

2 Building a Realistic Honeypot

A review of the state-of-the-art of ICS honeypots carried out during the initial phases of the project (see for example [3]), showed that there were common pitfalls that should be avoided right from the start. A brief list of the most relevant among them follows:

- ICS honeypots tend to be over-simplistic when it comes to industrial processes. The reviewed cases didn't match any realistic process and, what's more, consisted only in software simulations running in a computer which had some common ICS protocols ports open.
- Physical equipment was lacking or scarce. A typical configuration was that of a single PLC (Programmable Logic Controller) communicating with a computer.
- Typically, ICS honeypots are too simplistic to allow any complex interaction with a potential attacker, thus preventing any sophisticated actions from taking place.
- A tendency to over-promote the honeypot on the Internet as a means to enhance its visibility and attract attackers, complemented with just too evident vulnerabilities put in place 'to let the bad guys in'.

Summing Up: Attackers with a sound knowledge of industrial processes and ICS technology are not likely to be deceived by the reviewed honeypots, which look far too much IT-inspired. The most probable 'victims' of these honeypots are casual or conventional attackers, biasing the data on malicious activity obtained in this way.

In order to answer the questions asked above, a brand new approach is required. So, right from the onset of the design activities, we defined some important basic premises:

- The simulated infrastructure must be a realistic one, comparable to those a modern society relies upon.

- The honeypot must be realistic enough, so as not to raise suspicion, not only in casual or IT focused attackers, but also in experts with experience in ICS and industrial processes.
- The honeypot must allow for a degree of interaction high enough for complex attacks to take place. More precisely: in order to keep an attacker engaged for as long as possible, the system must show some kind of response to malicious actions. In fact, this action/reaction behavior should match reality as close as possible. For example, if an attacker expects, as a result of his actions, a pump to stop, flow through the corresponding pipe should drop to zero smoothly, just as it would in a real world installation.
- Contrary to IT honeypots, cyber security monitoring must be almost invisible. The reason for this is, that currently most SCADA systems lack complex monitoring infrastructures. Finding complex security monitoring in operation may raise suspicion.

3   The iHoney ICS Honeypot

3.1   Design Process

Our *iHoney* honeypot has been designed, built and operated on these principles. From the beginning the project was planned and executed just as the ICS for an actual infrastructure would have been. The main milestones were:

1. **Fake infrastructure design.** For this project, a water treatment plant was selected. The design involved treatment process definition and associated calculations, equipment selection (pumps, blowers, instrumentation…). Summing up, the design process was the same as it would have been in the development of an actual plant.
2. **Automation and ICS system design.** In this step controllers, communication buses and protocols and the whole ICS architecture where designed.
3. **Graphic Interface Development for the SCADA HMI** (Human-Machine Interface). This task was carried out in a realistic manner, using the blueprints already designed in the previous phase. In addition to the plant layout, other common screens were also developed, such as alarms, historian, etc., in order to provide a very realistic system.
4. **Physical processes modeling by means of logical and mathematical expressions that involve the considered state variables.** In order to provide an action/reaction model, in which system manipulation results in realistic state changes in the system, a full system simulator was developed, which interacts with the PLC and SCADA system, just as the physical components in areal water treatment plant would behave.
5. **Cyber security monitoring subsystem design.** In this step, the hidden monitoring architecture was developed, in terms of soft-ware, communication net-works and connection to the Internet. A set of hardware and soft-ware components were deployed for monitoring purposes. Monitoring activities were designed from the

beginning to be integrated into the companies live iSOC in the same way the industrial infrastructure of real clients are monitored.

6. **ICS system implementation.** In this final step, the ICS hardware was deployed and programmed as an actual system would have been. This task was accomplished with help from a specialized contractor.

3.2 Honeypot Architecture

The iHoney ICS honeypot consists of three differentiated modules:

- The **ICS system**, composed of an SCADA server/HMI, a control network of PLC that regulates the several processes and the associated industrial communication protocols. Figure 1 shows an example screen of the actual SCADA HMI.

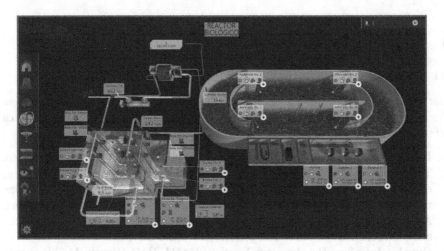

Fig. 1. SCADA HMI

- The **simulation system**, that evaluates the process status variables in real-time and interacts with the ICS inputs (legitimate or not) generating the appropriate outputs (as the actual system would). This system provides 'plant operators' with an interface that enables them to interact with the physical system: physical buttons and switches to operate manually, drives and panels, local interfaces to manually change set points, etc.
- The **cyber security monitoring infra-structure**, which obtains information about the behavior of honeypot attackers. This is composed of two elements: a NIDS (Network Intrusion Detection System) which monitors all the network traffic looking for threats, and a HIDS (Host-based Intrusion Detection System) installed on the exposed SCADA server/HMI, which monitors the activities of the system looking for suspicious activity.

NIDS: A passive solution was chosen for the transmission of all network traffic to the monitoring system. This solution is based on the use of TAP devices (Fig. 2). These devices are placed between the two hosts and replicate the traffic to our custom built monitoring probe, *argos*, which forms part of the companies monitoring tool stack. *argos* is the logical core where all the packets that pass through the TAPs are treated.

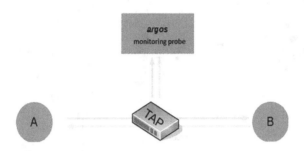

Fig. 2. Connection of the TAP with argos

The chosen TAPs are completely invisible for an attacker because they are not manageable and they do not have a physical address (MAC) and IP address. Figure 3 shows how the TAPs are deployed in the system.

When the replicated traffic arrives at the *argos* monitoring probe, this has different agents that analyze its different characteristics in real time. These include the SNORT NIDS and the Modbus [5] and S7Comm [6] industrial protocol dissecting agents (dissectors). SNORT is based on signatures that identify different patterns within a network packet, so that when a packet or set of network packets with certain characteristics matches the patterns defined in an implemented signature, it allows to log, alert or discard that packet. These patterns are defined from rules, which are the ones that define the situations to be detected. SNORT has a generic package of generic rules that detect different situations and attacks. In addition, a series of specific signatures were added for the detection of different actions against the devices present in the system, including actions carried out using typical IT protocols and actions carried out using the Modbus and S7Comm industrial protocols. On the other hand, the function of the dissectors is to dissect all the Modbus and S7Comm packets according to the specification of each protocol, in order to analyze in detail all the actions carried out by them.

HIDS: The function of the HIDS installed in the SCADA server/HMI is to alert of different actions that are carried out against the own server. Access to certain folders, user creation or files deletion could be an example. To do this, HIDS consults the Windows Event Viewer (where this information is located) and sends this information to *argos*.

Software that the attacker could not recognize is used, in order for the HIDS to go unnoticed. To this end, an ad-hoc HIDS was created for the occasion. The HIDS hides behind the appearance of a legitimate program whose function is to check the status of communications with PLCs.

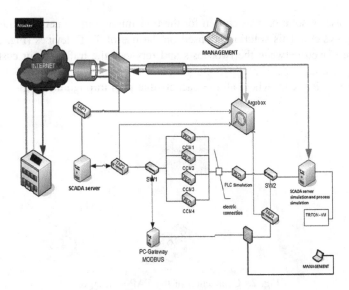

Fig. 3. TAPs deployed in the control system

3.3 Challenges

During the project execution some important issues have required special attention. Here follows a list of the most relevant:

- Some compromises were necessary to ensure, on the one hand, a realistic enough fake system and, on the other hand, an adequate level of complexity. So some simplification has been made in the mathematical relations between physical variables. Of course, there is a limit to this imposed by the need to keep the system simple but realistic.
- Choosing an infrastructure prone to be cyber-attacked. This is kind of a goldilocks problem: attractive enough but not so notorious that it raises suspicion. For example, choosing a big airport may not be such a good idea as it seems: it is difficult to simulate in a realistic manner; it is not likely that serious attackers take a singular infrastructure overexposed on the internet for the real thing; the possible impact of a casual attack on such a notorious thing may dissuade most individuals.
- Implementing the honeypot so as to render the simulation module invisible. One of the key factors to achieve this is the use of 24 V DC signals in the communication between the ICS and the simulating module.
- Simulating the response of physically driven relays built in some actual equipment (for example, overheat emergency switches in submersible pumps) and safety interlocks.
- Developing a high quality set of layout blueprints as a template for the SCADA HMI interfaces.

- Integrating the simulation module and the ICS one accounting for the tight requirements of ICS systems regarding real time processing, stability and network latency.
- Customizing the monitoring system to conceal the generation and exfiltration of information on attacks (logs, etc.).

Once the design and construction stages were over, the iHoney honeypot entered the operational phase. A maintenance and operation plan was designed that included activities such as:

- Scheduled maintenance stops.
- Scheduled operations (on a daily, weekly and monthly basis).
- Scheduled equipment failure simulation.

This plan was put in place to keep the infrastructure 'alive', as any potential attacker would expect from an actual plant.

4 Intelligence Obtained

4.1 Lessons Learned During Exposure

The iHoney system has been exposed to the Internet for over two years providing valuable lessons to our security team and intelligence data to be used by our analysts and monitoring toolchain.

Some basic insights observed so far can be highlighted:

- The system was attacked almost instantly, and, when connected, is being attacked on a daily basis. The actual volume of attacks has been much higher than expected. See below for detailed statistics.
- Most of the registered attacks are automated and are directed towards the IT components of the SCADA system.
- When properly configured and updated, it is not easy for attackers to get into the system. So, the importance of a good security management can hardly be overstated. In fact, this is prompting attackers to explore other ways in, such as social engineering (see next paragraph).
- A certain number of attacks were more advanced and directed against the operators behind the machines. Since human operators are the weakest link in the cyber security chain, this is a factor that cyber security analysts must account for.

4.2 Data Analysis

In order to analyze and visualize incidents a data analytics frame work has been defined.

There are several information sources for the analysis:

- **Network traffic:** It is the main information source for the different monitoring agents and is collected through the TAP devices of the system.

- **Snort Alerts:** They are sent to the correlator and stored in the system to allow the technician to access that information.
- **Logs from S7COMM & Modbus dissectors:** They allow to have a detailed register of all S7COMM & Modbus network packets, including all the fields of every petition and response of the protocol.
- **Logs of the SCADA server:** It gathers information from the Windows Event Viewer of the SCADA server. The logs give data in real time about the state of the equipment.
- **Logs of the Modbus slave simulator:** The Modbus slave simulator has the ability to keep a record of all Modbus petitions addressed to it.
- **Alerts generated by the correlator:** The information generated by the IDS, the industrial protocol dissecting agents and the HIDS, is correlated to detect more complex situations that could not be identified using another way. That allows to discern whether the actions are due to a legitimate use or an attack.
- **Other information sources:**
  - **Industrial devices:** The specifications of an industrial device, the way it is programmed, operated and maintained.
  - **Industrial protocols:** The structure of communication of industrial protocols. This allows to understand the communications between the different devices located in an infrastructure.
  - **Industrial applications:** Anomaly detection criteria can be established understanding how this kind of applications work.

To perform the analytics, a modified ELK (Elasticsearch Logstash Kibana) pile is used [4]. The captured traffic contained in files is loaded into a virtual machine. The IDS processes the network packets and generates alerts that are stored in an Elasticsearch database. Finally, the data is visualized using a Kibana personalized dashboard. Figure 4 shows this process.

The histogram in Fig. 5 shows the total number of IDS alerts that were handled by the iHoney during an initial exposure period (from July 2015 to September 2016).

The large number of alerts in the first months of study are due the Remote Desktop Protocol we used, which generated many replicated alerts due to the IDS signatures functioning. In order to reduce the volume of replicated data, the RDP service was substituted by a Virtual Network Computing service. We have chosen to maintain the high number of replicated alerts in this analysis, in order to highlight the difficulty of security monitoring in such an environment and because it serves as an example of unexpected lessons that can be learned in honeypot deployment.

Attack attempts came from all over the world, mainly from countries like USA (13% of IDS alerts), Netherlands (11%), UK (10%) and Romania (10%). It is important to point out that the locations studied are the exit points to the Internet of the IPs that produced the alerts, but they are not necessarily the geographic location of the IT equipment used to make the action (Fig. 6).

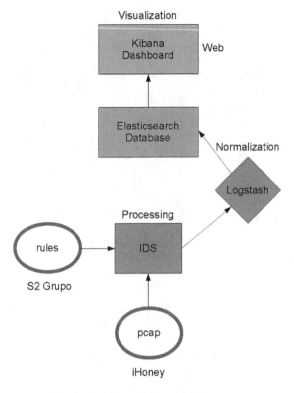

Fig. 4. Structure of the analysis process

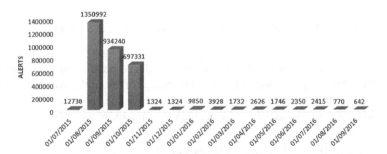

Fig. 5. Alerts histogram by month (July 2015–September 2016)

Studying the time distribution of the IDS alerts caused by IP addresses, different behavioral profiles are identified. On the one hand, there are IPs that concentrate the attack in a short time span. On the other hand, there are directions that have a continuous rate of alerts maintained for months (Fig. 7).

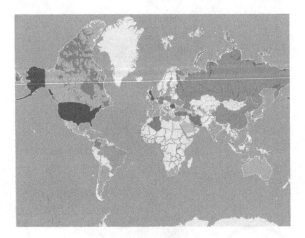

Fig. 6. Heat map of alerts

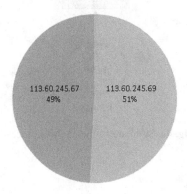

Fig. 7. Sectorial graph of alerts by IP of the group 113.60.245.67 & 113.60.245.69

One of the most interesting discoveries was evidence pointing to the existence of coordinated attacks against the iHoney honeypots. For example, we compared the octets of all the attackers IPs, looking for coincidences in the first two or three of them and considering it as an indicator of a potentially common origin range.

4.3   Input into Daily Monitoring Operation

The iHoney honeypot is continuously providing intelligence and insights for our daily business as a managed cyber security service provider.

The flowing is a lists of benefits gained in our daily operation:

- **IDS signatures.** Signatures of observed attacks are continuously being integrated into the IDS systems that for part of our ICS monitoring toolchain.
- **Event/Alert Correlation Rules.** Our monitoring toolchain includes advanced event correlation, which helps reducing the number of events to be dealt with by a

security analyst by identifying related alerts. The observations made by analyzing iHoney continuously leads to a better understanding of correlation of certain alerts, which are expressed as correlation rules and fed to our correlation engine.

- **Anomaly detection module development.** Attacks observed have led to the development of new modules for our anomaly detection capabilities. One simple example of such module is the development of a capability to discern between manual and automated actions from a potential attacker in SCADA HMIs. To achieve this, the detection of mouse clicks and movements that hardly could be imitated by an automated software has been developed. This module has been proven in the industrial environment with positive detection results.

- **General Awareness of the cyber threat landscape.** Apart from the above inputs to our toolchain, the honeypot provides important information on current developments in cyber security attacks, which leads to improved training and wariness of our cyber security analysts.

5   Conclusion

Honeypots are an efficient way of obtaining cyber security threat intelligence. However, designing a realistic honeypot simulating industrial control systems is not a trivial task.

In this paper we have described our approach to designing such an industrial control system honeypots, which is currently used to feed intelligence to real world ICS cyber security monitoring services. Furthermore, the results of more than two years of exposure of the system have been reproduced.

References

1. Ukranian power supply attack: BBC News (2016). http://www.bbc.com/news/technology-38573074
2. WannaCry cyber attack: Symantec Security Center (2017). https://www.symantec.com/security_response/writeup.jsp?docid=2017-051310-3522-99
3. Wilhoit, K.: Who's Really Attacking Your ICS Equipment?. TrendMicro (2013). https://www.trendmicro.de/cloud-content/us/pdfs/security-intelligence/white-papers/wp-whos-really-attacking-your-ics-equipment.pdf
4. Elasticsearch Kibana: https://www.elastic.co/products
5. Modbus Industrial Protocol Specificacion. http://www.modbus.org/specs.php
6. Siemens S7Comm Protcol. https://support.industry.siemens.com/cs/document/26483647/what-properties-advantages-and-special-features-does-the-s7-protocol-offer-?dti=0&lc=en-WW

A Comparison of ICS Datasets for Security Research Based on Attack Paths

Seungoh Choi[(✉)], Jeong-Han Yun, and Sin-Kyu Kim

The Affiliated Institute of ETRI, Daejeon, Republic of Korea
{sochoi,dolgam,skkim}@nsr.re.kr

Abstract. Industrial control systems (ICSs) are widely deployed in various domains of critical infrastructure. In recent years, security threats targeting an ICS are increasing. However, developing or verifying security technology at actual operation sites is quite difficult due to constraints that must be in place for non-disruptive operation and high availability of the control system. In addition, there is also a limit in obtaining datasets for security research. To overcome these limitations, several experimental studies have been conducted to build an ICS testbed for an experimental environment. Based on the testbed, datasets have been captured and released publicly. To properly apply datasets to fulfill the research objectives, the datasets should be analyzed in advance, because each dataset has different characteristics based on domains and security concerns. In this paper, we introduce the results of comparative analysis of various ICS datasets focusing on attack scenarios and discuss considerations of applying datasets to an ICS security research. It is expected that our results will help further researchers deal with datasets for their individual purposes.

Keywords: Security · Dataset · Attack path
Industrial control system

1 Introduction

Industrial control systems (ICSs) are widely deployed in critical infrastructure such as those power plants, water treatment, and gas. ICSs provide the features of measurement, monitoring, and control for various field devices [2]. In addition, the ICS is extended to the industrial field like a digital twin as part of Industry 4.0. It is connected with heterogeneous devices to monitor a wide range of state information and analyze data. As the operating environment of the ICS becomes complicated, due to the scalability and openness of the connection heterogeneous components have with each other in a network, the attack surfaces are exposed to various security threats.

Since the ICS directly controls a physical system such as the field device, it is essential to prepare a security countermeasure in case a cyber-attack occurs, as it may cause not only destruction of the device but also physical damage due to

© Springer Nature Switzerland AG 2019
E. Luiijf et al. (Eds.): CRITIS 2018, LNCS 11260, pp. 154–166, 2019.
https://doi.org/10.1007/978-3-030-05849-4_12

a secondary explosion. In fact, the US Department of Homeland Security ICS-CERT reported 257 ICS-related vulnerabilities in 2016, and they are expected to continue to grow in the future [17].

To respond to these security threats targeting ICSs, a security technology reflecting the ICS operating environment is needed. Moreover, an ICS research with big data analysis techniques has recently increased. It is based on integrated studies such as machine learning to strengthen diversity and complexity in ICS security. However, it is very difficult to deal with technology for the real world because we cannot accurately predict the effect of new technology or guarantee high availability during consistent operation of the actual ICS. Therefore, an experimental environment similar to the actual environment should be created to ensure that ICS security is elaborate.

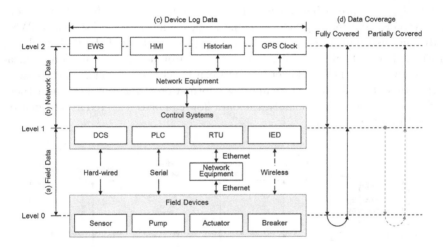

Fig. 1. Experimental environment to obtain dataset in critical infrastructures

In general, the ICS experimental environment consists of a Level 0 layer representing field devices, a Level 1 layer performing the computation and processing for the ICS control process, and a Level 2 layer handling the control process and operation information with a human-machine interface (HMI). Devices should be located and set up when building the environment. In addition, a system for collecting various data is arranged during the ICS operation. Once the setup is complete, the operation scenario is configured according to the purpose of the test and used for testing and verification. Based on the hierarchical architecture, the environment for providing datasets is actively studied [4,10,14–16,23]. The environment for ICS dataset collection should simulate the actual control system operating environment, taking into account scalability. Thus, related works used emulation or simulation methods appropriately to construct the field devices, programmable logic controller (PLC), network, etc.

We analyze the sharable datasets related to ICS for security research. In this paper, we present our result based on attack methods and paths. In addition, we discuss limitations and considerations related to performing security research based on the surveyed datasets. It is expected that applying datasets suitable for further dataset-driven ICS security research to our results will be useful and informative for comparison and considerations.

The rest of this paper is organized as follows. Section 2 addresses the background of ICS experimental environment and scenario of normal operation. Section 3 presents an overview on the datasets in ICS. In Sect. 4, we describe our comparative analysis of each dataset in terms of attack scenarios. In Sect. 5, we discuss the considerations of datasets. We conclude this paper in Sect. 6.

2   Background

Generally, when preparing the experimental environment, the field devices, control systems, and management systems (e.g., engineering workstation (EWS), HMI, and historian) are configured according to each level of the ICS, as shown in Fig. 1. For vertical data collection in the environment, there are communications between Level 0 and Level 1 or between Level 1 and Level 2. In the case of horizontal data collection, state and log information is generated by constituent devices at all levels. Additionally, the data flow can be considered as information moves through each level.

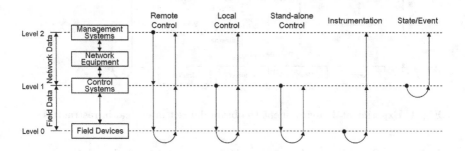

Fig. 2. Scenarios of normal operations in critical infrastructures

In a typical control system, the normal operating scenario is as shown Fig. 2. Normal operating scenarios are divided into control, instrumentation, and state/event. First, the control scenario consists of remote control, field control, and stand-alone control. Remote control is used to control the field device using the HMI from a remote site. Remote control can acquire data at both the field and network levels. In case of field control, unlike remote control, the control system does not perform control according to the upper command: it performs the control itself and transmits the result to the management system. The stand-alone control architecture is not used widely at present, but it is supported by a control system. It is composed of the pair of a control system and field device to perform the control process as well as to store or discard the information without sending it to another system. Second, the measurement scenarios are connected with feed-back, feed-forward, and cascade control by mainly transmitting the measurement information (e.g., temperature, pressure, and flow rate) of the sensor to the control and management systems. Lastly, a state or an event scenario refers to a state operated by using the functions of the device and alarm information embedded in the control system.

Table 1. Public ICS datasets to be analyzed in this paper

Dataset ID	Data domain	Year of release	Data source	Related works
Morris-1	Power System	2014	[13]	[5, 18–20]
Morris-2	Gas Pipeline	2013	[13]	[1]
Morris-3	Gas Pipeline, Water	2014	[13]	[14]
Morris-4	Gas Pipeline	2015	[13]	[16]
Morris-5	EMS	2017	[13]	-
Lemay	SCADA	2016	[9]	[10]
SWaT	Water	2016	[6]	[4, 11]
Rodofile	Mining Refinery	2017	[22]	[23]
4SICS	Complex	2015	[8]	-
S4x15CTF	Complex	2015	[21]	-
DEFCON23	Complex	2015	[3]	-

3   Public ICS Datasets

In this section, we briefly describe each dataset as shown in Table 1 prior to the comparison of the datasets. Each dataset is collected from their own experimental environment in specific or complex domain. To specify our target of analysis, we limited our study to the ICS-related datasets that can be accessed publicly.

3.1   Data Type

We have identified data type previously described in Fig. 1 as well as the file extension for each dataset as shown in Table 2. The Morris dataset provides five datasets as csv or arff[1] files, which include field data, network data, and device log data. In the case of the Lemay, Rodofile, 4SICS, S4x15CTF, and DEFCON23 datasets, the original dataset containing raw network data is provided in the pcap format. The Lemay and Rodofile datasets also include csv files to provide label information. The SWaT (Secure Water Treatment) dataset contains only field

---

[1] This is an abbreviation of attribute-relation file format, which represents a list of instances with a set of attributes using the Weka machine learning software.

Table 2. Type of datasets

Dataset ID	Target of data collection			Data Format
	Field Data	Network Data	Device Log	
Morris-1	O	-	O	csv, arff
Morris-2	-	O	-	csv
Morris-3	-	O	-	arff
Morris-4	-	O	-	arff
Morris-5	-	-	O	csv
Lemay	-	O	-	csv, pcap
SWaT	O	O	-	csv
Rodofile	-	O	O	csv, pcap
4SICS	-	O	-	pcap
S4x15CTF	-	O	-	pcap
DEFCON23	-	O	-	pcap

data and network data collected during the same time, and it provides all the data in csv and pcap file formats; however, we analyzed only the csv type in this study. Table 3 shows a summary of datasets where the file includes network traffic. As the table shows, the SWaT dataset has the longest duration and the largest packet volume.

3.2 ICS-related Protocols

We have verified that datasets contain various ICS protocols as shown in Table 4. The Modbus protocol was included in most datasets (i.e., Modbus/RTU, Modbus/ASCII protocol in Morris-2, and Modbus/TCP protocol in the other datasets). EtherNet/IP (Common Industrial Protocol, CIP) was used in SWaT, 4SICS, and S4x15CTF datasets. Since the 4SICS dataset contains the largest number of ICS protocols, they can be considered as priority for the research of ICS protocol. The DEFCON23 dataset is uniquely characterized by including all types of PROFINET protocols: PROFINET DCP, PROFINET PTCP, and PROFINET IO. Moreover, the S4x15CTF dataset includes BACnet, which is mainly used in a building control system. Therefore, it can be used for research related to direct digital control devices.

3.3 Brief Description of Datasets

Morris et al. Datasets. Morris et al. [14–16] have released five different datasets related to power generation, gas, and water treatment for their intrusion detection research. Since the Morris datasets provide labels in common, they can be considered as datasets for machine learning in the development of intrusion detection systems. The Morris-1 dataset consists of 37 power system event scenarios that consider the intelligent electronic device (IED) operation count,

Table 3. Network traffic in the dataset

Dataset ID	Sub-data	Num. of Pkts	Byte of Pkts	Duration
Lemay	Run8	72,186	6,035,064	1 h
	Run11	72,498	5,989,226	1 h
	Run1 6RTU	134,690	15,017,158	1 h
	Run1 12RTU	238,360	16,191,008	1 h 3 m
	Run1 3RTU 2 s	305,932	20,330,477	1 h
	Polling only 6RTU	58,325	3,441,247	59 m
	Moving two files 6RTU	3,319	200,189	3 m
	Send a fake command 6RTU	11,166	657,840	1 h 1 m
	Characterization 6RTU	12,296	761,587	1 h 5 m
	CnC uploading exe 6RTU	1,426	160,547	1 h 1 m
	6RTU with operate	1,856	1,129,078	1 h 1 m
	Channel 2d 3 s	383,312	22,816,188	1 h 6 m
	Channel 3d 3 s	255,668	15,218,187	44 m
	Channel 4d 1 s	414,412	24,595,619	1 h 12 m
	Channel 4d 2 s	266,387	15,833,346	46 m
	Channel 4d 5 s	107,577	6,421,852	19 m
	Channel 4d 9 s	60,295	3,619,845	11 m
	Channel 4d 12 s	44,977	2,712,015	9 m
	Channel 5d 3 s	143,809	8,559,985	25 m
SWaT	Network(pre-processed)	19,761,714	5,498,545,489	11d
Rodofile	Master	1,802,757	173,836,593	9 h
	HMI	448,655	61,956,933	9 h
	Attacker	1,373,938	114,462,713	9 h
4SICS	GeekLounge	3,773,984	314,562,089	1d 22 h 7 m
S4x15CTF	Advantech	307	35,293	1 m
	BACnet FIU	100,934	7,378,656	N/A
	BACnet Host	21,285	1,486,618	N/A
	iFix Client	5,149	818,114	N/A
	iFix Server	86,897	10,607,624	N/A
	MicroLogix	65,668	7,959,426	N/A
	Modicon	4,193	816,137	3 m
	WinXP	26,068	2,975,574	3 m
DEFCON23	ICS Village	1,368,167	92,193,653	1d 5 h 39 m

as well as normal/abnormal events in the power system testbed composed of generators, IEDs, breakers, switches, and routers. The Morris-2, Morris-3, and Morris-4 datasets include communication between the control device and the HMI with the Modbus protocol by connecting the RS-232 or Ethernet interface

Table 4. ICS-related protocols in datasets

Dataset ID	Modbus	S7Comm	DNP 3.0	PROFINET	EtherNet/IP
Morris-1	-	-	-	-	-
Morris-2	O	-	-	-	-
Morris-3	O	-	-	-	-
Morris-4	O	-	-	-	-
Morris-5	-	-	-	-	-
Lemay	O	-	-	-	-
SWaT	O	-	-	-	O
Rodofile	-	O	-	-	-
4SICS	O	O	O	-	O
S4x15CTF	O	-	-	-	O
DEFCON23	O	-	-	O	-

in the gas pipeline testbed. Each dataset contains network data information that removes some header information such as TCP and MAC of raw packets. In particular, the Morris-3 dataset also provides separate network data information for the water storage tank. The Morris-5 dataset is relatively large and is collected from an actual energy management system for over 30 days, which is the longest time in comparison with other datasets. This dataset contains information on the event ID, priority code, device, and event message. Some of the information is anonymized due to security issues.

Lemay et al. Dataset. Lemay et al. [10] provided the network traffic dataset related to covert channel command and control in the supervisory control and data acquisition (SCADA) field. To construct the test environment, SCADA network was constructed using SCADA Sandbox, a public tool, and two master terminal units were implemented using SCADA BR. The dataset includes Modbus/TCP by connecting three controllers and four field devices per controller. The dataset has diversity as it reflects various scenarios. For example, the dataset is obtained by changing the number of controllers and the polling cycle, ensuring manual operation by the operator, etc. Most datasets provide labels to distinguish between normal and abnormal data.

SWaT Dataset. Datasets released by the SWaT collected sensors, actuators, PLC input/output (I/O) signals and network traffic during seven days of normal operation and four days of the attack scenario. In particular, the SWaT datasets provide the largest amount of data in a large testbed. SWaT defined the device and physical points to be attacked and designed each attack to construct a total of 36 attack scenarios related to field signals and network traffic [4]. Attack scenarios are based on the principles of the physical system to determine the normal operation. When the physical system operates differently, it is considered as an attack [11]. In addition, since the datasets are separated by the network and a physical layer, they can be used in the research for monitoring analog I/O and digital I/O, which are signals in the field layer.

Rodofile et al. Dataset. Rodofile et al. [23] used the Siemens S7-300 and S7-1200 PLCs to obtain the S7Comm Dataset on the mining refinery. The experimental environment consists of a conveyor, wash tank, pipeline reactor field device, master PLC, and slave PLC. To create an attack scenario, an attacker is allowed to access the PLC through the network and to perform a process attack that creates malfunctions in the control process. Rodofile et al. have released datasets on about nine hours of network traffic including S7Comm as well as HMI and PLC logs.

4SICS Dataset. The 4SICS dataset is collected from the ICS Lab's environment where Siemens S7-1200, Automation Direct DirectLogic 205 PLC, and Industrial Network Equipment including Hirchmann EAGLE 20 Tofino, Allen-Bradley Stratix 6000, and Moxa EDS-508A are deployed. Because heterogeneous ICS devices in the same environment are networked, various ICS-related protocol traffic such as S7Comm, Modus/TCP, EtherNet/IP, and DNP 3.0 are included in the dataset.

S4x15 ICS Village CTF Dataset. Unlike the other datasets, this dataset (hereinafter S4x15CTF) is the network traffic collected during the capture-the-flag (CTF) in the ICS Village, provided by DigitalBond [21]. Therefore, the dataset includes various attacks attempted by many CTF participants that focus on the components of the ICS Village (e.g., Advantech PLC, Modicon PLC, and MicroLogix PLC). Each dataset is grouped according to the components of the ICS Village, but no label is provided.

DEFCON 23 ICS Village Dataset. This dataset (hereinafter DEFCON23) includes network traffic collected by running the ICS Village, provided at DEF CON23. ICS Village is composed of various control systems and communication protocols are used. In particular, the PROFINET PTCP, DCP, and IO protocols are included but labels are not provided.

4 Attack Scenarios in the Public ICS Datasets

The ICS datasets are a collection of information generated based on normal operating scenarios or attack scenarios. As described in Fig. 2, a normal operating scenario consists of necessary actions or situations. Table 5 shows the analysis results, except for the datasets that do not contain either the data label of attack or attack scenario. Due to the lack of space, we combined the individual sub-data of each dataset to describe the normal and attack data. In fact, we identified that seven out of eleven datasets were provided with labels. The attack data were generally smaller than normal data, but in the case of the Morris-1 dataset and some of the attacks of the Lemay dataset, the attack data occupied a higher proportion than the normal data. In addition, some datasets are provided with less than 5% attack data. For conducting attack scenarios, we divided them into modification, fabrication, interruption, and interception [24].

Table 5. Statistics of normal and attack data in the labeled datasets

Dataset ID	Num. of normal data (%)	Num. of attack data (%)
Morris-1	22,714 (29.98)	55,663 (71.02)
Morris-2	140,382 (97.32)	3,867 (2.68)
Morris-3	233,871 (70.10)	99,627 (29.90)
Morris-4	643,740 (78.13)	180,144 (21.87)
Lemay	16,362 (92.09)	1,405 (7.91)
SWaT	395,298 (87.86)	54,621 (12.14)
Rodofile	1,137,294 (63.09)	665,463 (36.91)

- **Modification.** The information is not only intercepted but also modified by an attacker while in transit from the source to the destination (e.g., man-in-the-middle attack).
- **Fabrication.** An attacker injects fake data into the system without having the sender do anything (e.g., relaying and masquerading attack).
- **Interruption.** A system becomes unavailable due to resource exhaustion or destroyed physically. This attack targets the specific system or communication path (e.g., denial-of-service (DoS) attack).
- **Interception.** An attacker gets the information by intercepting information from the communication channel (e.g., wiretapping).

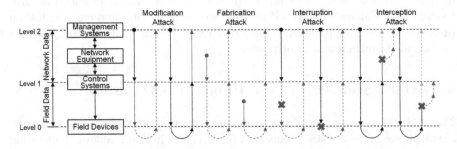

Fig. 3. Attack scenarios with attack paths (Color figure online)

Figure 3 shows attack scenarios described that attacks can occur in different attack paths. The solid red line stands for attack path. The dashed red line means that the attack could affect the information afterwards. The attack path in the same communication level means that the attack takes place at a device itself. For example, an attacker may change setting of control system directly. We assigned an attack scenario ID for each dataset through an attack scenario analysis. Table 6 shows the attack scenario IDs to identify the four general attack methods at communication paths between levels, as described in Fig. 3. We expressed each attack and path through symbols. For instance, 'F3' means that attack scenarios include fabrication attack from level 1 to level 0

We have limited that the attack scenarios of the labeled datasets in ICS represented by Table 6 while various ICS attack and its real exploitation have been introduced [12]. We identified that each dataset includes modification, fabrication, and interruption, except interception. In particular, the attacker injects data or command through the connection between Level 1 and Level 2 as the attack scenario. The specific attack scenarios targeting ICSs are as follows. First, reconnaissance (e.g., scanning) attacks are performed for preliminary work to collect information such as on control system services. For example, in the case of PLCWorm, scanning was performed to identify available service ports. Second, in the case of a DoS attack trips a field device by sending a trip command, resulting in a DoS, or by exploiting a Modbus communication vulnerability to cause a DoS through resource exhaustion. Third, as a representative example of Stuxnet, the response injection attack (i.e., HMI spoofing attack) injects the response contents so that the operator does not correctly recognize the HMI device information of the field device. Lastly, in the case of a command/data injection attack, the field device caused a trip or fault by manipulating or injecting the command with an abnormal value that is out of the threshold. As shown in Table 7, modification and fabrication attacks through all levels are the major attack scenario in the public ICS datasets. In the datasets, the ICS attack scenarios tend to focus on the malfunction of a field device by sending abnormal data to control systems.

Table 6. Categories of attack scenarios based on attack paths and methods

Attack path	Attack method			
	Modification	Fabrication	Interruption	Interception
Level 0→0	M1	F1	R1	C1
Level 0→1	M2	F2	R2	C2
Level 1→0	M3	F3	R3	C3
Level 1→1	M4	F4	R4	C4
Level 1→2	M5	F5	R5	C5
Level 2→1	M6	F6	R6	C6

Table 7. Classification of attack scenarios in datasets

Dataset ID	Modification						Fabrication						Interruption						Interception					
	1	2	3	4	5	6	1	2	3	4	5	6	1	2	3	4	5	6	1	2	3	4	5	6
Morris-1	-	-	-	O	-	-	-	-	-	-	O	O	-	-	-	-	-	-	-	-	-	-	-	-
Morris-2	-	-	-	O	-	-	-	-	-	-	O	O	-	-	-	O	-	-	-	-	-	-	-	-
Morris-3	-	-	-	O	-	-	-	-	-	-	O	O	-	-	-	O	-	O	-	-	-	-	-	-
Morris-4	-	-	-	O	-	-	-	-	-	-	O	O	-	-	-	O	-	O	-	-	-	-	-	-
Lemay	-	-	-	O	-	-	-	-	-	-	-	-	O	-	-	-	-	-	-	-	-	-	-	-
SWaT	-	-	-	O	-	-	-	-	-	-	-	-	O	-	-	-	-	-	-	-	-	-	-	-
Rodofile	-	-	-	O	-	-	-	-	-	-	-	-	O	-	-	-	-	-	-	-	-	-	-	-

5   Consideration for Generating ICS Datasets

– **Timing issues.** The synchronization of I/O and internal information acquisition time may not match when OLE for process control (OPC) is used to collect information from various control systems such as PLC and distributed control system. Even if OPC is not used, the S4x15CTF dataset are provided with '1970-01-01 00:00:00' as time information because time synchronization between the devices was not applied. Therefore, it is preferable to use time synchronization of information such as through network time protocol so that information generated at the near time can be identified easily.
– **Criteria of abnormal states.** In a dataset, it is important to display the label at the time of abnormal action (e.g., attack) during normal operation of control systems. When machine-learning and detection techniques distinguish between normal and abnormal states, the label marked for each record in the dataset can be used. If a dataset does not correctly provide both normal and abnormal labels reflecting the characteristics of the control devices, both machine-learning and detection can not be performed properly. Even though the label is marked as normal, the actual data may show a different pattern than the normal state. In case of the SWaT dataset, some researches have excluded the data collected during initial operation of the experiment environment from the learning since the sensor was not stabilized at that period [7]. In addition, after finishing attacks, the sensor information may not be stabilized immediately but may gradually return to the normal state.
– **Same attack in different environments.** ICSs react differently depending on the time, target, and operational state of the attack, even if the same attack occurs. To test an attack scenario against anomaly detection on machine-learning based techniques, it is essential to test the same attack several times in different states of target system. To provide diverse datasets, it is necessary to consider constructing a system that can reproduce the attack situation generated by the user at a desired time.

6   Conclusion

We analyzed various aspects of datasets obtained publicly. We broke down attack scenarios with the attack methods and paths, then identified attack scenarios of each dataset. As a result, the ICS datasets are biased towards a specific attack paths. This paper presented additional considerations when generating datasets for ICS security research. We expect that our results can be used as an index when using and generating ICS datasets for security research.

References

1. Beaver, J.M., Borges-Hink, R.C., Buckner, M.A.: An evaluation of machine learning methods to detect malicious scada communications. In: 2013 12th International Conference on Machine Learning and Applications, vol. 2, pp. 54–59 (2013). https://doi.org/10.1109/ICMLA.2013.105
2. CIPedia©. https://publicwiki-01.fraunhofer.de/CIPedia/index.php. Last Accessed 30 Apr 2018
3. DEFCON23: compilation of ICS PCAP files indexed by protocol. https://media.defcon.org/DEFCON23/DEFCON23villages/DEFCON23icsvillage/DEFCON23ICSVillagepacketcaptures.rar. Last Accessed 30 Apr 2018
4. Goh, J., Adepu, S., Junejo, K.N., Mathur, A.: A dataset to support research in the design of secure water treatment systems. In: Havarneanu, G., Setola, R., Nassopoulos, H., Wolthusen, S. (eds.) CRITIS 2016. LNCS, vol. 10242, pp. 88–99. Springer, Cham (2017). https://doi.org/10.1007/978-3-319-71368-7_8
5. Hink, R.C.B., Beaver, J.M., Buckner, M.A., Morris, T., Adhikari, U., Pan, S.: Machine learning for power system disturbance and cyber-attack discrimination. In: 2014 7th International Symposium on Resilient Control Systems (ISRCS), pp. 1–8 (2014). https://doi.org/10.1109/ISRCS.2014.6900095
6. iTrust: Swat datasets. https://itrust.sutd.edu.sg/dataset/. Last Accessed 30 Apr 2018
7. Kravchik, M., Shabtai, A.: Detecting cyberattacks in industrial control systems using convolutional neural networks. ArXiv e-prints, June 2018
8. ICS Lab: 4SICS ICS lab PCAP files. https://www.netresec.com/?page=PCAP4SICS. Last Accessed 30 Apr 2018
9. Lemay, A.: SCADA network datasets. https://github.com/antoine-lemay/Modbus_dataset. Last Accessed 30 Apr 2018
10. Lemay, A., Fernandez, J.M., Montréal, É.P.D.: Providing SCADA network data sets for intrusion detection research. In: Usenix Cset (2016)
11. Mathur, A.P., Tippenhauer, N.O.: SWaT: a water treatment testbed for research and training on ICS security. In: 2016 International Workshop on Cyber-physical Systems for Smart Water Networks (CySWater), pp. 31–36 (2016). https://doi.org/10.1109/CySWater.2016.7469060
12. McLaughlin, S., Konstantinou, C., Wang, X., Davi, L., Sadeghi, A., Maniatakos, M., Karri, R.: The cybersecurity landscape in industrial control systems. Proc. IEEE 104(5), 1039–1057 (2016). https://doi.org/10.1109/JPROC.2015.2512235
13. Morris, T.H.: Industrial control system (ICS) cyber attack datasets. https://sites.google.com/a/uah.edu/tommy-morris-uah/ics-data-sets. Last Accessed 30 Apr 2018

14. Morris, T., Gao, W.: Industrial control system traffic data sets for intrusion detection research. In: Butts, J., Shenoi, S. (eds.) ICCIP 2014. IAICT, vol. 441, pp. 65–78. Springer, Heidelberg (2014). https://doi.org/10.1007/978-3-662-45355-1_5

15. Morris, T.H., Srivastava, A., Reaves, B., Gao, W., Pavurapu, K., Reddi, R.: A control system testbed to validate critical infrastructure protection concepts. Int. J. Crit. Infrastruct. Prot. **4**(2), 88–103 (2011). https://doi.org/10.1016/j.ijcip.2011.06.005

16. Morris, T.H., Thornton, Z., Turnipseed, I.: Industrial control system simulation and data logging for intrusion detection system research (2015)

17. NCCIC: ICS-CERT year in review. https://ics-cert.us-cert.gov/Year-Review-2016. Last Accessed 30 Apr 2018 (2016)

18. Pan, S., Morris, T., Adhikari, U.: Classification of disturbances and cyber-attacks in power systems using heterogeneous time-synchronized data. IEEE Trans. Ind. Inform. **11**(3), 650–662 (2015). https://doi.org/10.1109/TII.2015.2420951

19. Pan, S., Morris, T., Adhikari, U.: Developing a hybrid intrusion detection system using data mining for power systems. IEEE Trans. Smart Grid **6**(6), 3104–3113 (2015). https://doi.org/10.1109/TSG.2015.2409775

20. Pan, S., Morris, T.H., Adhikari, U.: A specification-based intrusion detection framework for cyber-physical environment in electric power system. I. J. Netw. Secur. **17**, 174–188 (2015)

21. Peterson, D., Wightman, R.: Digital bond S4x15 ICS village CTF PCAP files. https://www.netresec.com/?page=DigitalBond_S4. Last Accessed 30 Apr 2018

22. Rodofile, N.R.: S7comm datasets. https://github.com/qut-infosec/2017QUT_S7comm. Last Accessed 30 Apr 2018

23. Rodofile, N.R., Schmidt, T., Sherry, S.T., Djamaludin, C., Radke, K., Foo, E.: Process control cyber-attacks and labelled datasets on S7Comm critical infrastructure. In: Pieprzyk, J., Suriadi, S. (eds.) ACISP 2017. LNCS, vol. 10343, pp. 452–459. Springer, Cham (2017). https://doi.org/10.1007/978-3-319-59870-3_30

24. Stallings, W.: Network Security Essentials: Applications and Standards. Pearson Education India, Kindersley (2000)

Advancements in Governance and Resilience of Critical Infrastructures

PPP (Public-Private Partnership)-Based Cyber Resilience Enhancement Efforts for National Critical Infrastructures Protection in Japan

Kenji Watanabe[✉]

Graduate School of Engineering, Nagoya Institute of Technology, Aichi, Japan
watanabe.kenji@nitech.ac.jp

Abstract. Emerging vulnerability of the national critical infrastructures (CIs) against to the cyber risk including cyberattacks and unintentional large-scale information system or network failures have increased frequency and the scale of socioeconomic impacts to our society. As dependencies among critical infrastructures have increased rapidly, the impact of a single cyber incident at a certain critical infrastructure tends to spread very quickly and widely to external systems and networks in other critical infrastructures or areas through widely connected networks. Considering the situation, PPP (Public-Private Partnership) efforts between critical infrastructure service providers and responsible governmental agencies have become very important to protect critical infrastructures from cyber risks. Based on this recognition, PPP-based cybersecurity exercises for critical infrastructure protection (CIP) have been executed for the last decade in Japan. This paper summarizes the over 10 years joint efforts of the Japanese government and critical infrastructure service providers and discusses the lessons learned and challenges to be shared with other countries to collaborate in the cybersecurity field.

Keywords: PPP (Public-Private Partnership)
BCM (Business Continuity Management) · Cross-sector exercise

1 Background of the Critical Infrastructure Protection (CIP) in Japan

In the last few decades, remarkable developments in ICT (Information and Communication Technology) and OT (Operational Technology) have been promoted and a variety of hardware, software or networks have been implemented to the operations and controls of the national critical infrastructure (CI) services. In addition to this trend, many CI service providers have been aggressive in introducing outsourcing, multi-platform technologies, open-architecture design, cloud computing, big data analysis, or IoT (Internet of Things) to achieve more effective and flexible operations with less costs and more efficiency. As a result, our society is enjoying higher value-added and flexible CI services but at the same time, the dependency of CI operations and service delivery on ICT and OT have been increased dramatically. We have started to experience critical disruptions of CI services caused by ICT and/or OT failures and also by intentional cyberattacks.

© Springer Nature Switzerland AG 2019
E. Luiijf et al. (Eds.): CRITIS 2018, LNCS 11260, pp. 169–178, 2019.
https://doi.org/10.1007/978-3-030-05849-4_13

Direct causes for the ICT and OT disruptions vary by case but root causes can be considered as increase of systems complexity, enlarged patchy systems, open or networked system architectures and interdependency among systems. With those concerns, the Japanese Government established the National Information Security Center (NISC) in 2005 and defined critical infrastructures to be protected. The original "NISC" turned into the National center of Incident readiness and Strategy for Cybersecurity (NISC) in 2015 along with the enforcement of the "Basic Act on Cybersecurity". The NISC defined the current set of 13 CI sectors [1] (see Table 1).

Table 1. Defined 13 critical infrastructure sectors and major systems (Cybersecurity Policy for Critical Infrastructure Protection, 2017)

CI sectors		Applicable CI operators [Note 1]	Applicable critical information system examples
Information and communication services		- Major electronic communications operators - Major terrestrial base broadcast operators - Major cable television operators	- Network systems - Operation support systems - Organization/operation systems
Financial services	- Banking services	- Banks, credit unions, labor credit unions, agricultural cooperatives, etc.	- Accounting systems - Financial securities systems
	- Life insurance services	- Financial settlement agencies - Electronic credit record agencies	- International systems - External connection systems
	- General insurance services	- Life insurance services - General insurance services	- Financial institution internetwork systems - Electronic credit record agency systems
	- Securities services	- Securities firms - Financial product exchanges - Money transfer agencies - Financial product clearing agencies etc.	- Insurance service systems - Securities trading systems - Exchange systems - Money transfer systems - Clearance systems etc.
Aviation services		- Major scheduled air transport operators	- Flight systems - Reservation/boarding systems - Maintenance systems - Cargo systems
Railway services		- Major railway operators including JR companies and major private railway companies	- Railway traffic control systems - Power supply control systems - Seat reservation systems
Electric power supply services		- General electric power transmission and distribution operators and major power producers, etc.	- Electric power control systems - Smart meter systems
Gas supply services		- Major gas supply operators	- Plant control systems - Remote monitoring and control systems
Government and administrative services		- Various ministries and government offices - Local governments	- Various ministry and local government information systems (handling of e-government and e-municipalities)
Medical services		- Medical facilities (Excluding small scale facilities)	- Medical examination record management systems, etc. (electronic patient record systems, remote diagnostic imaging systems, electric medical equipment, etc.)
Water services		- Water service operators and city water service providers (Excluding small scale facilities)	- Water utility and water supply monitoring systems - Water utility control systems, etc.
Logistics services		- Major logistics operators	- Collection and delivery management systems - Cargo tracking systems - Warehouse management systems
Chemical industries		- Major petrochemical facilities	- Plant control systems
Credit card services		- Major credit card services operators, etc.	- Credit card payment systems
Petroleum industries		- Major petroleum refinery facilities and petroleum wholesalers	- Sales order management system - Product management system - Shipping management system etc.

The 10 of the current set of 13 CI sectors were originally defined in 2005 as below;

(1) Information and Communication Services
(2) Financial Services (Banking/Insurance/Securities)
(3) Aviation Services
(4) Railway Services
(5) Electric Power Supply Services
(6) Gas Supply Services
(7) Government and Administrative Services
(8) Medical Services
(9) Water Services
(10) Logistics Services (Freight and Shipping)

In 2016, the following three CI sectors were added considering increasing socioeconomic impact of its disruptions;

(11)   Chemical Industries
(12)   Credit Card Services
(13)   Petroleum Industries

and Airport Services (including terminal operations, ground handling, and immigration/customs operations) will be added as the 14th CI in 2018 which are separated from the Aviation Services, the third defined CI.

2   Challenges of the PPP (Public-Private Partnership) and Intensive Efforts Through Annual Cross-Sector Cybersecurity Exercises

The NISC started arrangement of PPP-based cross-sector cybersecurity exercises. The first exercise was held in 2006. The objective of the first three exercises based on the National CI Information Security Measures Action Plan I (1st Edition) was establishment and feasibility building of the PPP structures in CIP (see Table 2).

Table 2. Overview of the cross-sector cybersecurity exercises in 2006–2008 (based on published data from NISC)

National CI Cybersecurity Action Plan I (2006–2008)

Objective	Enhancement of PPP(Public–Private Partnership)	
Actions	Establish PPP structure, improve PPP functionalities, and increase feasibility of PPP	
	Improve PPP functionalities	
	Increase feasibility of PPP	
Year	Participants	Theme
2006	90	ICT failures along with large–scale national disaster
2007	120	ICT failures caused by intentional cyberattacks
2008	136	Defining intentional cyberattacks by information sharing among stakeholders

In the 2006 exercise, 90 people participated from the original ten CI sectors and their regulatory agencies. The motivation of the participating CI service providers was not so high because of the presence of their responsible regulatory agencies.

The next series of the cross-sector cybersecurity exercises were held between 2009 and 2013. Those exercises focused on interoperable capability among CIs within their framework of BCM (Business Continuity Management) [2] (see Table 3).

The exercises which were held in this period also included cascading effects (dependencies) among the CIs and their widely distributed supply chains. Some of the exercise scenarios were based on the research done by NISC's assigned Technical Committee for Interdependency Analysis in 2007 that reported increasing dependencies among CIs as were verified by several researches on the natural disaster such as 2007 Niigata Chuetsu-Oki Earthquake case study. (Aung and Watanabe 2009) [3] (see Fig. 1).

Table 3. Overview of the cross-sector cybersecurity exercises in 2009–2013 (based on published data from NISC)

National CI Cybersecurity Action Plan II (2009-2013)		
Objective	Assurance of feasibility and issues of CI service provider's BCPs	
Actions	Increase awareness of CI service providers on shred threats across CIs	
	Enhance CI response capabilities by recognizing other CI's response ability	
	Enhance effectiveness of operations for PPP-based information sharing	
Year	Participants	Theme
2009	116	Wide-area critical electric power outages
2010	141	Wide-area critical telecommunication failures
2011	131	Cascade failures among energy-related CIs (electric power and gas)
2012	148	Cascade failures in electric power and telecommunications followed by cyberattacks
2013	212	Large-scale information security incidents

The case study analyzed cascaded incidents among CIs after the earthquake hit and evaluated interdependency of each CI and dependencies among CIs. (The solid arrows indicate clearly recognized dependencies and the dotted arrows indicate partially recognized dependencies)

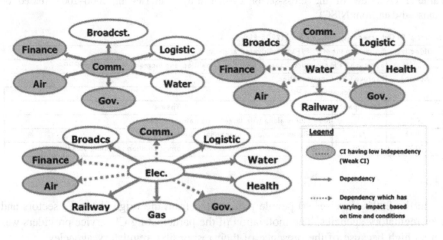

Fig. 1. Result of dependencies among CIs (NISC, 2007 translated by Z. Aung.)

The committee's analysis works examined and utilized the existing frameworks and methodologies including an analytical planning framework for hypothesizing, formulating, and mitigating vulnerability in CIs [4, 5].

The next period between 2014 and 2016 focused more on the capabilities and interoperability in incident responses among CIs and their regulatory agencies (see Table 4).

Table 4. Overview of the cross-sector cybersecurity exercises in 2014–2016 (based on published data from NISC)

National CI Cybersecurity Action Plan III (2014–2016)		
Objective	Enhance protection capability of overall CI service providers through execution of information security solutions and its feasibility confirmations	
Actions	Enhance CI service providers' capability in incident response	
	Raise the level of readiness at overall CIs	
	Enhance and maintain the partnerships among CI stakeholders	
	Assure governmental support for CI service providers' autonomic and continuous efforts	
Year	Participants	Theme
2014	348	Validate feasibility of ICT incident response structure including information sharing with items and frameworks related to ICT failure responses
2015	1,168	
2016	2,084	

Following to the three editions of national policy, the Japanese Government issued the Cybersecurity Policy for Critical Infrastructure Protection (4th Edition) in 2017 with the following objectives:

- Maintenance and Promotion of the Safety Principles
- Enhancement of Information Sharing System
- Enhancement of Incident Response Capability
- Implement Risk Management Framework and Preparation of Incident Readiness
- Enhancement of the Basis for CIP

and The Cybersecurity Strategic Headquarters strongly recommended CI service providers to apply PDCA (Plan-Do-Check-Act) management cycle in their cybersecurity enhancement efforts with BCM (Business Continuity Management) framework and at the same time, the annual cross-sector cybersecurity exercises have been aggressively enriched in scenario and operations. The fundamental objectives of the exercises were almost same and included information sharing among stakeholders in the public and private sectors related to the CIs. The establishment of interoperability for the coordinated incident responses was promoted.

Each CI sector has their own information sharing structure called CEPTOR (Capability for Engineering of Protection, Technical Operation, Analysis and Response). Inbound/outbound information flows are integrated into NISC in the Cabinet Secretariat through responsible government agencies for each industry sector to share information during an incident [1] (see Fig. 2).

The cross-sector cybersecurity exercise 2017 was held on December 13th, 2017 with over 2,600 participants from the defined 13 CI sectors and their responsible governmental agencies on sites in Tokyo, Osaka, and Fukuoka and additionally, on private remote sites at each organization that shared the same scenario and timeline. The participants used the same synchronized set of scenarios such as DDoS (Denial of Service) attacks, Malware Infection at network devices, and Malware Infection at SCADA (Supervisory Control And Data Acquisition) systems. However, they could add any original scenario as extension based on their real situations and business

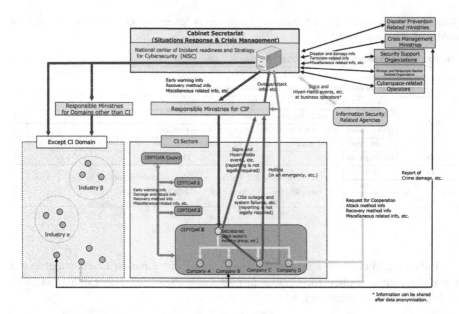

Fig. 2. "To Be" structure for Information Sharing and Shared Incident Response (Cybersecurity Policy for Critical Infra-structure Protection, 2017)

environment. A "hot wash" session was held following to the exercise and their lessons learned were shared among participants such as:

– Need to learn how to devise a wide range of response patterns based on limited information
– Need to consider response with limited resources to attacks that occur late at night or in the weekend
– Need to apply lessons identified in the exercises to improve CIP or CIIP (Critical Infrastructure Information Protection) at each CI service provider.

Those outcomes have been reflected on the Developing Guideline for Safety Standards at Critical Infrastructures to Assure Information Security [6].

3   Limitations of NISC's Cross-Sector Cybersecurity Exercises and Alternative Approaches that Complement It

NISC's over ten years' arrangement for the cross-sector cybersecurity exercises have had limitations in designing advanced scenarios for experienced CI service providers and in dynamic on-site scenario arrangements along with each response of the exercise players. This is because the basic scenario of NISC's exercise is to raise awareness on the necessity of building PPP-based interoperability in cyber incident responses with broadening the horizon of participants from CI service providers. As a result, the scenario which is used at the exercises has been pre-set and shared with all participants with a few options which will be provided by sub-controllers assigned for each CI sector.

On more thing is the lack of aspect of "region" because the basic structure of the exercise arrangements are made by industry in collaboration with their applicable responsible governmental agencies. This situation makes it difficult to assure interoperability across the CIs in responding to chained cyber incidents caused by dependencies among CIs in a specific region.

In order to compliment the limitations, CIs in Nagoya (4th largest city in Japan) district have started region-focused cross-sector cybersecurity exercises with dynamic dependent scenario while working with local police and municipal governments. The range of participants is wider than NISC's definition and include major manufacturing industries (mainly automotive) which the area heavily depend on to keep up its economy and employment. Their first exercise was on the same date of the NISC's exercise in 2017 and based on NISC's scenario but many customized additional scenarios injected. One of the major injection forced one of the CIs to shut down their system proactively and required the CI to notify other CIs and also local governments to evacuate and shelter the citizens.

Basically the operations and systems for CIs have been designed and implemented with the requirements such as;

- Stability: Stable services with expected quality and state
- Robustness: Capable of performing without failure under a wide range of conditions
- Availability: Assured quality or state of being available
- Expandability: Capacity to increase the extent, number, volume, or scope
- Safety: Condition of being safe from external intrusions and internal leakages
- Flexibility: Ready capability to adapt to new, different, or changing requirements
- Reliability: Quality or state of being reliable

to have resilience of its operations even in the severe incidents caused by natural disasters, system failure, human errors or cyberattacks (see Fig. 3).

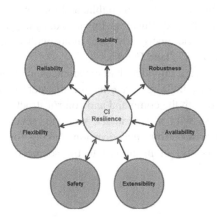

Fig. 3. Functional requirements for CI operations and systems

In the natural disaster cases, CIs basically try to keep their systems using the aspects of robustness and availability with business continuity framework to recover CI services as soon as possible (Fig. 4). In the cyberattack cases especially in those targeting control systems (such as SCADA), however, CI operators sometimes have to make decisions to shut down their critical systems proactively to keep their social responsibility in stability, reliability, and safety (Fig. 5). The decision to stop CI services are sometime difficult for CI service providers because of its critical socioeconomic impact. However, they have to stop their services certainly before losing system control by cyberattacks.

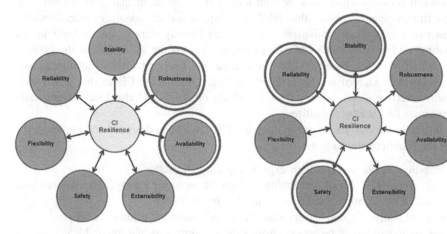

Fig. 4. Functional requirements in the case of natural disasters

Fig. 5. Functional requirements in the case of cyberattacks targeting CI control systems

In the Nagoya's exercise, planning members tried to put injections into the scenario to force the participants to escalate symptoms to higher management, to share with other local CIs and local police (cyber police division), and to take necessary immediate actions in risk communication to the public and local governments. Each decision required their processes of BIA (Business Impact Analysis) and SIA (Social Impact Analysis) to decide about the emergency level along with their pre-determined command and control structure [7] (see Fig. 6).

Many Japanese CI service providers had experiences in emergency response to the severe situations caused by the large-scale natural disasters in the past such as earthquake, typhoon, or flood with the command and control structure headed by their CEO. However, in the exercise with a cyberattack scenario, several hesitations had been observed in escalation or reporting, and decision making for proactive shutdown of their control systems because of its impact to the socioeconomic activities and the citizen's life.

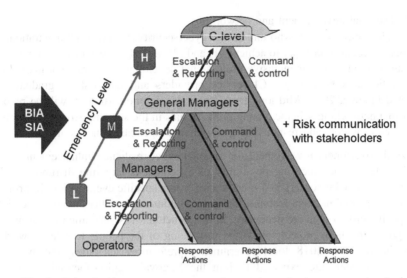

Fig. 6. Cyber incident response structure by pre-determined emergency level

4   Conclusions and the Next Steps and Challenges of CIP with PPP-Based Cyber Resilience Enhancement in Japan

With the intensive efforts in the CIP lead by the Japanese Government, readiness for cybersecurity incidents in CIs has been enhanced during the last over ten years. However, at the same time, CIs' dependencies on ICT and OT have increased and cyberattack techniques have advanced. The Japanese PPP-based efforts for cybersecurity in CIs are facing the following challenges for which the CI service providers and government sectors have to work together more tightly to make next steps dynamically to enhance cyber resilience of our society:

(1) Dynamic and interoperable PPP-based operations

Need more organic and trust–based information sharing and coordinated incident responses among stakeholders in the CI service providers, responsible government agencies, and major CI users. Bilateral CI-CI exercises and region-focused exercises such as the Nagoya's exercise addition to the centralized NISC's exercises will be effective to make the PPP-based operations more dynamic and interoperable.

(2) Proactive incident response structure at CI service providers

Leverage existing CSIRTs (Computer Security Incident Response Teams) and SOCs (Security Operation Centers) in the process of BIA (Business Impact Analysis) and SIA (Social Impact Analysis) and make them as "interpreters" between cybersecurity operational level and enterprise management judgement level. Some of the CI service providers have already integrated their incident response operations for cybersecurity and for natural disasters.

(3) Professional development and networking

Develop professionals who understand cybersecurity, business administration, and emergency response in order to achieve (1) and (2). In 2017, the Japanese Government has launched an one year intensive professional development course that invited full-time participants from major CI service providers and the first 50 graduates are expected in June, 2018. Mid-long term career development strategy will be required and also a networking scheme among professionals in the stakeholder organizations of CI service providers and responsible governmental agencies is necessary.

(4) Local government involvement for regional cyber resilience enhancement

Considering the emerging possibility of cyberattacks targeting disruptions of CI services and social disorders in a specific city or in a specific event period, information sharing and shared incident response structure with interoperability among stakeholders in a specific city or area are necessary. In this structure, it is very important to involve local governments to protect safety and well-being of the people (residents, workers, and visitors) [8]. In 2018, local governments (prefectures and cities) and more local police departments are expected to join the Nagoya's region-focused cross-sector exercise.

References

1. Cybersecurity Strategic Headquarters (Government of Japan): The Cybersecurity Policy for Critical Infrastructure Protection (4th Edition, Tentative Translation), 18 April 2017. https://www.nisc.go.jp/eng/pdf/cs_policy_cip_eng_v4.pdf
2. ISO 22301:2012 Societal security – Business continuity management systems—Requirements, International Organization for Standardization (2012)
3. Aung, Z.Z., Watanabe, K.: A framework for modeling interdependencies in japan's critical infrastructures. In: Palmer, C., Shenoi, S. (eds.) ICCIP 2009. IAICT, vol. 311, pp. 243–257. Springer, Heidelberg (2009). https://doi.org/10.1007/978-3-642-04798-5_17
4. Hellström, T.: Critical infrastructure and systemic vulnerability: towards a planning framework. Saf. Sci. 45, 415–430 (2007)
5. Zimmerman, R.: Decision-making and the vulnerability of interdependent critical infrastructure, CREATEREPORT, Report#04-005 (2004)
6. Cybersecurity Strategic Headquarters (Government of Japan): The Developing Guideline for Safety Standards at Critical Infrastructures to Assure Information Security, 5th edn. (2018). (in Japanese)
7. ISO/TS 22317:2015 Societal Security – Business continuity management systems – Guidelines for business impact analysis (BIA)
8. Watanabe, K., Hayashi, T.: PPP (Public-Private Partnership)-Based Business Continuity of Regional Banking Services for Communities in Wide-Area Disasters. In: Rome, E., Theocharidou, M., Wolthusen, S. (eds.) CRITIS 2015. LNCS, vol. 9578, pp. 67–76. Springer, Cham (2016). https://doi.org/10.1007/978-3-319-33331-1_6

Governance Models Preferences for Security Information Sharing: An Institutional Economics Perspective for Critical Infrastructure Protection

Alain Mermoud[1,2]([✉])[iD], Marcus Matthias Keupp[2,3],
and Dimitri Percia David[1,2]

[1] Department of Information Systems, Faculty of Business and Economics
(HEC Lausanne), University of Lausanne (UNIL), 1015 Lausanne, Switzerland
alain.mermoud@unil.ch
[2] Department of Defense Management, Military Academy at ETH Zurich,
8903 Birmensdorf, Switzerland
[3] Institute of Technology Management, University of St. Gallen (HSG),
9000 St. Gallen, Switzerland

Abstract. Empirical studies have analyzed the incentive mechanisms for sharing security information between human agents, a key activity for critical infrastructure protection. However, recent research shows that most Information Sharing and Analysis Centers do not perform optimally, even when properly regulated. Using a meso-level of analysis, we close an important research gap by presenting a theoretical framework that links institutional economics and security information sharing. We illustrate this framework with a dataset collected through an online questionnaire addressed to all critical infrastructures ($N = 262$) operating at the Swiss Reporting and Analysis Centre for Information Security (MELANI). Using descriptive statistics, we investigate how institutional rules offer human agents an institutional freedom to self-design an efficient security information sharing artifact. Our results show that a properly designed artifact can positively reinforces human agents to share security information and find the right balance between three governance models: (A) public-private partnership, (B) private, and (C) government-based. Overall, our work lends support to a better institutional design of security information sharing and the formulation of policies that can avoid non-cooperative and free-riding behaviors that plague cybersecurity.

Full paper submitted for double-blind peer-review to the 13th International Conference on Critical Information Infrastructure Security (CRITIS 2018) under topic 2: Advances in C(I)IP organization: Policies, good practices and lessons learned. Economics, investments and incentives for C(I)IP.

E. Luiijf et al. (Eds.): CRITIS 2018, LNCS 11260, pp. 179–190, 2019.
https://doi.org/10.1007/978-3-030-05849-4_14

Keywords: Economics of information security
Security information sharing · New Institutional Economics
Information Sharing and Analysis Center
Critical infrastructure protection · Information assurance

1 Introduction

In recent years, critical infrastructures (CIs) have grown more dependent on
Supervisory Control and Data Acquisition (SCADA) systems and the Internet
network to operate properly [3]. Therefore, the cybersecurity of CIs is increasingly recognized as a public good that is essential in the daily life of human
agents, organizations, and governments [17]. Thus, the need for managing critical infrastructure protection (CIP) is of vital importance for national security
because cascading effects caused by mutual dependencies across different CIs
and their services are considered to be a systemic risk [16,19,24].

Previous research has shown that security information sharing (SIS)[1] is a
key activity for producing information security for CIP [12,15]. SIS is widely
acknowledged by policy-makers and industrial actors, as it can reduce risks, deter
attacks, and enhance the overall resilience of CIs [13]. For the last two decades,
Information Sharing and Analysis Centers (ISACs) have been the preferred way
for CIs to organize and coordinate SIS[2]. Even though no empirical evidences
demonstrate the link between the SIS activity and an observed enhancement of
information security, most scholars and practitioners are convinced that such an
activity contributes to foster cybersecurity and social welfare as a whole [9,12].

Although empirical studies have investigated the incentive mechanisms that
support voluntary SIS at a micro-level (i.e., between human agents), most ISACs
do not perform at their theoretical Pareto-optimal level[3], even when properly
regulated [18]. This leads to the following research question: What are the most
efficient institutional rules for designing a SIS artifact? To the best of our knowledge, no scientific study has investigated this aspect. To address it, we propose
a set of institutional rules for the design of efficient SIS artifacts at a meso-level,
i.e., a theoretically "ideal" SIS center. Using descriptive statistics from a primary set of field-data, we present three generalizable SIS governance models,
thus suggesting how human agents would self-organize SIS if these particular
rules are implemented.

---

[1] SIS is an activity consisting of human agents exchanging cybersecurity-relevant information on vulnerabilities, malware, data breaches, as well as threat intelligence analysis, best practices, early warnings, expert advice and general insights.

[2] ISACs are non-profit organizations that provide a central resource for gathering
information on cyber threats by providing a two-way sharing process, often involving
both the private and the public sector.

[3] Pareto efficiency describes a state of allocation of resources from which it is impos-
sible to reallocate so as to make any human agent better off without making at least
one human agent worse off.

The remainder of this paper is structured as follows: In Sect. 2, we survey related work and connect different streams of economic theories in order to generate a novel theoretical framework. In Sect. 3, we conceptualize a set of institutional rules linked to an SIS artifact. We document our population and how the dataset was collected in Sect. 4. In Sect. 5, we present descriptive statistics illustrating our framework in the context of CIP. Concluding remarks, limitations and future work are presented in Sect. 6.

2   Theoretical Framework and Related Work

This paper is premised on the belief that a computer security-based approach, although necessary, is not sufficient to handle information security issues of CIs. Therefore, in this section we connects different streams of theories from institutional economics and security of information systems in order to create a multi-disciplinary theoretical framework.

2.1   An Institutional Economics Perspective of SIS

The driving forces leading to the creation of the ISAC differ; in some cases, the private sector takes the lead, whereas in others, the public sector brings all stakeholders together[4]. In both cases, it is crucial for the ISAC to find the right balance of collaboration between the public and private sectors, usually formalized into a public-private partnership (PPP)[5] [7]. Our research is premised on the idea that ISACs are institutions that were not designed in the most efficient way, because they were historically initiated and regulated by governments that are more focused on complying to security principles, rather than on ensuring a security efficiency [2].

From an organizational-theory perspective, ISACs perform differently as they operate under different institutional rules [6]. With each industry or government being free to set up their ISAC, those sharing institutions widely differ in quality, structure, and in how they are funded, managed and operated [4, 22]. Consequently, by applying an economic perspective on ISACs, it is possible to understand the quality, performance and problems of this particular institution. An institutional economic analysis can reveal why human agents behave differently depending on how the sharing institution is designed. This can explain why

---

[4] Some EU legislation nourishes the existing ISACs and the creation of new ones. For example, in December 2015, the European Parliament and Council agreed on the first EU-wide legislation on cybersecurity, adopting the EU Network and Information Security (NIS) Directive. The EU General Data Protection Regulation (GDPR) aims to harmonize and unify existing EU privacy-breach reporting obligations. On the other hand, some regulations, such as the US Freedom of Information Act might represent a barrier to SIS.

[5] A PPP is a cooperation between two or more private and public sectors. In this study, we do not differentiate whether the public or the private sector are owning and/or managing the PPP.

suboptimal performance appears to be pervasive, even in the next generation of ISACs, for instance in Information Sharing and Analysis Organization (ISAOs) or so-called "fusion centers" [20,21,25], which are supposed to aggregate and manage the flow of information across all levels and sectors. To address this problem, we propose a set of institutional rules for the design of efficient SIS artifacts, i.e., a theoretically "ideal" SIS center designed at a meso-level.

The New Institutional Economics (NIE) literature offers insights on how legal norms and rules (i.e., institutions) underlie an economic activity, such as SIS [26]. The NIE theory describes how rules affect human behavior, as institutions have different political, economic and social conditions [8,23]. Institutions set the rules on how an economic system is working and create incentives and threats to orient human agents' actions such as for SIS [1]. Thus, human agents cannot be expected to voluntarily engage in SIS, unless they are provided with a safe and conducive institutional design that facilitates SIS [18]. As a result, the decisive criteria for SIS performance are not related to funding or regulations, but rather to the design of "good" institutions. As there is an ongoing global debate about whether SIS should be mandatory, our research contributes to the formulation of policies based on voluntary SIS that can avoid non-cooperative and free-riding behaviors that plague cybersecurity [14].

3   Research Models and Set of Rules

In this section, we develop an SIS artifact based on a set of institutional rules.

3.1   Institutional Design of an SIS Artifact

Design science research (DSR) focuses on the creation, development and performance evaluation of artifacts typically including research models, algorithms, knowledge and human-computer interfaces [10]. We use the DSR theory to conceptualize our SIS artifact as a generic "information center" which is not necessarily related to ISACs as such. In our study, we use the NIE literature to design a theoretical "ideal" SIS artifact with the intention of improving the functional performance iteratively. Figure 1 presents nine institutional rules which can generate institutional incentives for SIS. Depending on how the rules are implemented, the performance and governance models will differ, because human agents can self-organize SIS and "select" the right balance of partnership between the public and private sector. The lack of cooperation between the public and private sector remains a major pitfall for SIS and the global security [22], especially in a "post-Snowden" context where trust has been broken.

3.2   Set of Universal Rules for SIS

Using a free-market economy approach, we suggest that, if human agents can self-design an SIS artifact, the market will select the best model on the long run [11]. Previous research suggests that nine universal institutional rules are particularly relevant for a design-efficient SIS artifact [6,7]:

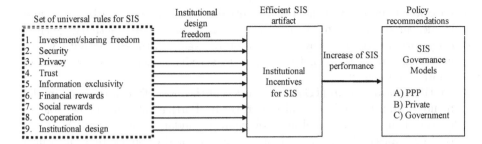

Fig. 1. Describes a set of institutional rules that offer human agents an institutional freedom to design an efficient SIS artifact. The artifact positively reinforces human agents to share security information in three generic governance models; (A) public-private partnership, (B) private, and (C) government-based.

1. **Investment/sharing freedom** guarantees that participation in SIS is voluntary and not forced by any regulations and/or constraints. Participants can determine what they share and are allowed to leave the artifact at any time.

2. **SIS security** is guaranteed that the artifact is built, managed and audited with the highest cybersecurity standards. An application program interface (API) should be designed to enable tokenization, in order to facilitate a secured SIS process and meet the security requirements of US and European regulators (e.g., regarding sensitive customer data).

3. **SIS privacy** is guaranteed by the participants' ability to seclude themselves, or information about themselves, thus engaging in SIS selectively. Therefore, participants can access, modify and delete their (meta)data at any time and have a "right to be forgotten". Participants can determine with whom they share security information according to the circle theory (e.g., participants can choose to share information only with the government or only with their industry) [17]. Upon request, the (meta)data can be anonymized in order to protect the participants' identities. The data will not be used for other purposes than producing information security.

4. A **trust** mechanism process is implemented in order to build trust among participants (e.g., with workshops or events). Trust can also be built on existing relationships or collaborations.

5. **Information exclusivity** is a rule that ensures that the shared information is timely, relevant, actionable and exclusive, thus making the artifact more attractive for participants.

6. **Financial rewards** are organized in order to motivate participants with a financial reward mechanism that recognizes their involvement in the SIS activity.

7. **Social rewards** are organized in order to motivate participants with a reciprocal altruism mechanism. As in the "tit-for-tat" strategy, evolutionary biology defines reciprocal altruism as a behavior where an organism acts in a manner that temporarily reduces its fitness while increasing another organism's fitness, with the expectation that the other organism will act in a similar manner, and eventually increase its own fitness.

8. **Cooperation** is implemented by altruistic punishment mechanisms and is measured by the frequency and intensity of the SIS activity. Such a cooperation is triggered by the intention to engage in the SIS activity, which was triggered by the belief that the SIS activity is performing in terms of information security.

9. **Institutional design (ID)** guarantees that the most efficient rules are implemented, audited and controlled iteratively. Participants should be able to choose their organizational and governance standards, for instance between: (9a) centralized sharing model such as a relational database (e.g., a forum) and (9b) decentralized sharing model such as a distributed database (e.g., a blockchain). This rule is also defined by (9c) formalization and (9d) standardization. Formalization is the extent to which work roles are structured in an organization, and the activities of the participants are governed by rules and procedures. Standardization is the process of implementing and developing technical standards based on the consensus of different parties.

4   Application to Critical Infrastructure Protection

In this section, we present how our data set was collected and three different generic governance models that can be applied to CIP.

4.1   Population and Data Collection

We conducted our study with the Swiss Reporting and Analysis Centre for Information Security (MELANI). The center was created in 2005 as PPP between the federal government and the private industry. It operates an ISAC (MELANI-Net) that brings together over 150 CI operators from all sectors in Switzerland. The questionnaire[6] was sent to the 424 participants of that closed SIS user group. These human agents freely decide whether to share information, such that their individual behavior also determines the behavior of the CIs they represent. The closed user group comprises senior managers from diverse industries; all are in charge of providing cybersecurity for their respective firms.

Data collection began on October 12, 2017 and finished on December 1, 2017. Two reminders were sent on October 26 and November 9, 2017. When data collection ended, 262 responses had been collected, of which 189 fully completed questionnaires (72%). Overall, the survey response rate was 63%.

4.2   Possible Governance Models for SIS

We posit that human agents - positively reinforced by institutional rules - will self-organize SIS and find the right balance between three main generic SIS governance models based on previous studies [5,6]:

---

[6] The full questionnaire with items and scales is available from the corresponding author or can be downloaded at the following address https://drive.switch.ch/index.php/s/DgYt2lWZcgVSyMP.

(A) **The public-private partnership** model typically brings together cybersecurity stakeholders to organize SIS. Therefore, a strong cooperation between CIs and governments is needed in order to address cybersecurity issues. In this model, trust is hard to achieve, because of the high cultural heterogeneity. This governance model is the result of a mixed economy, i.e., a system bringing together elements of free market and planned economies. The government often has a role of facilitator but is not the driving force behind the governance model.

(B) **The private industry model** is typically a sector-specific model focusing on organizing SIS for CIs within the same sector, in order to generate sectorial knowledge and trend analysis. This governance model is likely to be joined by highly competitive international industries, such as banking and finance or air transport. This governance model is the result of a market economy, because the driving force is the private industry.

(C) **The government model** is typically a country-centered approach focusing on gathering public CIs and cybersecurity agencies, such as governmental computer emergency response team (CERTs). This governance model is often funded by government subsidies where participation is either mandatory or voluntary for both public and private CIs (e.g., mandates stemming from EU directives, such as breach reporting mentioned at the art. 13a of the Telecom Law). This governance model is usually the result of a planned economy, because the driving force is the government.

5 Results

In this section, we present descriptive statistics illustrating an application of our framework in the context of CIP. Using the collected field-data, we investigated correlations between governance models preferences and institutional rules. We extended our pre-analysis to four other control variables in order complement the preferences analysis: organization size, participations in trust building events, and sector of activity.

5.1 Correlations Between Institutional Rules and Governance Model Preferences

Table 1 shows the correlation coefficients between the governance model preferences and the nine rules measured at a micro-level. These latter are represented by proxies that have been gathered through specific psychometric questions[7]. Our results show relatively low correlations between pre-established institutional rules and human agents' preferences for respective generic governance models,

---

[7] *T*-test and analysis of variance (ANOVA) were performed in order to analyze the differences and statistical significance among group means. The detail of those analysis and proxies selection are available upon request from the corresponding author.

namely PPP-, private-, or government- ISACs. Moreover, only a few correlations (seven out of thirty-six) are statistically significant. Concerning the following rules, namely: (2) Security, (4) Trust, (5) Information exclusivity, PPP are preferred (positive signs). Yet, despite statistically significant results, those correlation coefficients remain at low levels. However, rule (8) Cooperation is highly statistically significant for the PPP preference, despite remaining at a relatively low level as well. This rule also shows a statistically significant correlation coefficient for the Private model preference, but also remains at a low level. Rule (3) Privacy is interestingly showing a negative and statistically significant correlation between the Government model and the Privacy rule. Despite an also low level, it instinctively indicates trust suspicions between human agents and the government. Due to the correlation coefficients low levels, and the general lack of statistically significant results, at this stage, no direct link between institutional rules and preferred generic governance models can be deducted. Therefore, future work on what defines governance model preferences is needed at the meso-level.

Table 1. Shows the governance model preferences ($N_1 = 137$) correlated with a set of rules measured at a micro-level, represented by proxies that have been gathered through specific psychometric questions. Each response score was measured on a scale anchored at 1 (lowest score, e.g., "never", "not content at all") to 5 (highest score, e.g. "always", "highly content"). Hence, the larger the score in the table, the greater the satisfaction or involvement with the specific governance model. For corresponding significance levels: $*p < 0.1$, $**p < 0.05$, $***p < 0.01$.

Set of universal rules for SIS	(A) PPP	(B) Private	(C) Government
(1) Investment/sharing freedom (Q7)	−0.09	−0.02	0.06
(2) Security (Q15)	0.15*	−0.00	−0.03
(3) Privacy (Q95)	0.10	0.01	−0.15*
(4) Trust (Q16)	0.15*	0.04	−0.09
(5) Information exclusivity (Q17)	0.15*	0.05	0.03
(6) Financial rewards (Q48)	−0.02	−0.01	0.05
(7) Social rewards (Q51)	0.11	0.05	−0.02
(8) Cooperation (Q54)	0.26***	0.15*	0.03
(9a) ID: centralization (Q56)	0.08	0.00	−0.02
(9b) ID: decentralization (Q57)	0.06	0.00***	0.12
(9c) ID: formalization (Q58)	0.09	0.10	0.00
(9d) ID: standardization (Q59)	−0.10	0.06	0.01

5.2   Governance Model Preferences by Organization Size

Figure 2 shows the governance model preferences ($N_2 = 260$) related to the organization size. This confirms that PPP-based and private-based governance models are generally preferred. Overall, private-based and PPP-based governance models are preferred. Large organizations (>250 employees) slightly prefer private-based and PPP-based governance models. Such a result can be explained by the fact that larger organizations are likely to be international organizations that are more subject to experiencing more competitive environment, thus are more familiar with a free market setup. As such a setup has the tendency of obeying fewer regulations, a private-based governance model would be a better fit for them. According to their experience, most participants perceive the number of participants in the their closed circle to be optimal (45%) and sometimes too large (24%) or too small (31%).

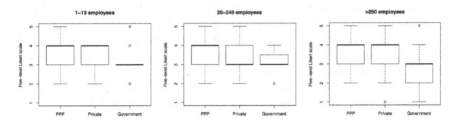

Fig. 2. shows governance model preferences ($N_2 = 260$) related to the organization size measured by the number of employees. Each response score was measured on a scale anchored at 1 (lowest score, e.g., "strongly disagree" to 5 (highest score, e.g., "strongly agree").

5.3   Governance Model Preferences by Participation in Trust Building Events

We measured the governance model preferences ($N_2 = 260$) related to the participation in trust building events, such as workshops. Each response score was measured on a dichotomous scale anchored at 1 ("Yes") to 2 ("No"). Our results show no clear differences between governance model preferences between operators who have participated in workshops and those who have not. However, participating in such events helps build trust among operators. The slight preference for private-based governance models of operators who have participated in workshops (3.75) with respect to those who have not (3.51) might be explained by this participation in trust building events. They might prefer privately-based SIS or in PPPs (3.70), instead of government-based SIS (2.88) as the trust they create among themselves is not directly related to the government. This shows, however, that the government is important for creating initial trust and setting the rules for a conducive environment for the SIS activity.

5.4   Governance Model Preferences by Sector of Activity

Figure 3 shows sector-wide governance model preferences trends. Surprisingly, among the administration population ($N_3 = 36$), private-based and PPP-based governance models are preferred over the government-based models. PPP-based models is the most preferred option, and the private-based option is not far behind. Such statistics are relevant as the administration is part of the government. This can be explained by the fact that the information-security expertise of the private sector is an attribute that administrators are keen to take advantage of by sharing the knowledge between the private industry and the government. Among those in the banking and finance population ($N_4 = 57$), private-based and PPP-based governance models are also preferred with respect to government-based models. Such statistics are not surprising as the banking and finance sector is highly competitive and obeys to a free-market setup. Moreover, a government-based option is the least preferred, corroborating the idea that less regulation is better for that specific sector. In the transport and logistic sector ($N_5 = 7$), the PPP governance model is the preferred one, probably because this specific industry has a long history of collaboration between the private and public sector. Furthermore, this sector is predominantly composed of fully state-owned limited companies regulated by public law. Further research could investigate the relationship between shareholding and governance model preferences, in order to develop sector-wide tailored policy options.

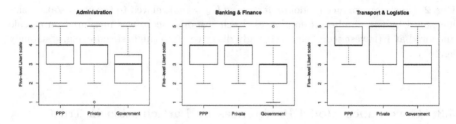

Fig. 3. Shows sector-wide governance model preferences trends. Each response score was measured on a scale anchored at 1 (lowest score, e.g., "strongly disagree" to 5 (highest score, e.g., "strongly agree").

6   Concluding Remarks, Limitations and Future Work

To the best of our knowledge, this work is the first study linking institutional rules with a conducive environment that could foster SIS at a meso-level. Using descriptive statistics from a primary set of field-data, we have presented three preferences generic SIS governance models, suggesting how human agents could self-organize SIS if these particular rules are implemented. Our results suggest that a properly designed artifact may positively reinforces human agents to share security information and find the right balance between three governance models. Overall, our work lends support to a better institutional design of SIS and the formulation of policies that can avoid non-cooperative and free-riding behaviors that plague cybersecurity.

This study has some limitations. First, we recognize socioeconomic biases, such as an overrepresentation of male respondents. Second, in some cases we note a tension between the micro-level measurements and some analysis performed at a meso-level. However, the analysis of those two distinct levels is meticulously distinguished. Even though respondents' answers are measured at a micro-level, their preferences shed some light on their meso-level preferences.

Our research could be extended in several ways. First, our model could be generalized to other contexts, for instance, cross-border information sharing among intelligence agencies, which remains a major pitfall for fusion centers established after the 9/11 attacks [22]. As the presented rules are universal, they could probably be implemented in other cultures and contexts, for instance, in information exchanges between tax authorities. Second, engaging in the SIS economy is not only a matter of incentives and institutional design. As SIS is a human activity (even when partially automatized) that takes place only if it is perceived as effective by those who are likely to implement it. A positive performance perception that SIS can bring to information security is thus a *sine qua non condition* for engaging in SIS. Such a motivational approach could *in fine* also support the information security of CIs.

References

1. Bauer, J., van Eeten, M.: Cybersecurity: stakeholder incentives, externalities, and policy options. Telecommun. Policy **33**(10–11), 706–719 (2009)
2. Boettke, P., Coyne, C., Leeson, P.: Comparative historical political economy. J. Inst. Econ. **9**(3), 285–301 (2013)
3. Eden, P., et al.: A cyber forensic taxonomy for SCADA systems in critical infrastructure. In: Rome, E., Theocharidou, M., Wolthusen, S. (eds.) CRITIS 2015. LNCS, vol. 9578, pp. 27–39. Springer, Cham (2016). https://doi.org/10.1007/978-3-319-33331-1_3
4. European Union Agency for Network and Information Security (ENISA): Cyber Security Information Sharing: An Overview of Regulatory and Non-regulatory Approaches. Report/Study, Heraklion (2015)
5. European Union Agency for Network and Information Security (ENISA): Information Sharing and Common Taxonomies Between CSIRTs and Law Enforcement. Report/Study, Heraklion (2016)
6. European Union Agency for Network and Information Security (ENISA): Information Sharing and Analysis Center (ISACs) - Cooperative Models. Technical report, Heraklion (2018)
7. European Union Agency for Network and Information Security (ENISA): Public Private Partnerships (PPP) - Cooperative models. Report/Study, Heraklion (2018)
8. Furubotn, E., Richter, R.: Institutions and Economic Theory: The Contribution of the New Institutional Economics. University of Michigan Press, Ann Arbor (2005)
9. Gordon, L., Loeb, M., Lucyshyn, W., Zhou, L.: Externalities and the magnitude of cyber security underinvestment by private sector firms: a modification of the Gordon-Loeb model. J. Inf. Secur. **06**(01), 24–30 (2015)
10. Gregor, S., Hevner, A.: Positioning and presenting design science research for maximum impact. MIS Q. **37**(2), 337–356 (2013). https://doi.org/10.25300/MISQ/2013/37.2.01

11. Hayek, F.: The Road to Serfdom. Institute of Economic Affairs, London (2005)
12. Laube, S., Böhme, R.: The economics of mandatory security breach reporting to authorities. J. Cybersecur. **2**(1), 29–41 (2016)
13. Laube, S., Böhme, R.: Strategic aspects of cyber risk information sharing. ACM Comput. Surv. **50**(5), 77:1–77:36 (2017)
14. Luiijf, E., Kernkamp, A.: Sharing cyber security information: good practice stemming from the Dutch public-private-participation approach (2015)
15. Luiijf, E., Klaver, M.: On the sharing of cyber security information. In: Rice, M., Shenoi, S. (eds.) ICCIP 2015. IAICT, vol. 466, pp. 29–46. Springer, Cham (2015). https://doi.org/10.1007/978-3-319-26567-4_3
16. Luiijf, E., Nieuwenhuijs, A., Klaver, M., van Eeten, M., Cruz, E.: Empirical findings on critical infrastructure dependencies in Europe. In: Setola, R., Geretshuber, S. (eds.) CRITIS 2008. LNCS, vol. 5508, pp. 302–310. Springer, Heidelberg (2009). https://doi.org/10.1007/978-3-642-03552-4_28
17. Mermoud, A., Keupp, M.M., Ghernaouti, S., Percia David, D.: Using incentives to foster security information sharing and cooperation: a general theory and application to critical infrastructure protection. In: Havarneanu, G., Setola, R., Nassopoulos, H., Wolthusen, S. (eds.) CRITIS 2016. LNCS, vol. 10242, pp. 150–162. Springer, Cham (2017). https://doi.org/10.1007/978-3-319-71368-7_13
18. Mermoud, A., Keupp, M.M., Huguenin, K., Palmié, M., Percia David, D.: Incentives for human agents to share security information: a model and an empirical test. In: 17th Workshop on the Economics of Information Security (WEIS), Innsbruck, Austria, pp. 1–22, June 2018
19. Percia David, D., Keupp, M.M., Ghernaouti, S., Mermoud, A.: Cyber security investment in the context of disruptive technologies: extension of the Gordon-Loeb model and application to critical infrastructure protection. In: Havarneanu, G., Setola, R., Nassopoulos, H., Wolthusen, S. (eds.) CRITIS 2016. LNCS, vol. 10242, pp. 296–301. Springer, Cham (2017). https://doi.org/10.1007/978-3-319-71368-7_25
20. PricewaterhouseCoopers (PwC): study and considerations on information sharing and analysis organizations. Technical report (2015)
21. PricewaterhouseCoopers (PwC): Information sharing and analysis organizations: putting theory into practice. Technical report (2016)
22. Prieto, D.: Information sharing with the private sector: history, challenges, innovation, and prospects. In: Seeds of Disaster, Roots of Response: How Private Action Can Reduce Public Vulnerability (2006)
23. Richter, R.: Essays on New Institutional Economics. Springer, Cham (2015). https://doi.org/10.1007/978-3-319-14154-1
24. van Eeten, M., Nieuwenhuijs, A., Luiijf, E., Klaver, M., Cruz, E.: The state and the threat of cascading failure across critical infrastructures: the implications of empirical evidence from media incident reports. Publ. Adm. **89**(2), 381–400 (2011)
25. Weiss, E.: Legislation to facilitate cybersecurity information sharing: economic analysis. Technical report, Congressional Research Service, June 2015
26. Zenger, T., Lazzarini, S.G., Poppo, L.: Informal and formal organization in new institutional economics. Technical report, Social Science Research Network, September 2002

Conceptual Framework for Hybrid Situational Awareness in Critical Port Infrastructures

Stefan Schauer[1]([✉]), Benjamin Rainer[1], Nicolas Museux[2], David Faure[2],
Javier Hingant[3], Federico Jesús Carvajal Rodrigo[3], Stefan Beyer[4],
Rafael Company Peris[5], and Sergio Zamarripa Lopez[4]

[1] Austrian Institute of Technology, Vienna, Austria
stefan.schauer@ait.ac.at
[2] Thales, 1 av. Augustin Fresnel, Palaiseau cedex 91167, France
[3] Universitat Politècnica de València, Valencia, Spain
[4] S2 Grupo, Ramiro de Maeztu 7, Valencia, Spain
[5] Fundación Valenciaport, Valencia, Spain

Abstract. Over the last years, critical infrastructures have become the target of highly sophisticated attacks causing severe damage to economic and social life. In most cases, such attacks are utilizing combined attack vectors from both the physical and the cyber domain. The magnitude of the consequences is often increased by cascading effects in both domains, even further amplifying each other. In this article, we present a framework implementing a holistic approach towards situational awareness for critical infrastructures. This Hybrid Situational Awareness (HSA) combines information coming from the physical as well as from the cyber domain and is able to identify potential cascading effects of an incident. In this context, the hybrid approach particularly focuses on the inter-domain propagation of a failure, i.e., the effects of a physical incident on the cyber domain and vice versa. We will show how such a Hybrid Situational Awareness can be implemented and illustrate its functionality based on a complex attack scenario.

Keywords: Physical situational awareness
Cyber situational awareness · Incident propagation
Cascading effects · Markov chains

1 Introduction

In recent years, coordinated and increasingly complex attacks on critical infrastructures have been encountered. Due to the progressive digitalization of the industrial sector and many critical infrastructures (CIs), the impact of a coordinated physical attack, a deliberate disruption of critical automation and control systems or even a combined scenario including both kinds of attacks, has severe consequences for the economy and the social well-being of European member

© Springer Nature Switzerland AG 2019
E. Luiijf et al. (Eds.): CRITIS 2018, LNCS 11260, pp. 191–203, 2019.
https://doi.org/10.1007/978-3-030-05849-4_15

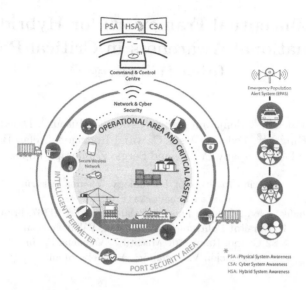

Fig. 1. Conceptual overview on the general idea behind the SAURON project.

states. The repeated hacking of the Ukrainian power grid in 2015 [16,33] and 2016 [10] or the effects of the WannaCry malware on health care systems [8,9] showed how vulnerabilities in software systems can have impact on the physical domain. In particular, maritime ports as one of Europe's main critical infrastructures are taking a special position in this context, since both the physical and the cyber domain represent a prominent factor in their daily operation. Due to the interrelations between both domains, vulnerabilities in one domain can affect and cause problems in the other domain, including, for example, the hiding of drugs in containers and redirecting these containers unnoticed to retrieve the drugs later on [6]. Further, shipping companies systems have been hacked to identify the loaded goods of specific vessels to find the most valuable targets and prepare piracy attacks later on [3]. Also the WannaCry and (Not-)Petya malware affected port operators' and logistic companies systems, resulting in business interruptions in container terminals [15,25] (Fig. 1).

Technical solutions to detect and counter such attacks are at hand and port infrastructures as well as all critical infrastructures use them in their everyday business life. Physical Situational Awareness (PSA) systems provide operators with the required overview on the prevailing situation of their physical assets, aggregating information from video surveillance, access control or fire detection systems. Similarly, Cyber Situational Awareness (CSA) systems provide details on the current status of the cyber systems, utilizing network traffic analyzers, intrusion detection systems (IDS) or log file analyzers. However, if an incident is detected, none of these systems is capable of identifying and analyzing cascading effects, particularly with regards to the respective other domain. Furthermore, combined attacks, i.e., attacks using both physical and cyber attack vectors, cannot be detected by either of those systems, in general. Therefore, a holistic overview on relevant incidents originating in one of the domains and their effects on both domains is required.

In this article, we present a conceptual framework for such a Hybrid Situational Awareness (HSA), developed in the context of the SAURON project for maritime port infrastructures. This HSA is capable of determining the potential consequences of any relevant incident detected either by the PSA or the CSA and will show the potential cascading effects in the two different domains. Therefore, the HSA generates a graph representation of all assets (physical as well as cyber) within the port infrastructure, also taking their intra- and inter-domain relations into account. Using mathematical models based on Markov chains and computer simulation techniques, the HSA can calculate how an incident will propagate through this graph and which assets are most likely to be affected. To identify combined attacks, the HSA is equipped with a correlation engine which associates incidents from the physical and the cyber domain and identifies potential threats using a rule-based approach. The HSA, as described here, is designed to work within port infrastructures but can also be applied to any other critical infrastructure operating large physical premises and complex cyber systems.

2   Related Work

Situational awareness (SA) is regarded as *"the perception of the elements in the environment within a volume of time and space, the comprehension of their meaning, and the projection of their status in the near future"* [11]. In this relation, PSA systems consist of those providing a complete knowledge of the situation to the decision makers by preventing and detecting any kind of physical threat in real-time. Besides the classical sensors to support a PSA (e.g., video surveillance systems, smoke or presence detectors), positioning systems have become more and more important to obtain a precise overview on the organization's premises and the location of security personnel within. For example, a 3D mapping and real-time provision of aerial images are earth observation techniques supporting crisis management [20]. However, it has been demonstrated that typical SA measurement techniques appear to be inefficient for command & control, communication, computer and intelligence systems.

In the context of critical maritime port infrastructures, the PSA is of particular importance due to the large physical premises operated by ports. A general overview on the existing different approaches in this field are given in [4,5]. Some implemented solutions for both US and EU port scenarios are introduced in [17,22], respectively. Finally, a cyber-physical collaborative self-assessment and management system for protecting port facilities is presented in [23].

Whereas there are several theoretical approaches and many practical implementations for physical and cyber situational awareness systems, there are little to no solutions looking at the interlink between those two domains to identify cascading effects among them. However, there are several methodologies already present in the literature for analyzing cascading effects in general. One of the first was the Cross Impact Analysis (CIA) [13,30], which generally describes the relation between events and how one event would affect another one in the future. A more recent extension to CIA, called Cross Impact Analysis and Interpretative Structural Model (CIA-ISM) [7], is extensively used in emergency management to analyze the interaction between critical events and obtain a reasonable view on potential future consequences (cf. [31] and the references cited therein for a more detailed overview on CIA and CIA-ISM).

The CIA and its extension are based on a rather high-level model, using conditional probabilities to describe the relations between specific events. Such stochastic processes are also used in several other approaches, in particular, the application of randomness improves the modeling of sometimes unknown dynamics between these events. One example for this is percolation theory from the field of epidemics spreading [28,29], which can also be applied in cyber security to analyze the propagation of malware spreading within an ICT and SCADA network [19]. Another approach are Interdependent Markov Chains (IDMCs) which have been originally used in the energy sector to analyze overload scenarios and to take care of the probability for a blackout [27,32]. The most recent advances of modelling cascading effects in power systems is surveyed in [14]. The IDMCs have been extended to model the propagation of cascading effects within an infrastructure [26].

3   Physical Situational Awareness

The PSA application of the SAURON system is responsible for providing continuous SA to the decision makers in case of a declared physical attack. It is linked with both the port's security and responder teams and, in combination with the CSA, the PSA helps the commanders evaluating the current situation. This will support more accurate decisions for mitigating the consequences of a crisis. In particular, the PSA application consists of a real-time SA system adapted to the EU ports' requirements for their protection against any type of physical threat. This includes novel capabilities as dynamic assets and resource locations, management and monitoring of the sensors deployed on the ports. In addition, it provides innovative video processing techniques, which will improve both the access control to critical areas and the security inside the port facilities, that will be integrated in the system.

The PSA application is mainly composed of three internal modules: the Security & Privacy module is responsible for ensuring the PSA system's security in terms of access control. The Communications Interface module is composed of several logical interfaces that ensure the integration of different types of data (e.g. video-cameras flow, units on field's alerts, other sensor's alerts, etc.). Further, the Physical Situation Awareness module includes the different internal sub-modules that provide the specific PSA application features. Moreover, the system will prepare the received sensor data to be displayed in a proper way in the PSA Human–Machine–Interface (HMI), avoiding information overflow for the PSA application operators and decision makers. The PSA collects information from different sources, e.g., video-cameras, units on field, geo-location (GIS) systems and other sensor, and stores everything in the central Data Management Module. The information is then analyzed in the System Kernel Module, where anomalies are identified, processed and finally visualized using the HMI Module. Based on the resulting information, the PSA users can trigger alerts which will then be sent to the HSA application for analyzing potential cascading effects (cf. Sect. 5 below).

4   Cyber Situational Awareness

Cyber Situational Awareness (CSA) refers to a system which allows to prevent and detect threats and, in case of a declared attack, mitigate the effects of the identified infection/intrusion. In SAURON, this is achieved by combining traditional cyber security monitoring tools with innovative visualization techniques and threat hunting capabilities based on anomaly detection. The CSA provides its detection capabilities by means of a cyber security monitoring platform, which is able to monitor, process and analyze data coming from multiple information sources. These sources are classified as both cooperative and non-cooperative environments, depending on the information coming from the ports' own infrastructure or from other open sources, respectively. Data from both the cooperative and non-cooperative environment is sent to the CSA Correlation Module to generate contextualized alerts, which support SAURON operators to take decisions based on the resulting risk level. In this way, the CSA aims to identify any situation that might boil down to a potential threat for any of the port authority's assets. The CSA is implemented using a modular layered approach consisting of a Sensoring Module, a Correlation Module and an Alert Module. In the Sensoring Module, coordinated cyber security sensors gather relevant information from different sources on a real-time basis using an agent-based architecture. These data sources include IDS, system availability signals, network usage and bandwidth monitoring as well as active vulnerabilities in the current technological infrastructure.

The collected data is further processed by the Correlation Module. The module aims are to normalize, aggregate and reduce the information towards a list of alerts pinpointing what is really relevant in terms of cyber security threats. When an event is received on this correlation platform, a set of rules is executed in the Correlation Module in real-time in order to match relevant compromised situations based on severity, alert classification, type of attack and criticality of the affected assets. When the Correlation Module determines that a particular situation is relevant for the port's security, all gathered information about the current situation is received as an alert by the Alerts Module, helping the operators to manage alerts and make decisions. The alert is also sent to the HSA for evaluating potential cascading effects (cf. Sect. 5 below). Based on the criticality of the detected alerts and taking the information data flow into account. Therefore, the alerts are used to identify both impact and probability of a set of predefined threat groups. Additionally, the CSA system includes new visualization paradigms for the cyber space, which consist of a section in the Alerts Module showing the attack affected assets as well as the external affected IP addresses showing the attack.

5 Hybrid Situational Awareness

The Hybrid Situational Awareness (HSA) application incorporates inputs from the physical and the cyber domain and analyzes existing interdependencies. Its main goal is to indicate the cascading effects of an incident in both domains. Further, it will detect combined attacks on the port infrastructure, i.e., attacks that utilize vulnerabilities in the physical and the cyber domain. Therefore, the HSA consists of two main modules: the Event Correlation Engine and the Threat Propagation Engine (cf. also Fig. 2).

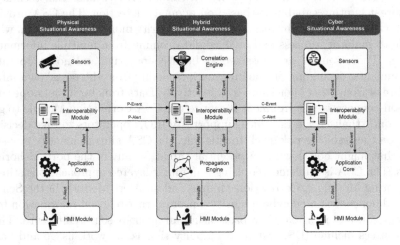

Fig. 2. Illustration of the interplay between PSA, HSA and CSA.

5.1 Event Correlation Engine

The purpose of the Event Correlation Engine (ECE) is to interpret the detections and events provided by both the PSA and the CSA in a higher level of situational context. As the HSA receives information from both the physical world and the cyber world, it has a more comprehensive overview on the current situation. Therefore, the ECE is based on a complex event processing approach [12,21] that intents to recognize, in real-time, specific patterns of event-objects within a flow, coming from heterogeneous sources, and triggers the corresponding actions. In this paradigm, an event-object (also shortly called *event*) is defined as a record of something that happens. It has a semantic representation that can be processed by a computer, is timestamped and may have a duration and a spatial localization. Its representation is not unique and is related to the purpose of its processing.

The ECE is based on Drools Fusion [24] and follows its inference rule syntax. Thus, the standard logic operators are used together with the temporal logic ones, as described in [1,2]. Additionally, any boolean constraints can be applied on the attributes of an event in order to check contextual conditions (relatively one event to the others or to general conditions). Lastly, when the event types are defined from a hierarchical type modeling (an ontology, a class hierarchy or similar), the embedded *is-a* inheritance relationship is then useful to factorize definition of rules. When an event-pattern is applied for a certain type of event, it is also applicable (without any explicit marker) to all of its sub types. Therefore, the descriptive capability offered is very large and may encompass most of the threat situations the ECE has to recognize. It is stimulated each time a new event is received and is a candidate to at least one rule. All stimulated rules are latent until a satisfiability decision can be made (i.e., the event-pattern is satisfied or can't be satisfied anymore). The rules defined in the ECE must be compliant to the necessary prior risk analysis of the port infrastructure. As the correlations are not discovered or learned but recognized, it is important to design them accordingly to the detections capabilities and the rational of the detections sources deployment. Further, it is obvious not to wait for events or patterns that never occur because neither the PSA nor the CSA are able to detect events feeding the expected schema. This is not only true for the inputs, but also for the outputs of the ECE. When some rules are triggered by a series of events, the ECE creates a Hybrid Alert, which is then sent to the Threat Propagation Engine and also displayed to the security officer.

5.2   Threat Propagation Engine

The Threat Propagation Engine (TPE) identifies the potential cascading effects of incidents coming from the physical domain, indicated as Physical Alerts, and the cyber domain, indicated by Cyber Alerts (cf. also Fig. 2). Moreover, Hybrid alerts coming from the ECE are also considered. To achieve that, the TPE builds upon a graph representation of the port's infrastructure. The nodes in this infrastructure graph represent all assets, physical as well as cyber, within the port. The (directed) edges represent the different types of interdependencies between these assets, i.e., they describe how the assets are linked together. In the physical domain, such a dependency can mean that a machine is placed within a specific room or some rooms are located next to each other within a building. In the cyber domain, this can mean that an application is running on a specific server or two services are exchanging data for operation. Regarding dependencies between the physical and cyber domain, these can represent that an operating system is installed on a physical server, which stands in a certain room, or a service controls some physical machinery within a specific area of the port.

Each alert received by the TPE contains the information about which asset is directly affected by it. The TPE now inspects the infrastructure graph and evaluates which other assets (physical or cyber) might become affected by the incident. This evaluation builds upon a mathematical model using Markov chains previously described in a similar context [18]. Markov chains do fit the purpose quite well because, in general, cascading effects do not depend on the history but *only* on the current situation. Each asset itself is modeled as Markov chain which reflects the status of the asset in terms of likelihood to be affected by an incident. This likelihood and the state of each asset is represented by the labels, e.g., "normal operation", "partly affected" or "completely affected". The state of an asset depends on the states of its neighboring assets in the infrastructure graph. The probability that an affected asset has an effect on another dependent asset is again modeled by a *Transfer* Markov Chain. State changes are probabilistic and described by the transition matrix of the Markov chain; thus the non-deterministic behavior, which we regularly see in realistic scenarios, can be captured by the model.

In other words, if the TPE receives an alert, it changes the state of the affected asset; based on the model's transition matrix, the assets next to it might become affected, too, due to their dependencies and change their status accordingly. In a next step, the dependencies between the newly affected assets and their neighbors are evaluated and additional assets change their state. This describes how an incident propagates step-by-step through the port's physical and cyber infrastructure. The TPE simulates this propagation several times to obtain a list of the affected assets together with an estimation of their likelihood to become affected by the initial incident. As a main results of the TPE this list is then visualized for the security officer in the HSA's HMI to support their mitigation actions.

6   Use Case Application

The use case we are focusing on here is one of two scenarios covered in the SAURON project and evolves around a terrorist group using combined attack vectors (from the physical and cyber domain) to enable a physical attack on the port's infrastructure.

Scenario Description. The scenario takes place in a large port infrastructure, located inside a metropolitan area, operating a large container terminal. A terrorist group plans to access the port's Terminal Operating System (TOS), which stores all container movements and their position, as well as the Port Community System (PCS), which runs all the communications between the port and their stakeholders. The main goal is to change the ID of a specific container arriving later on at the port ensuring that it is hidden within the container terminal and not subject to inspection. In this container, a small bomb equipped with some radiological substance is located. Upon arrival of the container, some members of the attacker group access the cargo area and activate the bomb. Thus, the plan is to infiltrate the TOS and the PCS by remote access or social engineering, to enter the port's premises by exploiting weak spots in the port's physical security and activating the bomb using a timer. The detonation on the next day would not only affect the whole port facilities due to the physical damage but also affect a large part of the city due to the spreading of the radiological substance.

Hybrid Analysis of Scenario. The described scenario combines attacks in the cyber and the physical domain. Hence, all three applications of the SAURON system, i.e., the CSA, PSA and HSA will be involved in the detection. First, the infiltration of the TOS by the attacker group leaves some traces in the network or system log files, e.g., if some exploits of the TOS are used to gain access remotely. These anomalies are detected by the sensors attached to the CSA and the CSA's Correlation Module. Thus, an event is triggered and sent to the operator for a check as well as to the HSA for further evaluation in the ECE. In case the CSA operator identifies the event as malicious, an alert is triggered and sent to the TPE within the HSA. The cascading effects are analyzed.

In a similar way, the infiltration of the PCS and the tampering of the container's ID by the attacker group later on can also be detected by the CSA, causing an event to be created and displayed to the CSA's operator as well as sent to the HSA. If the CSA operator decides to create an alert, the TPE calculates the potential cascading effects of the infiltration. In detail, the TPE links the tampered data to the physical container and its location within the port, indicating that this physical asset is affected by the cyber attack. This information is also displayed to the PSA operator via the HSA's HMI and additional personnel is sent to inspect the container as a mitigation action. In case no cyber alert is triggered, the ECE within the HSA can correlate the two events based on its predefined rule set, identify the anomalies in the TOS and the PCS as a potential malicious behavior and trigger a Hybrid Alert. For this alert, the TPE calculates the potential cascading effects and everything together is presented to the operators via the HSA's HMI.

Looking at the physical part of the attack (and assuming that the attack has not been mitigated, yet), the intrusion of the attackers into the port's premises is not detected by a surveillance camera. However, a presence sensor captures the attacker's motion further within the premises. The received event is displayed in the system's HMI and sent to the HSA's ECE. Once verified by the PSA operator, a physical alert is created and sent to the HSA. Within the HSA, the TPE calculates the potential cascading effects of an intrusion in that area, e.g., listing the containers located there. As a mitigation action, the PSA's GIS capabilities help to determine which security units are closest to the event location and, through the messaging module of the PSA, they are committed to move and inspect the identified area. Even if the PSA's operator does not trigger an alert, e.g., because the signal from the presence detector is considered as a false alarm, the ECE correlates the detection event with the two events coming from the CSA. The tampering of the container's ID in the PCS together with the signal from the presence detector in the same area where the container is located can be enough to trigger a Hybrid Alert. The alert is communicated to the operators using the HSA's HMI and the potential cascading effects are calculated by the

TPE. Thus, the operators get a hint that thought false alarm is a real alarm and with maybe severe impact.

Hence, the SAURON system is able to identify the cyber and the physical aspects of the attack individually. Moreover, in case the events triggered from the PSA and CSA are misinterpreted by the respective operators, the ECE within the HSA is also able to identify the combined attack. In this scenario, the main advantage of the hybrid view introduced by the HSA is its ability to associate the individual events as part of one sophisticated attack. Knowing this, the operator is then able to better coordinate the response and prioritize the mitigation actions. Further, the TPE allows to identify the consequences of such an attack in the physical and the cyber domain, which is very difficult if a holistic view is missing.

7   Conclusion

In this paper, we presented a framework for a Hybrid Situational Awareness system developed in the SAURON project. The HSA integrates information on security alerts coming from the physical and the cyber domain to identify cascading effects and related combined attacks. In this way, the HSA framework brings current physical and cyber situational awareness one step further towards a fusion of both domains.

As a major benefit of this system, CSA operators receive alerts regarding their domain based on the cascading effects from the physical world and PSA operators receive alerts issued from the cyber world. This allows them, on the one hand, to be aware of incidents that originate in the respective other domain but have an impact on their own infrastructure. On the other hand, the system indicates potential combined attacks which would not be detected by either a PSA or a CSA system alone. Therefore, the HSA provides a holistic overview on the overall infrastructure and supports the security officers from both domains in their decision making process.

Nevertheless, we still foresee some open issues of our approach at this time. The first potential bottleneck is the capability for a system to manage the whole security of an infrastructure. Since critical infrastructures are in general very large and rather complex organizations, there are numerous physical and cyber assets to manage. Therefore, the algorithms for implementing the ECE and the TPE (as well as other specific tasks of the HSA) need to be efficiently designed. Another issue might be the maintenance of the asset infrastructure information. In such a big organization, the configuration of assets and the inter-dependencies between them might change frequently. Another aspect that needs maintenance is the rulse set of the ECE. Thus, the SAURON system needs to guarantee that the analyses are carried out on the most accurate infrastructure configuration.

A more organizational concern evolves around the training of the operators. For the moment, there is training for physical security and training for cyber security, both carried out separately most of the time. Hence, there is no "mixed" or "hybrid" training. However, facing an increasing number of combined attacks and a respective HSA solution, operators that are trained to manage physical alerts, cyber alerts are required in both domains. The operators need to be trained to identify and manage the cascading effects from one domain to the other to reach the concept of a holistic security solution.

In general, the future of security situational awareness foresees the removal of the boundaries between these two worlds. In the past, the protection of critical infrastructures was very much connected to the physical world, in particular when it comes to maritime port infrastructures. With the increase of cyber attacks in recent years, cyber security has become more important. Therefore, the interplay and cascading effects between the physical, cyber and combined attacks - and thus a more holistic "hybrid" view - have to be considered more thoroughly in the future.

Acknowledgments. This work was supported in part by the EC in the context of the SAURON under the HORIZON 2020 Framework (Grant No. 740477).

References

1. Allen, J.F.: An interval-based representation of temporal knowledge. IJCAI **81**, 221–226 (1981)
2. Allen, J.F.: Maintaining knowledge about temporal intervals. Commun. ACM **26**(11), 832–843 (1983)
3. Allianz Global Corporate & Specialty SE: Allianz Global Risk Barometer Top. Business Risks (2017). http://www.agcs.allianz.com/assets/PDFs/Reports/Allianz_Risk_Barometer_2017_EN.pdf
4. Andritsos, F.: Port security and access control: a systemic approach. In: IISA 2013, Piraeus, Greece, pp. 1–8 (2013)
5. Andritsos, F., Mosconi, M.: Port security in EU: a systemic approach. In: 2010 International WaterSide Security Conference, Carrara, Italy, pp. 1–8 (2010)
6. Bateman, T.: Police warning after drug traffickers' cyber-attack (2013). www.bbc.com/news/world-europe-24539417
7. Bañuls, V.A., Turoff, M.: Scenario construction via Delphi and cross-impact analysis. Technol. Forecast. Soc. Change **78**(9), 1579–1602 (2011)
8. BBC News: NHS cyber-attack: GPs and hospitals hit by ransomware (2017). http://www.bbc.com/news/health-39899646
9. CBS News: Global cyberattack strikes dozens of countries, cripples U.K. hospitals (2017). https://www.cbsnews.com/news/hospitals-across-britain-hit-by-ransomware-cyberattack/
10. Condliffe, J.: Ukraine Power Grid Gets Hacked Again, a Worrying Sign for Infrastructure Attacks (2016). www.technologyreview.com/s/603262/ukraines-power-grid-gets-hacked-again-a-worrying-sign-for-infrastructure-attacks
11. Endsley, M.R.: Design and evaluation for situation awareness enhancement. Proc. Hum. Factors Soc. Ann. Meet. **32**(2), 97–101 (1988)
12. Etzion, O., Niblett, P., Luckham, D.C.: Event Processing in Action. Manning, Greenwich (2011)
13. Gordon, T.J., Hayward, H.: Initial experiments with the cross impact matrix method of forecasting. Futures **1**(2), 100–116 (1968)

14. Guo, H., Zheng, C., Iu, H.H.C., Fernando, T.: A critical review of cascading failure analysis and modeling of power system. Renew. Sustain. Energy Rev. **80**, 9–22 (2017)

15. Hern, A.: Wannacry, petya, notpetya: how ransomware hit the big time in 2017 (2017). https://www.theguardian.com/technology/2017/dec/30/wannacry-petyanotpetya-ransomware

16. ICS-CERT: Cyber-Attack Against Ukrainian Critical Infrastructure (2016). https://ics-cert.us-cert.gov/alerts/IR-ALERT-H-16-056-01

17. Koch, D.B.: PortSim-A port security simulation and visualization tool. In: 2007 41st Annual IEEE International Carnahan Conference on Security Technology, Ottawa, Canada, pp. 109–116 (2007)

18. König, S., Rass, S.: Stochastic dependencies between critical infrastructures, Rome, Italy, pp. 106–110 (2017)

19. König, S., Schauer, S., Rass, S.: A stochastic framework for prediction of malware spreading in heterogeneous networks. In: Brumley, B.B., Röning, J. (eds.) NordSec 2016. LNCS, vol. 10014, pp. 67–81. Springer, Cham (2016). https://doi.org/10.1007/978-3-319-47560-8_5

20. Lechner, K., Gähler, M.: Earth observation based crisis information - emergency mapping services and recent operational developments. In: 4th International Conference on Information and Communication Technologies for Disaster Management (ICT-DM), pp. 1–7 (2017)

21. Luckham, D.: The Power of Events, vol. 204. Addison-Wesley, Reading (2002)

22. Orosz, M., Chen, J., Maya, I., Salazar, D., Chatterjee, S., Wei, D.: Protecting our Nation's ports with the port security risk analysis and resource allocation system (PortSec 3.0). In: 2013 IEEE International Conference on Technologies for Homeland Security (HST), Waltham, USA, pp. 38–42 (2013)

23. Papastergiou, S., Polemi, N.: Harmonizing commercial port security practices & procedures in Mediterranean Basin. In: IISA 2014, the 5th International Conference on Information, Intelligence, Systems and Applications, Chania, Greece, pp. 292–297 (2014)

24. Proctor, M.: Drools: a rule engine for complex event processing. In: Schürr, A., Varró, D., Varró, G. (eds.) AGTIVE 2011. LNCS, vol. 7233, p. 2. Springer, Heidelberg (2012). https://doi.org/10.1007/978-3-642-34176-2_2

25. PTI: New malware hits JNPT operations as APM Terminals hacked globally|The Indian Express (2017). http://indianexpress.com/article/india/cyber-attack-new-malware-hits-jnpt-ops-as-apm-terminals-hacked-globally-4725102/

26. Rahnamay-Naeini, M., Hayat, M.M.: Cascading failures in interdependent infrastructures: an interdependent markov-chain approach. IEEE Trans. Smart Grid **7**(4), 1997–2006 (2016)

27. Rahnamay-Naeini, M., Wang, Z., Ghani, N., Mammoli, A., Hayat, M.M.: Stochastic analysis of cascading-failure dynamics in power grids. IEEE Trans. Power Syst. **29**(4), 1767–1779 (2014)

28. Salath, M., Jones, J.H.: Dynamics and control of diseases in networks with community structure. PLOS Comput. Biol. **6**(4), e1000736 (2010)

29. Sander, L.M., Warren, C.P., Sokolov, I.M., Simon, C., Koopman, J.: Percolation on heterogeneous networks as a model for epidemics. Math. Biosci. **180**(1), 293–305 (2002)

30. Turoff, M.: An alternative approach to cross impact analysis. Technol. Forecast. Soc. Change **3**, 309–339 (1971)

31. Turoff, M., Bañuls, V.A., Plotnick, L., Hiltz, S.R., Ramrez de la Huerga, M.: A collaborative dynamic scenario model for the interaction of critical infrastructures. Futures **84**, 23–42 (2016)
32. Wang, Z., Scaglione, A., Thomas, R.J.: A Markov-transition model for cascading failures in power grids. In: 45th International Conference on System Sciences, pp. 2115–2124 (2012)
33. Zetter, K.: Everything We Know About Ukraine Power Plant Hack|WIRED (2016). https://www.wired.com/2016/01/everything-we-know-aboutukraines-power-plant-hack/

Discovering Vulnerabilities in Heterogeneous Interconnected Systems

Luca Faramondi[1]([✉]) [iD], Gabriele Oliva[1] [iD], Stefano Panzieri[2] [iD], and Roberto Setola[1] [iD]

[1] Campus Bio-Medico University, Via Álvaro del Portillo 2, 00128 Rome, Italy
{l.faramondi,g.oliva,r.setola}@unicampus.it
[2] University Roma Tre, Via della Vasca Navale 79, 00146, Rome, Italy
panzieri@uniroma3.it

Abstract. The identification of vulnerabilities in critical infrastructure networks, especially in the event of an intentional attack, is a fundamental task to comprehend the behavior of such networks and to implement protection strategies with the purpose of raising their robustness and resilience. In this work, we characterize the network vulnerability with respect to an attacker that aims at destroying subsystems in a way that guarantees, at the same time, the maximization of the damage dealt and the minimization of the effort spent in the attack. To this end, we follow a topological approach and we characterize each subsystem as a node, while dependencies are modeled in terms of a directed edges. Moreover, each node is characterized by an intrinsic degree of importance and by the effort required to attack it. Such a differentiation of the nodes allows to capture the heterogeneous essence of the different subsystems in a Critical Infrastructure network. In this setting, we model the damage dealt by the attacker in terms of a weighted version of the pairwise connectivity, where the weights correspond to the nodes' importance; moreover we model the overall attack effort in terms of the effort required to attack the nodes. The proposed methodology aims at computing a criticality metric based on a multi-objective optimization formulation. Specifically, the criticality metric represents the frequency with which a given subsystem is attacked in the hypothetical attack plans belonging to the Pareto front. Finally, we complement our methodology by introducing upper and lower bounds on the overall attacker's effort, in order to specialize the proposed methodology to different classes of attackers. The feasibility of the proposed solution is tested on the US Airline Network as in 1997.

Keywords: Critical infrastructure · Connectivity measure
Critical nodes

1 Introduction

Due to the large number of natural and malicious events that may affect Critical Infrastructures, improving the robustness and resilience of such systems is a

© Springer Nature Switzerland AG 2019
E. Luiijf et al. (Eds.): CRITIS 2018, LNCS 11260, pp. 204–215, 2019.
https://doi.org/10.1007/978-3-030-05849-4_16

fundamental task. In this view, due to budget limitations (in terms of required effort), it is mandatory to identify the most critical elements of an infrastructure, in order to properly organize the available protection resources. In the last few years, the scientific community has been increasingly interested in developing effective strategies to identify the most critical elements of an infrastructure network (see, among others, [10,11]). A large fraction of the proposed methods identifies criticality subsystems in terms of their interconnection with the other subsystems, i.e., according to a topological perspective. Specifically, a typical approach is to study the degradation of important network parameters, such as node degree, clustering coefficient, or betweenness, upon iterative removal of nodes and/or edges, thus simulating the robustness/resilience of the network with respect to intentional attacks or natural disasters [12]. Moreover, existing literature does not make particular distinction among the particular nodes, i.e., they assume that the topological parameters completely describe the robustness/resilience of the network after an adverse event, irrespectively of which pairs of nodes are actually connected by a direct link or by a path. If such an assumption is legitimate for particular networks (e.g., for a power grid, where any node might be able to provide power to the nodes connected to it by a path), it seems less justified in other sectors, such as telecommunications or transportations, where nodes might have highly heterogeneous characteristics.

Among other descriptors of network connectivity, the *pairwise connectivity* (PWC) [9] represents a popular metric, it that it explicitly measures the number of pairs of nodes in the network that are connected via a path. By leveraging on the PWC metric, the identification of the critical nodes is typically done by solving the so-called *Critical Node Detection Problem* (CNP) [6–8], which aims at identifying which nodes should be attacked (up to a given limit k) in order to create the largest possible degradation. Such an approach, however, typically requires a large number of Boolean decision variables [7] and a number of constraints that can be non-polynomial in the number of nodes of the network [8]; these factors may limit the applicability of the standard CNP methodology.

Notice that the CNP problem typically introduces some a priori hypothesis on the attack, e.g., the number of attacked nodes is upper-bounded by a small integer or different constraints are introduced to narrow the otherwise overwhelming complexity of this problem. In [2] a strategy to avoid introducing such constraints is provided by adopting a multi-objective optimization perspective where each node is characterized in terms of the effort required to attack it; in particular the approach in [2] aims at identifying those nodes that, if attacked, minimize the residual network connectivity in terms of PWC and, at the same time, correspond to the minimum effort. Notably, no a priori assumption is made on the specific attack budget and number of targets.

1.1 Contribution

In this work we propose an approach that extends the one in [2] by characterizing each node not only in terms of the effort required by the attacker to target that node, but also considering the relevance or importance the node has.

Also in this case, no a priori assumption on the attacker psychology is made. In more detail, while PWC assigns the same relevance to any pair of nodes connected by a path in the network after the attack, in this paper we extend such an index by considering a different relevance for different pairs of nodes, thus accounting for the degree of heterogeneity of the network. Finally, we complement our methodology by introducing upper and lower bounds on the overall attacker's effort, in order to specialize the proposed methodology to different classes of attackers.

1.2 Paper Outline

The paper outline is as follows: In Sect. 2, for the sake of completeness, we collect some preliminary definitions. In Sect. 3 we provide the definition of our methodology by introducing a connectivity measure for heterogeneous networks and the proposed attacker model. Results and discussions are presented in Sect. 4, where a validation is carried out for a real network. Finally, some conclusive remarks are collected in Sect. 5.

2 Preliminaries

2.1 General Preliminaries

Let us denote by $|X|$ the cardinality of a set X; moreover, we represent vectors via boldface letters, and we use $\mathbf{k}_m$ to indicate a vector in $\mathbb{R}^m$ whose components are all equal to k. We denote by $0_{n,m}$ an $n \times m$ matrix whose entries are all 0, and by I_n the $n \times n$ identity matrix.

Let A be an $n \times m$ matrix and let B be an $p \times q$ matrix; the *Kronecker product* of A and B is the $np \times mq$ matrix

$$A \otimes B = \begin{bmatrix} A_{11}B & \dots & A_{1m}B \\ \vdots & \ddots & \vdots \\ A_{n1}B & \dots & A_{nm}B \end{bmatrix}.$$

The Hadamard product of two matrices A and B, with the same number of rows and columns, is defined as

$$A \circ B = \begin{bmatrix} A_{11}B_{11} & \dots & A_{1n}B_{1n} \\ \vdots & \ddots & \vdots \\ A_{n1}B_{n1} & \dots & A_{nn}B_{nn} \end{bmatrix}.$$

We denote by $X = sign(A)$ the entry-wise sign of the matrix A, i.e., $X_{ij} = sign(A_{ij})$.

2.2 Graph Related Definitions

Let $G = \{V, E\}$ denote a *graph* with a finite number n of nodes $v_i \in V$ and e edges $(v_i, v_j) \in E \subseteq V \times V$, from node v_i to node v_j. A graph is said to be *undirected* if $(v_i, v_j) \in E$ whenever $(v_j, v_i) \in E$, and it is said to be *directed* otherwise; in the following we will consider undirected graphs.

The *adjacency matrix* of a graph G is an $n \times n$ matrix A such that $A_{ij} = 1$ if $(v_j, v_i) \in E$ and $A_{ij} = 0$ otherwise.

A *direct path* over a graph $G = \{V, E\}$, starting at a node $v_i \in V$ and ending at a node $v_j \in V$, is a subset of links in E that connects v_i and v_j, respecting the edge orientation and without creating loops.

A graph $G = \{V, E\}$ is *connected* if each node can be reached by each other node by means of the links in E, regardless of their orientation. A directed graph that has a direct path from each vertex to every other vertex is said to be *strongly connected*.

The *out-degree* of a node is defined as the number of edges directed out of the node.

2.3 Pairwise Connectivity

The *pairwise connectivity* (PWC) [1] of G is an index that captures the overall degree of connectivity of a graph:

$$PWC(G) = \sum_{(v_i, v_j) \in V \times V, v_i \neq v_j} p(v_i, v_j), \tag{1}$$

where $p(v_i, v_j)$ is 1 if the pair (v_i, v_j) is connected via a direct path in G, and is zero otherwise. In other words, the pairwise connectivity is the number of pairs of nodes that are connected via a path over G. Noting that the maximum number of couples in a graph with n nodes is $n(n-1)$, the *normalized pairwise connectivity* (NPWC) is defined as

$$NPWC(G) = \frac{PWC(G)}{n(n-1)} \in [0, 1]. \tag{2}$$

Remark 1. $NPWC(G)$ is a measure of connectivity of the graph G; in fact, it is easy to note that

$$G \text{ strongly connected} \Leftrightarrow NPWC(G) = 1.$$

When $NPWC(G) < 1$, the graph is not strongly connected, but the larger $NPWC(G)$ is, the more G is "close" to a strongly connected graph.

2.4 Multi-objective Optimization

In this section we briefly review the key aspects of multi-objective optimization (MOO).

Given a vector $\mathbf{x} \in \{0,1\}^n$ representing n decision variables, a MOO problem can be expressed as follows

$$\min f(\mathbf{x}) = \min \quad [f_1(\mathbf{x}), f_2(\mathbf{x}), \ldots, f_k(\mathbf{x})]^T, \quad \text{subject to } \mathbf{x} \in \mathcal{F}, \qquad (3)$$

where $k \geq 2$ and the i-th objective is given by

$$f_i(\mathbf{x}) : \mathbb{R}^n \to \mathbb{R}, \quad \text{for } i = 1, \ldots, k,$$

while $f(\mathbf{x}) \in \mathbb{R}^k$ is the *multi-objective function*. The set $\mathcal{F}$ represents the set of *feasible solutions* for the problem at hand. Moreover, the *multi-objective space* is defined as

$$\mathcal{Z} = \{\mathbf{z} \in \mathbb{R}^k : \exists \mathbf{x} \in \mathcal{F}, \mathbf{z} = f(\mathbf{x})\}.$$

Within a MOO problem, therefore, the aim is to select a feasible solution $\mathbf{x}$ that minimizes at the same time all the different objectives f_i. Let us consider a solution $\mathbf{x}^*$ for which all the objectives $f_i(\mathbf{x}^*)$ are simultaneously minimized, and let us denote the associated multi-objective vector $f(\mathbf{x}^*)$ by $\mathbf{z}^{id}$. Note that, when there is no conflict among the objectives, we can solve Problem (3) by solving k scalar problems, thus obtaining $\mathbf{z}^{id}$ as the *ideal* multi-objective vector. Due to the conflicting nature of the objectives $f_i(\mathbf{x})$, however, it is realistic to assume that $\mathbf{z}^{id} \notin \mathcal{Z}$.

In most practical cases, therefore, there is a need to overcome the above naive definition of an optimal solution; a typical approach in the literature is to resort to the theory of *Pareto optimality* [4].

Let $\mathbf{z}^a$ and $\mathbf{z}^b \in \mathcal{Z}$; we say that $\mathbf{z}^b$ is *Pareto-dominated* by $\mathbf{z}^a$ ($\mathbf{z}^a \leq_P \mathbf{z}^b$) if:

$\mathbf{z}_i^a \leq \mathbf{z}_i^b$ for each $i = 1, 2, \ldots, k$ and
$\mathbf{z}_j^a < \mathbf{z}_j^b$ at least for a value of $j \in \{1, \ldots, k\}$.

A solution vector $\mathbf{x}^* \in \mathcal{F}$ is a *Pareto optimal solution* if there is no other solution $\mathbf{x} \in \mathcal{F}$ such that:

$$f(\mathbf{x}) \leq_P f(\mathbf{x}^*). \qquad (4)$$

The *Pareto front* $\mathcal{P}$ is the set of all possible Pareto optimal solutions $\mathbf{x}^*$ for the matter at hand, while we denote by $\mathcal{P}_f$ the set of values $f(\mathbf{x}^*)$, in the multi-objective space, which correspond to each $\mathbf{x}^* \in \mathcal{P}$.

3   Network Vulnerability Analysis

In this section we generalize the PWC indexes introducing the "weighted" PWC in order to discriminate among the different pairs of nodes and illustrate how such an index can be used in MOO-based framework to identify the most critical nodes. Moreover, we introduce a bound on the maximum budget for the attacker in order to discriminate different classes of attackers: criminal, terroristic and warfare scenario.

3.1 Weighted Pairwise Connectivity

As introduced in Sect. 2.3, the PWC and the NPWC consists of two indices able to estimate the degree of connectivity of a graph. In this section we generalize these indices in order to consider not only the number of the pairs of nodes, but also the relevance of each specific pair. To this end we introduce the weighted pairwise connectivity (WPWC).

Consider a directed graph $G = \{V, E\}$ and let us define $\mathbf{w} \in \mathbb{R}^n$, whose entries satisfy $w_i > 0$ represents a measure of the relevance of the nodes (e.g. number of users, dimension of the town, etc.). We define the weighted pairwise connectivity as an extension of Eq. 1

$$WPWC(G, \mathbf{w}) = \sum_{(v_i, v_j) \in V \times V, v_i \neq v_j} p(v_i, v_j) w_i w_j. \tag{5}$$

Analogously we define its normalized version as

$$NWPWC(G, \mathbf{w}) = \frac{WPWC(G, \mathbf{w})}{\sum_{(v_i, v_j) \in V \times V, v_i \neq v_j} w_i w_j}. \tag{6}$$

According to the definition in Eq. (5), it is possible to express the WPWC in terms of the weight vector $\mathbf{w}$ and considering the adjacency matrix A, i.e.,

$$NWPWC(A, \mathbf{w}) = \frac{\mathbf{1_n^T} \left[P \circ \left(\mathbf{w} \otimes \mathbf{1_n^T} \right) \circ \left(\mathbf{1_n} \otimes \mathbf{w^T} \right) \right] \mathbf{1_n}}{\mathbf{1_n^T} \left[\left(\mathbf{w} \otimes \mathbf{1_n^T} \right) \circ \left(\mathbf{1_n} \otimes \mathbf{w^T} \right) \right] \mathbf{1_n}}, \tag{7}$$

where $P = sign(\sum_{i=1}^{n-1} A^i) - I$ is the $n \times n$ matrix whose elements P_{ij} are equal to 1 if exists a direct path in G from i to j, 0 otherwise. The definition of matrix P derives from the results described in [3], and is based on the property that the (i, j)-th entry of the k-th power of the adjacency matrix is equal to the number of paths of length k among the nodes v_i and v_j.

3.2 Critical Nodes Detection

Let us consider a set of n heterogeneous interdependent systems, modeled as a directed graph $G = \{V, E\}$ whose nodes v_i represent the subsystems and each link in E consists of an interdependence relation among them.

Moreover, consider a vector $\mathbf{w} \in \mathbb{R}^n$; each entry w_i of $\mathbf{w}$ represents the degree of importance of the i-th subsystem. Let us also define a vector $\mathbf{c} \in \mathbb{R}^n$, whose elements c_i represent the attack cost for the i-th node, i.e., an estimate of the effort required for the attacker in order to make the i-th system completely inoperable. In the following, we assume that, when the i-th system is attacked, it is removed from the network within all its incident links. The malicious attacker aims at maximizing the damage dealt to the network, i.e., to minimize the network WPWC; at the same time, he/she wants to minimize his/her effort, i.e., minimize the total attack cost. In order to distinguish among different classes of attackers, we assume that the available total budget for the attacker can be significantly different in the case he/she is a criminal, a terroristic organization or a state-sponsored terroristic organization.

These two clashing requirements (maximizing damage and minimizing attack effort) can be formulated as a MOO problem with the aim to identify the most suitable nodes to attack, which are thus those nodes that deserve increased protection by the defendant. In particular, the proposed MOO formulation reads as follows

$$\min f(\mathbf{x}) = \min[f_1(\mathbf{x}), f_2(\mathbf{x})]^T,$$
$$\text{subject to} \quad B_L \leq \mathbf{c}^T \mathbf{x} \leq B_U \tag{8}$$
$$\mathbf{x} \in \{0,1\}^n$$

where $\mathbf{x} \in \mathbb{R}^n$ is the *attack vector* and has entries $x_i = 1$ if the i-th subsystem is attacked, and $x_i = 0$, otherwise. Morever, B_L and B_U are, respectively, the lower and upper bounds on the attack cost. Note that the upper bound B_U can be used to discriminate different attacker classes, while the lower bound B_L is a parameter that allows to filter non-realistic or trivial attack vectors corresponding to very limited damage/effort.

The two conflicting goals are summarized in the two following objective functions:

$$f_1 = NWPWC(\hat{A}, \mathbf{w}), \qquad f_2 = \frac{\mathbf{c}^T \mathbf{x}}{\mathbf{1}^T \mathbf{c}},$$

where $\hat{A}$, according to the definition in Eq. (9), represents the adjacency matrix of the graph once all the incident edges to the attacked nodes have been removed from the graph (i.e. all the entries of the associated row and columns are set to 0). In other words, it holds

$$\hat{A} = A \circ (\mathbf{1_n} - \mathbf{x}) \mathbf{1_n^T} \circ (\mathbf{1_n}(\mathbf{1_n} - \mathbf{x})^T) \tag{9}$$

Due to the conflicting nature of the two objective functions, we are unable to find a unique optimal solution. To overcome such a limit, we consider all the solutions which constitute the Pareto front. Each solution that belongs to the Pareto front is characterized by an attack cost and a connectivity value as defined in Eq. 3.2. In this way, we can implicitly consider a set of multiple attackers characterized by different preferences in terms of budget and attack strategy. Thanks to the analysis of each solution in the Pareto front, we are able to determine which nodes would be optimal to attack in attack plans in spite of attackers' preferences in terms of effects and budgets. As described in [2], we measure the frequency with which a given node is targeted in the solutions belonging to the Pareto front, and use this information to estimate the node criticality. Therefore, we adopt the *node criticality index* χ_i for a node v_i as

$$\chi_i = \frac{|\mathcal{P}_i|}{|\mathcal{P}|},$$

where $\mathcal{P}_i$ is the subset of solutions in the Pareto front where node v_i is attacked, i.e.,

$$\mathcal{P}_i = \{\mathbf{x} \in \mathcal{P} \mid x_i = 1\}.$$

while $\mathcal{P}$ is the set of all the solutions in the Pareto front.

The above index assigns greater criticality to those nodes v_i that are often attacked in a solution in the Pareto front, while the criticality of a node is small if it is attacked by only a few of the solutions in the Pareto front.

4   Case Study: U.S. Airport Network

In this section we validate the proposed methodology by analyzing the US Airline Network as in 1997 [5]. The network is represented by a directed graph with 332 nodes, which represents the US airports, and direct 4252 direct edges, which represent the existence of direct flights between the airports. As described in Sect. 3, we have defined for each node v_i of the graph a degree of importance w_i and an attack cost c_i. Without loss of generality, we assume that the value c_i is equal to the out-degree (i.e., the number of outgoing edges) of the i-th node. In other words, we assume that the larger the out-degree is, the higher the effort will be to disconnect the node from the network (i.e,. the attack cost is directly proportional to the number of direct flight routes from the airport to other destinations). Analogously, with respect to the definition of the importance degree, we assume that w_i is proportional to the betweenness centrality of the i-th node. We recall that for a node v_i the betweenness centrality is the fraction of shortest paths that pass through v_i (without considering v_i as source or destination of the paths). In this way, we associate a low importance to the airports with a low number of stopovers, while airports involved in high number of stopovers are considered essential for the network connectivity. For the sake of completeness, in Fig. 1, we report the distribution of out degree and betweenness centrality with reference to the analyzed network. Note that c_i and w_i can be estimated in different ways, e.g. c_i may be estimated on the basis of an assessment about the actual adopted security measure, and w_i on the base of the number of citizens living in the area of the i-th airport. In this paper we adopted the aforementioned selection because it can be estimated directly from the topology of the network.

According to the multi-objective formulation presented in Sect. 3.2, we compute the Pareto front by using an ant colony optimization algorithm [13]. We consider three different scenarios, each one evaluated by considering 10^6 generated solutions[1]. Specifically we consider the scenarios illustrated in Table 1 which represents different classes of attackers.

In Fig. 2 we report the Pareto front of the proposed problem in the case of an attacker belonging to a *state-sponsored organization*. This result is obtained by considering $B_L = 0$ and $B_U = 4252$ (i.e. the upper and lower bounds on the attack cost necessary to disconnect all the nodes from the network). Note that, as illustrated in the figure, the network is completely disconnected also when a budget of just 65% of B_U^{MAX} is used.

---

[1] An in depth analysis about the required computational complexity has been discussed in [2], where the time required to obtain suboptimal solutions has been studied with respect to large and small networks.

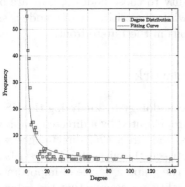
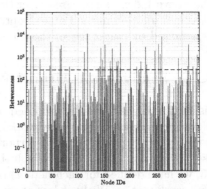

(a) Out-Degree frequency distribution (square markers) and fitting curve (solid line)

(b) Betweenness centrality for each node (blue bars), mean value (red dashed line)

Fig. 1. Degree and Betweenness distributions on US Airline Network.

Table 1. Attacker classes.

Class	B_U	% B_U^{MAX}	Scenario
State-sponsored organization	4252	100%	A
Terrorist group	1417	33%	B
Criminal organization	425	10%	C

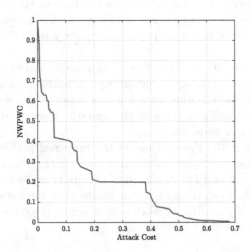

Fig. 2. Pareto front obtained for w_i proportional to the node betweenness centrality measures, and c_i proportional to the node degrees.

The Pareto front obtained via the proposed approximated technique is composed of 65 non-dominated solutions. In this view, each non-dominated solution represents a different attack plan, i.e., a different trade-off between the objectives. In order to highlight nodes that are recurrent in the different attack plans, in Fig. 3 we provide the frequency with which each node is involved in the 65 attack plans.

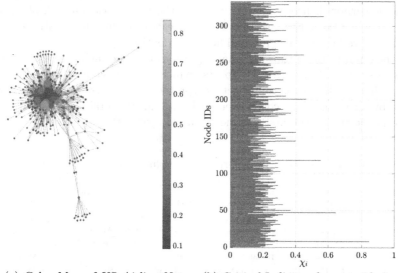

(a) Color Map of US Airline Network. The colors are related to the critical indices. The size of each node is proportional to the node attack costs c_i (i.e. the node degree).

(b) Critical Indices values considering c_i proportional to the nodes degree and w_i proportional to the nodes betweenness centrality.

Fig. 3. US Airline Network vulnerability analysis.

Looking at the figure, it is evident that the most critical node is the Anchorage Airport, which is involved in 84% of the generated hypothetical attack plans (this node is characterized by an attack cost $c_i = 29$ and an importance degree $w_i = 9288$ and its deletion disconnects the graph in several connected components.). The second most critical node is Seattle-Tacoma, which is involved in 64% of the attack plans (Seattle-Tacoma has an attack cost $c_i = 57$ and an importance degree of $w_i = 5069$). Note that Chicago O'Hare, although having the largest importance degree $w_i = 11377$, is involved only in 55% of the attack plans, i.e., it is ranked only fourth in terms of criticality. A reason for this lies in the high attack costs associated to it, which may imply that such an airport is too well protected and, consequently, it is not an appealing target for attackers that have limited resources. Data related to the first five most critical nodes is reported in Table 2, together with the results obtained for the other two scenarios.

In Scenario B, we consider an attacker belonging to a *Terrorist Group*. Terrorists, generally, can rely on considerable resources, although smaller than a *Sate-like entity*. Specifically, we impose, as illustrated in Table 1, an upper bound about the budget of the attacker equal to 33% of the maximum budget. Looking to Table 2 one can notice that the four most critical airports are the same as in Scenario A, but in this case they appear in considerably less attack plans (e.g., Anchorage airport is involved in only 76% of the hypothetical attack plans with respect to the 84% of Scenario A). This suggests that, in a terroristic scenario, the targets are larger hence more difficult to identify.

In the criminal organization scenario (Scenario C) one can notice that, except for the first three most critical airports (which are the same of the other scenarios), the attacker tends to neglect well protected airports (i.e., nodes characterized by an high attack cost), even with an high vulnerability (e.g., Chicago O'hare is not among the first five most critical airports).

Table 2. Most critical Airports in US Airline Network as in 1997.

Scenario A $B_L = 0\%$ and $B_U = 100\%$				Scenario B $B_L = 0\%$ and $B_U = 33\%$				Scenario C $B_L = 0\%$ and $B_U = 10\%$			
Airport	χ_i	c_i	w_i	Airport	χ_i	c_i	w_i	Airport	χ_i	c_i	w_i
Anchorage	0.84	29	9288	Anchorage	0.76	29	9288	Anchorage	0.79	29	9288
Seattle-Tacoma	0.64	57	5069	Seattle-Tacoma	0.58	57	5069	Seattle-Tacoma	0.62	57	5069
Honolulu	0.56	24	3721	Honolulu	0.48	24	3721	Honolulu	0.55	24	3721
Chicago O'hare	0.55	139	11377	Chicago O'hare	0.43	139	11377	San Francisco	0.41	68	5146
San Francisco	0.46	68	5146	Dallas/Fort Worth	0.41	118	8367	Salt Lake City	0.41	59	2662

5   Conclusions

In this paper we present a novel methodology for identifying network vulnerabilities. Specifically, we formulate a multi-objective optimization problem and based on the concept of weighted pairwise connectivity, with the aim to overcome the limitations of the other formulations which consider a single class of connected nodes without differences about their relevance in the network. The proposed methodology can be used to plan the allocation of limited protection resources, with the aim to globally improve the network's robustness. Future work will aim at applying the proposed methodology to multi-layer or hierarchical networks. Moreover, we will inspect the possibility to model the damage dealt by the attacker in terms of the reduction of flow over the network (e.g., for power or gas networks).

References

1. Arulselvan, A., Commander, C.W., Elefteriadou, L., Pardalos, P.M.: Detecting critical nodes in sparse graphs. Comput. Oper. Res. **36**(7), 2193–2200 (2009)
2. Faramondi, L., et al: Network structural vulnerability: a multiobjective attacker perspective. IEEE Trans. Syst. Man Cybern. Syst. (99), 1–14 (2018)
3. Fiol, M.A., Garriga, E.: Number of walks and degree powers in a graph. Discrete Math. **309**(8), 2613–2614 (2009)
4. Censor, Y.: Pareto optimality in multiobjective problems. Appl. Math. Optim. **4**(1), 41–59 (1977)
5. Rossi, R., Ahmed, N.: The network data repository with interactive graph analytics and visualization. In: AAAI, vol. 15, pp. 4292–4293, January 2015
6. Arulselvan, A., Commander, C.W., Elefteriadou, L., Pardalos, P.M.: Detecting critical nodes in sparse graphs. Comput. Oper. Res. **36**(7), 2193–2200 (2009)
7. Shen, Y., Nguyen, N.P., Xuan, Y., Thai, M.T.: On the discovery of critical links and nodes for assessing network vulnerability. IEEE/ACM Trans. Networking (TON) **21**(3), 963–973 (2013)
8. Di Summa, M., Grosso, A., Locatelli, M.: Branch and cut algorithms for detecting critical nodes in undirected graphs. Comput. Optim. Appl. **53**(3), 649–680 (2012)
9. Sun, F., Shayman, M.A.: On pairwise connectivity of wireless multihop networks. Int. J. Secur. Netw. **2**(1–2), 37–49 (2007)
10. Lalou, M., Tahraoui, M.A., Kheddouci, H.: The critical node detection problem in networks: a survey. Comput. Sci. Rev. **28**, 92–117 (2018)
11. Faramondi, L., Oliva, G., Setola, R., Pascucci, F., Esposito Amideo, A., Scaparra, M.P.: Performance analysis of single and multi-objective approaches for the critical node detection problem. In: Sforza, A., Sterle, C. (eds.) Optimization and Decision Science: Methodologies and Applications, ODS 2017. Springer Proceedings in Mathematics & Statistics, vol. 217, pp. 315–324. Springer, Cham (2017). https://doi.org/10.1007/978-3-319-67308-0_32
12. Lu, Z.M., Li, X.F.: Attack vulnerability of network controllability. PloS one **11**(9), e0162289 (2016)
13. Dorigo, M., Birattari, M.: Ant colony optimization. In: Sammut, C., Webb, G.I. (eds.) Encyclopedia of Machine Learning, pp. 36–39. Springer, Boston (2011). https://doi.org/10.1007/978-0-387-30164-8

Short Papers

RICS-el: Building a National Testbed for Research and Training on SCADA Security (Short Paper)

Magnus Almgren[1], Peter Andersson[2], Gunnar Björkman[3], Mathias Ekstedt[3], Jonas Hallberg[2], Simin Nadjm-Tehrani[4(✉)], and Erik Westring[2]

[1] Chalmers University of Technology, Gothenburg, Sweden
[2] FOI, Swedish Defence Research Agency, Linköping, Sweden
[3] KTH Royal Institute of Technology, Stockholm, Sweden
[4] Linköping University, Linköping, Sweden
simin.nadjm-tehrani@liu.se
http://www.rics.se

Abstract. Trends show that cyber attacks targeting critical infrastructures are increasing, but security research for protecting such systems are challenging. There is a gap between the somewhat simplified models researchers at universities can sustain contra the complex systems at infrastructure owners that seldom can be used for direct research. There is also a lack of common datasets for research benchmarking. This paper presents a national experimental testbed for security research within supervisory control and data acquisition systems (SCADA), accessible for both research training and experiments. The virtualized testbed has been designed and implemented with both vendor experts and security researchers to balance the goals of realism with specific research needs. It includes a real SCADA product for energy management, a number of network zones, substation nodes, and a simulated power system. This environment enables creation of scenarios similar to real world utility scenarios, attack generation, development of defence mechanisms, and perhaps just as important: generating open datasets for comparative research evaluation.

Keywords: Cyber security in C(I)I systems · Modelling · Simulation
Analysis and Validation approaches to C(I)IP
Training for C(I)IP and effective intervention

1 Introduction

Since the appearance of Stuxnet, a malware specifically targeting industrial control systems (ICS) in 2010, research on identifying new attack vectors and new

This work has been supported by the Swedish Civil Contingencies Agency (MSB) in the context of the RICS project.

© Springer Nature Switzerland AG 2019
E. Luiijf et al. (Eds.): CRITIS 2018, LNCS 11260, pp. 219–225, 2019.
https://doi.org/10.1007/978-3-030-05849-4_17

defence mechanisms on specific testbeds devoted to experimentation with ICS cyber security has accelerated [1–5]. However, the lack of environments in which realistic scenarios can be created, devices emulated, protocols tested, methods evaluated, and data collected, has been known for a long time. Efforts have been spent to reduce this gap, notably through European projects (e.g. CRU-TIAL [6]) or US national labs. Two recent surveys [7,8] provide an excellent overview of the existing testbeds. However, to the best of our knowledge none of the reviewed testbeds openly share data for comparative research, a critical feature for research quality.

A review of discussions in a recent NSF-funded workshop focusing on remotely accessible testbeds for cyber-physical systems security points out a "significant gap" between the theoretical foundations, small scale experimentations, and real deployments with societal impact [9].

An ideal research environment for enhancing cybersecurity should facilitate comparison of different methods in relevant scenarios, using access to common testbeds and parameter settings. This in turn requires structures for sharing knowledge and datasets [10]. Adapting the scenarios and testbed configurations to various stakeholders needs should be possible and efficiently repeatable. This will need to accommodate obvious confidentiality barriers, but also practical realisations.

The Swedish research centre on Resilient Information and Control Systems (RICS) works towards reducing this research gap by realising such an environment as one of its cornerstones since its start in 2015. RICS research leads to methods for security assessment, prevention and detection of cyber threats in ICS, with a focus on electricity, water, heating, and transportation sectors. The stakeholders closely collaborating with RICS include a major SCADA vendor, and 13 other enterprises (utility companies, security product vendors, security consultants, and a national regulating body).

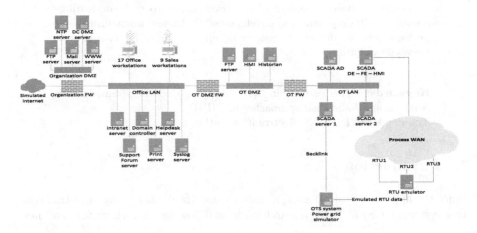

Fig. 1. Overview of the testbed zones, nodes, and connections

This paper presents an overview of RICS-el, a testbed for experiment-ing with supervisory control and data acquisition (SCADA) systems that has been realised in collaboration with RICS stakeholders and the Swedish defence research agency (FOI). Since the project is ongoing, the work is in an evolving state, but is already providing its first benefits to the collaborating universities in RICS.

In the following sections of the paper we first present an overview of the testbed, followed by a more detailed description of the architecture divided into the information technology (IT) and the operational technology (OT) subparts. The paper will also include a brief description of the utility of the testbed so far.

2   The RICS-el testbed

Our overall ambition with building the testbed is to make a simplified yet realistic copy of a utility's information and communication technology (ICT) infrastruc-ture. In the first iteration, we have focused on an electric power operator, as this domain is opting higher digitalisation and where attacks are also prominent. At the core of RICS-el we find a modern SCADA product for power system control from one of the large vendors in that segment (the top right part of Fig. 1). To model a power system, we use the operator training simulator module from the SCADA product that provides us with an emulated grid (the bottom right part of the figure). The test environment also features an office IT segment (the left part of the figure).

The testbed is built on top of the Cyber Range And Training Environment (CRATE) infrastructure at FOI which is a virtualized environment. The details of how it is typically used to create environments for training and security aware-ness can be found elsewhere[1]. Here, we focus on enhancement of the platform to enable SCADA experiments. All the hosts in RICS-el are run on virtual machines (VMs) using VirtualBox, including the emulation of the wide area network (WAN) that connects the remote terminal units (RTUs) included in the testbed. CRATE contains an in-house configuration tool where all organisations, networks, hosts with parameters are defined and stored in a database.

2.1   The Office IT Segment

As shown in Fig. 1, the office IT part of the testbed consists of two subnets, the demiliterized zone (DMZ) for the Organization and the Office LAN zone. The Organization DMZ contains servers for file transfer protocol (FTP), web, domain controller for DMZ, mail, and network time protocol (NTP). The exter-nal firewall filters traffic between the Organization DMZ, the Office LAN, and the CRATE Internet (cyber range emulated Internet). The Office LAN contains 10 office workstations, 9 office sales department workstations, and 6 other support

---

[1] https://www.foi.se/en/our-knowledge/information-security-and-communication/ information-security/labs-and-resources/crate-cyber-range-and-training-environment.html.

servers. Interesting from a security perspective, and also realistic, some of the sales and office workstations have been given credentials and a VPN connection to the OT DMZ, described next.

2.2   The OT Segment

The OT section of the RICS-el environment (the right segment in Fig. 1) is divided into four main parts: the demilitarized zone (OT DMZ), the OT LAN, the substation communication wide area network (Process WAN), and the power grid simulator, including the emulations of Remote Terminal Units (RTUs). This segment has been designed by vendor experts and researchers together.

The OT DMZ is included to isolate the OT LAN from the office LAN so that users in the office LAN will not be able to directly access the SCADA servers. Since certain SCADA data is of interest to the office users, a replicated Historian and an HMI are placed in the OT DMZ. By use of these replicated servers the office user can access SCADA data without having direct access to the SCADA server. It is possible for office users to view SCADA displays, e.g. real-time station diagrams, using the HMI in the OT DMZ.

In a similar way, certain data produced in the office environment is required in the SCADA zone. Examples are long-term generation schedules or load forecasts. Such data are sent as files to the FTP server in the OT DMZ where they can be picked up by the energy management system (EMS) or the distribution management system (DMS) applications in the SCADA system.

The OT LAN features two redundant SCADA servers with a real-time database for the process state as well as the two servers for DMS and EMS, with functionality such as state estimation, optimal power flow, and energy scheduling. Additionally, one host contains software modules for Human Machine Interface (HMI), data engineering (DE), and a communication front-end (FE), where the latter is a communication gateway to the WAN connecting the RTUs in the substations. Finally, there is an Active Directory (AD) host performing authorization of and granting access to the users in the zone.

The process WAN is built from 15 nodes forming a meshed communication network where each site (substation, electricity generation, main office) has an entry. Three RTUs are emulated using the RTU emulator and data from the power grid simulator. The communication between the SCADA front-end and the three emulated RTUs is performed by means of the IEC 60870-5-104 protocol routed through the process WAN to the front end (FE). If one of the communication nodes goes down the traffic is automatically rerouted using another route.

The power grid simulator is a key piece of the architecture to add realistic responses to any attacks or actions in the testbed. It is also instrumental for generating realistic traffic and events in the whole RICS-el environment. The simulator is using the Operator Training Simulator module (OTS) of the SCADA product. The OTS contains an extended power flow model that is designed to train grid operators for different operational scenarios in a realistic yet fictitious power grid. During operator training the OTS resides on the SCADA server, communicates directly with the SCADA database and the trained operators are acting over the HMI.

Within RICS-el, the OTS is used to give a realistic pseudo-dynamic model of the electrical process. The back bone of the OTS is a high voltage 400 kV grid with some twenty substations. Also some medium voltage transmission is included, but no low voltage parts. Hence, this corresponds to the business Transmission System Operator (TSO). Functionally the OTS operators can do all normal grid operation manoeuvres, e.g. open breakers, and the OTS model will respond by updating equipment states, power flows, etc. Scenarios of varying loads and production over a period of few days are used to give "life" to the emulated power flows. Since the OTS is developed with the purpose of training SCADA operators, grid emulation is updated on a higher level. This is the resolution on which the SCADA is normally managing the grid, so transients and other fast power system dynamics are not captured.

Using the operator training version of the product would be problematic in RICS-el, since the OTS in the original product operates directly on the SCADA database and does not generate any SCADA and substation traffic. For that reason we have made the OTS a stand-alone component by developing individual RTU emulation for three specific RTUs. The emulated power flows for these stations and corresponding power lines are then translated to IEC 60870-5-104 messages in the RTU emulator and sent to the SCADA front-end over the WAN as normal RTU traffic. These can therefore be potentially monitored by security components deployed in the testbed later. For the time being the other RTUs in the OTS use an internal backlink to update their status, but our intention is to completely remove this backlink in the future.

2.3   Emulated Users, Traffic and Scenarios

So far the structure of RICS-el has been described, but without any events this is an empty and deserted universe. For that reason, ongoing work is focused on adding realistic traffic to each segment in Fig. 1. The Office IT segment features a number of office worker bots, that send and read emails, surf the web, or open, edit, and close documents. Ongoing work includes emulating data exchanges over the SCADA DMZ, with the major inbound flow being load forecasts to the SCADA and the major outbound flow being the grid operation data sent from the SCADA to the Historian for further analysis by office users.

At the power grid end there are event generators in the form of scenarios provided as part of the OTS module from the vendor. These scenarios are 24 hour power generation and consumption profiles. The OTS also offers an interface (for the operator trainer) for introducing arbitrary power grid events. This means that traffic that flows over the substation communication network to the SCADA database and on to the HMI can be generated and such power grid operator bots are under construction. In their first version these bots will feature simple and rational behaviour similar to real grid events.

Note that by building RICS-el in the CRATE environment we are also able to generate arbitrary attack scenarios initiated on (the emulated) Internet including denial of service attacks. The Office LAN is connected to the OT DMZ via the firewall (OT DMZ FW) and via the OT DMZ and another firewall (OT FW) to the OT LAN. The OT DMZ can be removed by configuration to simulate some situations in real-life where office zones are connected to the SCADA systems via one (or no) firewall, making security vulnerabilities concrete.

3   Related Works

To our knowledge, all the testbeds mentioned earlier are either only accessible to those that created the testbed whereby the data generated therein is not available to other researchers, or include only IT related datasets. The closest testbed we are aware of is SWAT, a testbed within the iTrust initiative in Singapore [11] where a water treatment plant including elements from the SCADA and IT infrastructure is intended for performing security exercises and sharing data with other researchers. Other major testbeds for studying power generation problems, e.g. one at University of Strathclyde[2] of course exist, but do not extensively emulate the SCADA, WANs, and office environments, and not tailored for security related data generation (including attacks).

4   Summary: Current Work Using the Testbed

In this paper, we have described RICS-el, a virtualized testbed for SCADA security research and training. Key design goals were to make the environment realistic by including both IT and OT elements and involving vendor experts. The current version of the testbed has already proven itself useful by: (1) generating synthetic but realistic data to form a basis of understanding the traffic flows and testing anomaly detection mechanisms, and (2) creating a "realistic" environment as a backdrop to exercises that the FOI team organises in order to train various participants in national security training and awareness raising exercises.

Data Generation for Anomaly Detection. The emulated testbed has already been used to generate ten days of data flow with IEC 60870-5-104 packets captured as pcap files. This has helped us understand the distinction between the traffic patterns that are regular (request response patterns) and those that are generated by spontaneous events (some flows that use the spontaneous category in the above protocol setting). Preliminary work on anomaly detection for these types of flows has been reported elsewhere [12,13]. Our current work includes generating scenarios (using the OT and IT bots mentioned above) in which the pattern of spontaneous events in the SCADA elements can be systematically and repeatedly created for further studies.

---

[2] https://www.strath.ac.uk/research/subjects/electronicelectricalengineeringinstitute forenergyenvironment/industryengagementresearchcentres/thepowernetworksdemon strationcentre/.

Deployed in Exercises. A replica of RICS-el has been used for the iPilot exercise in October 2017. iPilot trained Swedish nuclear IT/OT operators to detect and defend against IT/OT attacks. The exercise was overseen and observed by IAEA with delegates from 30 countries present. The event was sponsored by the Swedish Radiation Safety Authority and the EU. There are plans to use RICS-el in future exercises during the rest of 2018 and also in coming years.

References

1. Reaves, B., Morris, T.: An open virtual testbed for industrial control system security research. Int. J. Inf. Secur. **11**(4), 215–229 (2012)
2. Genge, B., Siaterlis, C., Nai Fovino, I., Masera, M.: A cyber-physical experimentation environment for the security analysis of networked industrial control systems. Comput. Electr. Eng. **38**(5), 1146–1161 (2012)
3. Siaterlis, C., Genge, B., Hohenadel, M.: EPIC: a testbed for scientifically rigorous cyber-physical security experimentation. IEEE Trans. Emerg. Topics Comput. **1**(2), 319–330 (2013)
4. Redwood, O., Reynolds, J., Burmester, M.: Integrating simulated physics and device virtualization in control system testbeds. In: Rice, M., Shenoi, S. (eds.) Critical Infrastructure Protection X. IAICT, vol. 485, pp. 185–202. Springer, Cham (2016). https://doi.org/10.1007/978-3-319-48737-3_11
5. Adhikari, U., Morris, T., Pan, S.: WAMS cyber-physical test bed for power system, cybersecurity study, and data mining. IEEE Trans. Smart Grid **8**(6), 2744–2753 (2017)
6. Dondossola, G., Garrone, G., Szanto, J., Deconinck, G., Loix, T., Beitollahi, H.: ICT resilience of power control systems: experimental results from the crutial testbeds, pp. 554–559 (2009)
7. Holm, H., Karresand, M., Vidström, A., Westring, E.: A survey of industrial control system testbeds. In: Buchegger, S., Dam, M. (eds.) Secure IT Systems. NordSec 2015. LNCS, vol. 9417, pp. 11–26. Springer, Cham (2015). https://doi.org/10.1007/978-3-319-26502-5_2
8. McLaughlin, S., et al.: The cybersecurity landscape in industrial control systems. Proc. IEEE **104**(5), 1039–1057 (2016)
9. Egerstedt, M., Govindarasu, M.: Accessible remote testbeds: opportunities, challenges, and lessons learned, workshop report (2016)
10. Vasilomanolakis, E., Cordero, C.G., Milanov, N., Mühlhäuser, M.: Towards the creation of synthetic, yet realistic, intrusion detection datasets. In: IEEE/IFIP Network Operations and Management Symposium (NOMS), pp. 1209–1214, April 2016
11. Mathur, A.P., Tippenhauer, N.O.: SWaT: a water treatment testbed for research and training on ICS security. In: International Workshop on Cyber-physical Systems for Smart Water Networks (CySWater), pp. 31–36. IEEE (2016)
12. Lin, C.Y., Nadjm-Tehrani, S., Asplund, M.: Timing-based anomaly detection in SCADA networks. In: D'Agostino G., Scala, A. (eds.) CRITIS 2017. LNCS, vol. 10707, pp. 48–59. Springer, Cham (2018). https://doi.org/10.1007/978-3-319-99843-5_5
13. Lin, C.-Y., Nadjm-Tehrani, S.: Understanding IEC-60870-5-104 traffic patterns in SCADA networks. In: Proceedings of the 4th Cyber-Physical System Security Workshop (CPSS), AsiaCCS. ACM, June 2018

Efficient Analysis to Protect Control into Critical Infrastructures

Shuo Zhang$^{(\boxtimes)}$ and Stephen D. Wolthusen

School of Mathematics and Information Security,
Royal Holloway University of London, Egham TW20 0EX, UK
MYVA375@live.rhul.ac.uk, stephen.wolthusen@rhul.ac.uk

Abstract. To protect control into critical infrastructures against single component-dependency attacks or failures, we analyse the importance of any given dependency in maintaining controllability with a minimum set of inputs. Since people use critical, redundant and ordinary categories to clarify how an edge maintains controllability of linear time-invariant(LTI) dynamical networks, according to graph-based models of infrastructures and the minimum input theorem, we firstly use a *Erdős-Rényi* random digraph with a precomputed maximum matching to model some LTI and controllable infrastructures by a minimum set of inputs. We then efficiently analyse any given arc's category before and during single-arc removals, as a way to further confirm how related dependency keeps control into infrastructures. After running our label operations with linear time and space complexity, any edge-category analysis can be thus executed in $O(1)$ time in both cases.

Keywords: Network controllability · Modelling · Edge classification

1 Introduction

Malicious attacks or random failures on pairwise dependencies among critical infrastructure components might make critical infrastrucutres out of control, and may lead unavailability of purposed products and services in a large region for a significant length of time, which would cause severe economic impacts or life loss and limb [7]. Thus, efficient analysis on any given pairwise dependency between components in terms of keeping control into infrastructures is forward-looking to protect critical infrastructures. Given a controllable and linear time-invariant (LTI) critical infrastructure by a minimum set of inputs, according to the graph-based models of critical infrastructures [8] and the minimum input theorem used to control networks with LTI dynamics, to protect its controllability, we model this given infrastructure by a large, sparse *Erdős-Rényi* random digraph, which also contains a precomputed maximum matching, as an input graph [1]. Then, we solve the problem of efficient edge-category analysis on the input graph to classify any given edge into critical, redundant or ordinary categories before and during single-edge removals [6], so that how related pairwise

© Springer Nature Switzerland AG 2019
E. Luiijf et al. (Eds.): CRITIS 2018, LNCS 11260, pp. 226–229, 2019.
https://doi.org/10.1007/978-3-030-05849-4_18

dependency keeps control into critical infrastructure can be known. Specifically, removing a critical edge increases the minimum number of inputs; the absence of an ordinary edge only changes control structure rather than the minimum number of inputs; removing a redundant edge changes nothing [6]. Our edge-category analysis is executed through a bipartite graph mapped by the input graph. With this bipartite graph, we firstly introduce a generally static analysis, on which there is no edge removals. Based on our previous work [9], searching and labelling alternating cycles and paths related to a given maximum matching helps to confirm any edge's category. During the single-edge removal process, in addition of edge-category analysis, control into the residual network per edge removal should be recovered as well. With constrains on degree distribution of the input graph, label operations and control recovery are executed in $O(1)$ amortized time per edge removal. For our contribution, excluding the precomputed maximum matching of the input graph, by label operations executed in linear time and space complexity, category of any given edge of the input graph can be confirmed in $O(1)$ time. In the following paper: Sect. 2 models critical infrastructures and formulates research question; Sects. 3 and 4 executes static and dynamic edge-category analysis respectively; Sect. 5 gives conclusion.

2   Modelling

By control theory [4,5], an linear time-invariant infrastructure with external inputs can be described by a differential equation:

$$\dot{x}(t) = \mathbf{A}x(t) + \mathbf{B}u(t) \tag{1}$$

where $x(t) \in \mathbb{R}^N$ is the system state vector holding the state of each infrastructure component at time t, and $x(t) = (x_1(t), x_2(t), \ldots, x_N(t))^T$. $u(t) \in \mathbb{R}^M (M \leq N)$ is the control input vector, and $u(t) = (u_1(t), u_2(t), \ldots, u_M(t))^T$. System matrix $\mathbf{A} \in \mathbb{R}^{N \times N}$ shows the interactions among N components, while input matrix $\mathbf{B} \in \mathbb{R}^{N \times M}$ shows interactions among M inputs and N components. A system described by Eq. 1 is fully controllable if and only if the rank of the matrix $\mathbf{C} \in \mathbb{R}^{N \times NM}$, where $\mathbf{C} = [\mathbf{B}, \mathbf{AB}, \mathbf{A}^2\mathbf{B}, \ldots, \mathbf{A}^{N-1}\mathbf{B}]$, has full rank, noted by $rank(\mathbf{C}) = N$. Concerning graph-based model of the critical infrastrucutres [8], we model the infrastructure by a digraph defined below:

Definition 1 (Modelling Digraph). *Given a $\boldsymbol{A}$ of Eq. 1, let $G(\boldsymbol{A}) = (V_1, E_1)$ be a digraph, and $\alpha : \{\mathbf{A}\} \rightarrow G(\boldsymbol{A})$ be a bijection. For each non-zero entry $a_{ij} \in \boldsymbol{A}$, there are $\alpha : a_{ij} \rightarrow \overrightarrow{\langle v_j, v_i \rangle}$, where $\overrightarrow{\langle v_j, v_i \rangle} \in E_1$ and $\{v_i, v_j\} \subseteq V_1$.*

And controllability of $G(\mathbf{A})$ with a minimum set of inputs is confirmed by following theorem:

Theorem 1. (The Minimum Input Theorem [6]). *The minimum number of inputs to fully control a modelling digraph is one, if it has a perfect matching, where the input can directly drive any vertex. Otherwise, it equals to the number of unmatched nodes, which must be directly driven by the same number of inputs.*

In digraphs, a maximum matching is a set of arcs neither sharing common heads nor tails with highest cardinality [1]. When all nodes of a digraph are heads of arcs of a maximum matching, this digraph has a perfect matching. Also, there might be multiple maximum matchings in a same graph. By contrast, a maximum matching of a bipartite digraph is a set of vertex-disjoint edges with the highest cardinality. Above all, we define our modelling digraph, which is our input graph of following edge classification:

Definition 2 (Input Graph). *Let* $D = (V, E)$ *be a large, sparse and finite* Erdős-Rényi *digraph, where* $V = \{v_i | 1 \leq i \leq N\}(N > 3)$, $E = \{\overrightarrow{\langle v_i, v_j \rangle} | i \neq j, v_i, v_j \in V\}(|E| > 3)$. *$D$ excludes selfloops, parallel arcs and isolated nodes. Also, let M_D be a precomputed maximum matching of D by the algorithm of [3].*

With $D = (V, E)$ of Definition 2, efficiently analysing how any given dependency among infrastructure components maintains the control into the infrastructure with a minimum set of inputs, can be modelled into efficient edge-category analysis on D to confirm its any edge's category. Further more, we solve such analysis before and during the process of single-edge removals.

3   Generally Static Edge Analysis

This section confirms the category of any given arc of $D = (V, E)$ of Definition 2, when no arc is removed from D. A bipartite graph defined below to execute following edge-category analysis with items of Definition 4 and Corollary 1 and 2:

Definition 3 (B = (V$_\mathbf{B}$, E$_\mathbf{B}$)). *Given $D = (V, E)$ with M_D of definition 2, let $B = (V_B, E_B)$ be an undirected bipartite graph, β be a bijection. Also, let M_B be a maximum matching of B, and V_B^-, V_B^+ be two independent sets, where $V_B = V_B^- \cup V_B^+$. For any $\overrightarrow{\langle v_i, v_j \rangle} \in E$, $\beta : \overrightarrow{\langle v_i, v_j \rangle} \rightarrow (v_i^+, v_j^-)$, where $v_i^+ \in V_B^+, v_j^- \in V_B^-$ and $(v_i^+, v_j^-) \in E_B$. Besides, let M_B mapped by M_D.*

Definition 4 (Alternating Cycle & Alternating Path [9]). *Given $B = (V_B, E_B)$ with M_B of definition 3, a set of edges is either an alternating path or cycle, if it alternatively involves the same number of edges of M_B and $E_B \backslash M_B$.*

Corollary 1. *In $D = (V, E)$, let e be an edge of E, given $B = (V_B, E_B)$ and M_B, let e' be an edge of E_B and mapped by e. Then, e is a critical edge iff $e' \in M_B$ and out of any alternating cycles or paths related to M_B [9].*

Corollary 2. *In $D = (V, E)$, let e be an edge of E, given $B = (V_B, E_B)$ and M_B, let e' be an edge of E_B and mapped by e. Then, e is an ordinary edge iff $e' \in M_B$ and involved into an alternating cycle or path related to M_B [9].*

Thus, static analysis depends on finding all alternating paths and cycles related to M_B. Specifically, each identified edge is a mapped by an ordinary edge related to M_D of D, while each edge of M_B not identified corresponds to a critical edge of D. And any edge out of M_B and not identified is related to a redundant edge of D. To view related algorithms, please ask for the first author.

4   Conditionally Dynamic Edge Analysis

This section confirms the category of any given arc of residual network after removing single edges from $D = (V, E)$ of Definition 2, where control recovery per single-edge removal is also implemented. Solving this problem also depends on $B = (V_B, E_B)$ of Definition 3 during removing $p(1 \leq p < |E_B|)$ single edges. To increase efficiency, we assume that: (i)the number of in-degree and out-degree of any node of D should be less than or equal to 2; (ii) the average degree of D is bigger than one. By these assumptions, all paths and cycles can not share common vertex incident to M_B. Even though, several cases still should be concerned and related algorithms can be asked for the first author.

5   Conclusion

We use a digraph with a precomputed maximum matching to model a LTI controllable critical infrastructure with a minimum set of inputs, and execute efficient edge-category analysis, to confirm the importance of any given pairwise dependency in keeping controllability against removing single infrastructure dependency. We find and label alternating paths and cycles of a bipartite graph mapped by the graph model during continuous single-edge removals to support edge-category analysis. As a result, our entire operations cost linear time and space in the worst case for both static and conditionally dynamic edge analysis. Also, based on the aggregate analysis [2], an label operation per single-edge removal for conditionally dynamic edge analysis costs $O(1)$ amortized time. With those operations, category of any given arc can be confirmed in $O(1)$ time in both cases, which excludes label operations.

References

1. Chartrand, G., Lesniak, L., Zhang, P.: Graphs & Digraphs. CRC Press, Boca Raton (2010)
2. Cormen, T.H.: Introduction to Algorithms. MIT press, Cambridge (2009)
3. Hopcroft, J.E., Karp, R.M.: An n^5/2 algorithm for maximum matchings in bipartite graphs. SIAM J. Comput. **2**(4), 225–231 (1973)
4. Kalman, R.: On the general theory of control systems. IRE Trans. Autom. Control **4**(3), 110–110 (1959)
5. Kalman, R.E.: Mathematical description of linear dynamical systems. J. Soci. Ind. Appl. Math. Ser. A Control **1**(2), 152–192 (1963)
6. Liu, Y.Y., Slotine, J.J., Barabási, A.L.: Controllability of complex networks. Nature **473**(7346), 167–173 (2011)
7. Lopez, J., Setola, R., Wolthusen, S.D. (eds.): Critical Infrastructure Protection 2011. LNCS, vol. 7130. Springer, Heidelberg (2012). https://doi.org/10.1007/978-3-642-28920-0
8. Svendsen, N.K., Wolthusen, S.D.: Modelling approaches. In: Lopez, J., Setola, R., Wolthusen, S.D. (eds.) Critical Infrastructure Protection 2011. LNCS, vol. 7130, pp. 68–97. Springer, Heidelberg (2012). https://doi.org/10.1007/978-3-642-28920-0_5
9. Zhang, S., Wolthusen, S.D.: Security-aware network analysis for network controllability. In: 2018 32nd International Conference on Advanced Information Networking and Applications Workshops (WAINA). IEEE (2018)

Denial of Service Attacks: Detecting the Frailties of Machine Learning Algorithms in the Classification Process

Ivo Frazão[1], Pedro Henriques Abreu[1], Tiago Cruz[1(✉)], Hélder Araújo[2], and Paulo Simões[1]

[1] Centre of Informatics and Systems, Department of Informatics Engineering, University of Coimbra, Coimbra, Portugal
{icosteira,pha,tjcruz,psimoes}@dei.uc.pt
[2] Institute for Systems and Robotics, Department of Electrical and Computer Engineering, University of Coimbra, Coimbra, Portugal
helder@isr.uc.pt

Abstract. Denial of Service attacks, which have become commonplace on the Information and Communications Technologies domain, constitute a class of threats whose main objective is to degrade or disable a service or functionality on a target. The increasing reliance of Cyber-Physical Systems upon these technologies, together with their progressive interconnection with other infrastructure and/or organizational domains, has contributed to increase their exposure to these attacks, with potentially catastrophic consequences. Despite the potential impact of such attacks, the lack of generality regarding the related works in the attack prevention and detection fields has prevented its application in real-world scenarios. This paper aims at reducing that effect by analyzing the behavior of classification algorithms with different dataset characteristics.

Keywords: Denial of Service attacks · Intrusion detection systems Classifier performance

1 Introduction

Cyber-Physical System (CPSs) play an important role in today's society, particularly in the control of Critical Infrastructure (CIs), whose uninterrupted operation is essential for the safety and livelihood of a modern society [1].

A Denial-of-Service (DoS) attack is an attack on the quality and/or availability of a service that aims to disrupt the normal operation of an infrastructure by preventing or degrading the communication between its components. A Distributed DoS (DDoS) attack is a variant which further complicates its detection and prevention since it doesn't (or doesn't appear to) originate from a single source, making it very difficult to distinguish legitimate and illegitimate network traffic. Despite the relative abundance of published work in the field of intrusion detection devoted to DoS attacks, its bulk is mostly focused on the

© Springer Nature Switzerland AG 2019
E. Luiijf et al. (Eds.): CRITIS 2018, LNCS 11260, pp. 230–235, 2019.
https://doi.org/10.1007/978-3-030-05849-4_19

perspective of novel algorithms or domain-adaptation of known algorithms, preventing a proper generalization of their results and real-world applications. This article constitutes the first step to providing an insight at the frailties of ML algorithms in the classification process of DoS attacks, specifically by evaluating the impact that the size of the datasets and the relative scale of the attack traces within such datasets affects the performance of common algorithms. While performance comparisons are already available, they don't provide insights about how specific dataset characteristics relate to the performance obtained.

2   Related Work

Studies about the topic of DoS attack detection within the scope of common Internet infrastructures are abundant, such as the work in [3] (2003), where the authors performed a comparison between a comprehensive set of ML algorithms against the KDD dataset, which demonstrated that the classifiers were not capable of detecting all the attacks with high success, but, by using the best classifier for each type of attacks, a multi-classifier could be built, which outperformed every algorithm; or in [4] (2016), the authors proposed an ensemble-based multi-filter feature selection method for DDoS detection.

Domain-specific intrusion detection strategies for CPSs have also been proposed, encompassing diverse approaches to the subject, e.g., by implementing techniques derived from common defense mechanisms for Internet-exposed or ICT networks, such as the work in [5] (2005), where the author proposed an anomaly-based IDS, which makes predictions based in historical, exemplar observations of the traffic used for weighted distance calculation; or by modeling the system's behavior, as the work made in [6] (2013), where the authors presented a Deterministic Finite Automata to model the network, or in [7] (2014), where the authors use a variable-order Markov chain to determine the state of the system and detect anomalous occurrences, or even in [8] (2015), where the authors present a finite-state machine modeling technique for each type of register in a PLC to detect anomalous variances of the values. The effects of DoS attacks on these systems have been evaluated in works such as [9], where the authors analyzed the impact of a DDoS attack on the state of a simulated SCADA server, or in [10], where the authors simulated IP packet, TCP SYN, and IEC 60870-5-104 APCI packet flooding against an RTU and analyzed their impacts on the availability of the system. Such works are important to identify the relevant traffic features that can provide evidence about the existence of attacks, as well as the negative impact at a system-wide level, and not only on the component(s) directly affected by the attack. In [11] (2014), the authors performed an evaluation of the classification performance of multiple ML methods in order to explore the aptitude of such techniques for the detection of disturbances in the electrical grid, implementing three testing schemes, using multi-, three-, and binary-class classification of events, in 15 datasets. The first noteworthy result from this work showcased the consistency of the results for each learner, regardless of the dataset being used. Nevertheless, there can be no definitive conclusion on using different classification schemes, since each learner had a different response to each scheme.

3 Experimental Setup

The availability of datasets or network traces containing normal SCADA operations, as well as attacks aimed at those systems, is very limited. To overcome this limitation a testbed was used to generate those datasets, which emulates a CPS process controlled by a SCADA system using the MODBUS protocol. It consists of a liquid pump simulated by an electric motor controlled by a VFD, which in its turn is controlled by a PLC. The motor speed is determined by a set of predefined liquid temperature thresholds, whose measurement is provided by a MODBUS RTU device providing a temperature gauge, simulated by a potentiometer connected to an Arduino. The PLC communicates with the HMI controlling the system and horizontally with the RTU, providing insightful knowledge of how this type of communications may affect the overall system.

There are several types of DoS attacks that are effective against SCADA-based systems using the MODBUS over TCP protocol. For analysis purposes, a subset of the possible attacks was implemented in the testbed, namely ping flooding, TCP SYN flooding, and MODBUS Query flooding - Read Holding Registers, which targeted the PLC. While the first two attacks attempt to overwhelm the capacity of the network or the networking subsystem in the target device with requests (operating mostly at OSI layers 2 to 4), the third attack works at the SCADA protocol layer, flooding the device with read request operations which may lead to side effects such as device resource exhaustion, scan cycle latency deviations or loss of connectivity. The first two attacks were implemented using the *hping3* tool, using its ability to spoof the packet's IP address, whilst the last attack was implemented using an adaptation of the SMOD tool.

Concerning the aim of this work - to analyze the impact of the dataset size and the relative magnitude of the attack traces within such datasets on the behavior of machine-learned classifiers for DoS attacks - the following experiments were made: varying the time of the capture (30 min and 1 h of capture); and varying the time of the attack (1, 5, and 15 min of attack within each capture). The network captures were acquired from the testbed using the *tshark* network analyzer tool – for this purpose, the network switch that was used to interconnect the equipment was configured with a mirror port. This capture was then processed for feature extraction within Matlab, where a total of 68 features were extracted (packet timestamps, inter-packet arrival times, binary features defining which protocols were involved, and every field of the Ethernet, ARP, IP, ICMP, UDP, TCP and MODBUS over TCP headers). However, to generalize the captures for normal use of the system, the timestamps were removed from the datasets before the analysis.

Four of the most used classifiers were implemented in this analysis study, namely: k-Nearest Neighbors (kNN), Support Vector Machine (SVM), Decision Tree (DT), and Random Forest (RF), resorting to the Matlab implementations of the algorithms. In order to validate the models created, a cross-validation procedure was performed with a 70%/30% ratio for training and validation sets.

4 Results and Discussion

The results for the implemented algorithms are shown in Figs. 1 and 2 (full lines represent the accuracy, whilst dashed lines represent the F1-scores). The DoS attacks that were implemented are labeled as follows: (1) Ping DDoS Flood; (2) TCP SYN DDoS Flood; and, (3) MODBUS Query Flood.

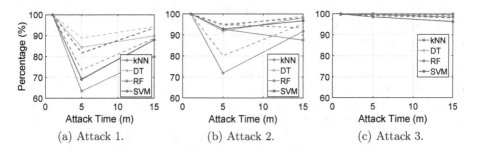

(a) Attack 1.   (b) Attack 2.   (c) Attack 3.

Fig. 1. Results of the implemented classifiers with 0.5 h of capture.

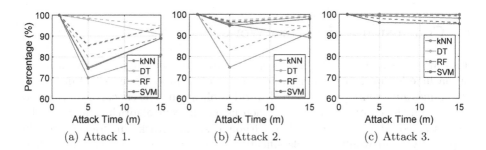

(a) Attack 1.   (b) Attack 2.   (c) Attack 3.

Fig. 2. Results of the implemented classifiers with 1 h of capture.

On a first approach, the analysis of the results reveals a trend for consistent high accuracy results for the smallest attack timespan. However, this is a misleading result, given the high imbalance in the data present in these situations, associated with the small variance of the attacks in such a small timespan. When the attacks increase in size, a decay of the performance can be observed, explained by the decrease of the aforementioned effects. The increasing attack timespan overcomes the imbalance within the dataset, allowing the algorithms to systematically learn more differences between normal and anomalous traces and improve the results – a similar effect is also accomplished with an increase in the size of the capture. Although the increase of the size of the capture increases the imbalance of the dataset, it also increases the number of packets available to differentiate the traces, improving the performance of the classifiers, as can be seen by the reduced decay in performance when the time of capture increases. The improvement of the results as a consequence of the increase in the relative size of the attack traffic is also reduced when the size of the capture increases.

The DT classifier presents the best results of all the studied classifiers. By analyzing the trees obtained, some of the attacks were classified by detection of the reduced inter-packet arrival times (a good metric for flooding attacks), however, when the inter-packet arrival times were not sufficient, the algorithm tended to overfit the data and, consequentially, exhibited higher performances but lacked generality. The RF algorithm aims to prevent these overfitting issues and, consequentially, showcases worse accuracy.

All the classifiers presented unusually good results for the third attack (the MODBUS query flood), prompting a deeper analysis of the dataset obtained. This allowed for the detection of a field with little variance during the attack, which allowed the algorithms to detect the attack with ease. Consequentially, inferring upon these results may be overreaching, requiring further analysis and an adaptation of the implemented attack in future works.

In conclusion, the effects of data imbalance on the classification process constitute a real problem that can lead to unintentional misleading when analyzing classifier performance. Moreover, this situation can be hard to detect since the datasets used for CPS security research are frequently restricted (and consequentially, difficult to analyze and characterize).

5   Conclusion and Future Work

This article constitutes the first step to providing an insight on the frailties of machine learning algorithms which may lead to proper generalization of the techniques and, consequentially, real-world application. The effects of varying the attack and the capture timespans, when using different algorithms and attacks were studied. It was inferred that, although small attack timeframes provide apparently good results, the classification accuracy starts to decrease as they grow in size and the imbalance of data starts to diminish. Once the data imbalance is overcome, the results start improving again. The overfitting problem is also detected and discussed.

As future work, the authors plan to further pursue this analysis effort, increasing the capture and attack timespans and also diversifying the types of implemented attacks. Finally, future developments of this work will also involve an analysis of how the feature selection process may affect both the time required to create the models for detection and the resulting classification performance.

Acknowledgements. This work was supported by the ATENA European H2020 Project (H2020-DS-2015-1 Project 700581).

References

1. Humayed, A., Lin, J., Li, F., Luo, B.: Cyber-physical systems security: a survey. IEEE Internet Things J. **4**(6), 1802–1831 (2017). https://doi.org/10.1109/JIOT. 2017.2703172

2. Zargar, S.T., Joshi, J., Tipper, D.: A survey of defense mechanisms against distributed denial of service (DDOS) flooding attacks. IEEE Commun. Surv. Tutor. **15**(4), 2046–2069 (2013). https://doi.org/10.1109/SURV.2013.031413.00127

3. Sabhnani, M., Serpen, G., More, K.K.: Application of machine learning algorithms to KDD intrusion detection dataset within misuse detection context. In: Proceedings of International Conference on Machine Learning: Models, Technologies, and Applications (MLMTA), January 2003, pp. 209–215 (2003). http://dl.acm.org/citation.cfm?id=1293805.1293811

4. Osanaiye, O., Cai, H., Choo, K.K.R., Dehghantanha, A., Xu, Z., Dlodlo, M.: Ensemble-based multi-filter feature selection method for DDoS detection in cloud computing. Eurasip J. Wirel. Commun. Netw. **2016**(1), 130 (2016). https://doi. org/10.1186/s13638-016-0623-3

5. Su, M.Y.: Real-time anomaly detection systems for Denial-of-Service attacks by weighted k-nearest-neighbor classifiers. Expert Syst. Appl. **38**(4), 3492–3498 (2011). https://doi.org/10.1016/j.eswa.2010.08.137

6. Goldenberg, N., Wool, A.: Accurate modeling of Modbus/TCP for intrusion detection in SCADA systems. Int. J. Crit. Infrastruct. Prot. **6**(2), 63–75 (2013). https://doi.org/10.1016/j.ijcip.2013.05.001

7. Yoon, M., Ciocarlie, G.F.: Communication pattern monitoring : improving the utility of anomaly detection for industrial control systems. SENT **14**(February), 110 (2014). https://doi.org/10.14722/sent.2014.23012

8. Erez, N., Wool, A.: Control variable classification, modeling and anomaly detection in Modbus/TCP SCADA systems. Int. J. Crit. Infrastruct. Prot. **10**, 59–70 (2015). https://doi.org/10.1016/j.ijcip.2015.05.001

9. Markovic-Petrovic, J.D., Stojanovic, M.D.: Analysis of SCADA system vulnerabilities to DDoS attacks. In: 11th International Conference on Telecommunications in Modern Satellite, Cable and Broadcasting Services, TELSIKS 2013, vol. 2, pp. 591–594 (2013). https://doi.org/10.1109/TELSKS.2013.6704448

10. Kalluri, R., Mahendra, L., Kumar, R.K.S., Prasad, G.L.G.: Simulation and impact analysis of denial-of-service attacks on power SCADA. In: National Power Systems Conference, NPSC 2016, vol. 1 (2017). https://doi.org/10.1109/NPSC.2016. 7858908

11. Hink, R.C.B., Beaver, J.M., Buckner, M.A., Morris, T., Adhikari, U., Pan, S.: Machine learning for power system disturbance and cyber-attack discrimination. In: 7th International Symposium on Resilient Control Systems, ISRCS 2014 (2014). https://doi.org/10.1109/ISRCS.2014.6900095

Author Index

Printed in the United States
By Bookmasters